Praise for

The Accidental Investment Banker

"The fashion world has *The Devil Wears Prada*. Hollywood has *You'll Never Eat Lunch in This Town Again*. Now Wall Street is getting a memoir-cum-tell-all that skewers some of the industry's most expensive egos. . . . [*The Accidental Investment Banker*] offers the public a rare, ringside seat inside the madcap and often egomaniacal world of Wall Street's Masters of the Universe [and] important insights into problems with Wall Street's often ruthless and conflicted culture."
—Andrew Ross Sorkin, *The New York Times*

"A wonderful primer for anyone who has wondered how Wall Street really works . . . Not since Michael Lewis's *Liar's Poker* has there been as good, as accessible or as pithy a look at the world of investment banking."
—*The Washington Post*

"[Jonathan Knee] has written the best account I've read on how the internet boom and bust was experienced inside the investment banking department of a big Wall Street firm."
—Michael Lewis, Bloomberg.com

"For anyone who remembers the crazy boom times, and the even crazier bust, Jonathan A. Knee's *The Accidental Investment Banker* is a must. . . . Reveals a world that rivals 24 in intrigue and drama."   —*Fortune*

"[Jonathan A. Knee] captures the glories and agonies of his profession. General readers will marvel at his discussion of banker pay, which, despite being slightly out-of-date, still seems glaringly huge. MBA students will linger over Mr. Knee's sardonic description of a 'sell side,' a mandate to auction a company. In step-by-step fashion, he shows how bankers give their clients the impression of running a 'secretive,' selective auction but in fact do quite the opposite."   —*The Wall Street Journal*

"This insider's chronicle brims with humor and insight as it depicts a world driven mad by money."   —*Fast Company*

"Studded with arresting details . . . and with often-trenchant insight."
—ROGER LOWENSTEIN, *The New York Times*

"As a memoir the book lies somewhere between Michael Lewis' crisp, and now classic *Liar's Poker* and the autobiographical hagigographies penned by Bruce Wasserstein or Alan 'Ace' Greenberg. . . . Articulate and funny . . . makes a compelling argument."   —MarketWatch

"Funny and knowing, this business memoir debut should appeal to a wide swath of business veterans."   —*Publishers Weekly*

"Most people know by now that investment bankers are rich, secretive and powerrful. But why? What do they really do? And why are they increasingly distrusted by their most powerful clients? Finally we have someone willing to lift the curtain."
—JAMES B. STEWART, author of *Den of Thieves* and
Disney War: The Battle for the Magic Kingdom

"Jonathan A. Knee takes a sharp look at the fundamental changes that have taken place in the investment banking business. It's an important story, and thanks to the skillful way Knee mixes in the tale of his own experience as a banker, it reads like a novel. The book is hard to put down."
—BETHANY MCLEAN, author of *The Smartest Guys in
the Room: The Amazing Rise and Scandalous Fall of Enron*

"A terrific book—engrossing and highly instructive."
—MARK GERSON, CEO, Gerson Lehrman Group

"*The Accidental Investment Banker* is a must-read for anyone in business who is impacted by Wall Street—and that is just about everyone."
—LEO HINDERY, JR., managing partner,
InterMedia Partners and former CEO of TCI

"Without a doubt, the deftest and most revealing thing I've read about investment banking."   —MICHAEL WOLFF, author of *Burn Rate*

THE ACCIDENTAL
INVESTMENT BANKER

THE ACCIDENTAL
INVESTMENT BANKER

Inside the Decade That Transformed Wall Street

JONATHAN A. KNEE

RANDOM HOUSE TRADE PAPERBACKS

NEW YORK

2007 Random House Trade Paperback Edition

Copyright © 2006 by Jonathan A. Knee

Published in the United States by Random House Trade Paperbacks,
an imprint of The Random House Publishing Group,
a division of Random House, Inc., New York.

RANDOM HOUSE TRADE PAPERBACKS and colophon
are trademarks of Random House, Inc.

Originally published in hardcover in the United States by
Oxford University Press, Inc., in 2006.

ISBN 978-0-8129-7804-9

LIBRARY OF CONGRESS CATALOGING-IN-PUBLICATION DATA
Knee, Jonathan A.
The accidental investment banker : inside the decade that transformed
Wall Street / Jonathan A. Knee.—1st Random House ed.
p.   cm.
Originally published: Oxford; New York: Oxford University Press, 2006.
Includes bibliographical references and index.
ISBN 978-0-8129-7804-9
1. Investment banking—United States. I. Title.
HG4930.5.K57 2007
332.660973—dc22   2007002088

Printed in the United States of America

www.atrandom.com

2 4 6 8 9 7 5 3 1

For Chaille Bianca and Vivienne Lael
and William Grant
who says he wants to be an investment banker

PREFACE

I WAS SITTING in a darkened theater over the Fourth of July holiday weekend during a late-night showing of *Superman Returns* when my Black-Berry began to vibrate, easily drawing my attention away from the screen. It was two months before the scheduled publication of *The Accidental Investment Banker*. I had spent more than three years wrestling with both my book's subject matter and its prospective publishers and was now quietly at peace with the final product. Through the book, I had sought to tell the history of investment banking in a way that would be accessible to a general audience but still speak to professionals working in and with the industry today. In an effort to reach both groups, I wove my own story into the narrative: how I accidentally fell into the business in 1994, and how I experienced the industry's dramatic transformation during the decade of boom-and-bust that followed. I had realized there might be some controversy over the use of real names and situations to bring the history to life, but felt confident that anything of that nature would be both minor and manageable. Without my book in mind, I looked down at the e-mail message that had set my BlackBerry aflutter.

"A Wall Street Exposé With an All-Star Index," read the headline of the article from the next day's Sunday *New York Times,* which a friend had helpfully forwarded to me. At first it did not even occur to me that what I was looking at had anything to do with my book. If the movie had been better, I might not have continued reading the description of my book and its likely impact by "DealBook" columnist Andrew Ross Sorkin: "The fashion world has *The Devil Wears Prada.* Hollywood has *You'll Never Eat*

Lunch in This Town Again. Now Wall Street is getting a memoir-cum-tell-all that skewers some of the industry's most expansive egos."[1]

What followed was an out-of-context catalog of the juiciest tidbits relating to the best-known names found in the index of my book. Sorkin reported that multiple "dog-eared, bootleg copies" of uncorrected book proofs had been circulating throughout the investment banking community for weeks. Financial industry blogs in subsequent days would not only confirm this, but describe how unfortunate young bankers were directed to spend the balance of the weekend procuring and summarizing the book for their superiors. Sorkin questioned my motivations for writing the book, seemed confident that it would make me an industry pariah, and was incredulous that a working investment banker would write such a book. "Mr. Knee may really never be able to eat lunch in this town again," wrote Sorkin.

I put down my BlackBerry and looked up at a cackling Lex Luthor on the screen. If I had been sitting in an aisle seat, I am confident I would have thrown up over the side.

Although it may seem obvious now that the book would have drawn this kind of attention, the fact is that, for a long time, *The Accidental Investment Banker* had been incapable of attracting any interest in the publishing community. I did eventually receive and accept an offer from a major trade house, but it became clear that this was based on the theory that I could be convinced to drop the history in favor of more salacious subject matter. "No one cares about Sidney Weinberg!" the exasperated editor shouted in our last conversation on the subject. Sidney Weinberg, the elfin former chimney sweep who built Goldman Sachs over forty years, is the hero of the book that follows. I returned the advance.

Although I had assumed the story would end there, my enterprising agent began showing the book to university presses, among them Oxford University Press, where *The Accidental Investment Banker* eventually found its home in hardcover. The folks at Oxford valued the book much more for its coverage of investment banking's recent tumultuous history than for any insider dish it could provide, and this was refreshing, to say the least, after my earlier experience. At the same time I knew that publishing with a university press, even a more commercially minded one like Oxford, would probably mean a small print run and publicity budget. But this was the book I wanted to write, and I was frankly thankful that *The Accidental Investment Banker* would see the light of day at all at that point.

Until that night in the movie theater, neither I nor my publisher was sure anyone would review the book, much less "break" the story of its impending publication, as *The New York Times* did. Sorkin's widely read article had a dramatic impact on both the profile of the book and, I believe, the nature and extent of the reaction to it.

The book's sales rank on Amazon.com jumped from somewhere below one million to number thirty-four in one day, based on pre-orders. Articles based on the Sorkin description of my book alone began to appear. This extended even to the United Kingdom, where I had not managed to find a publisher for the book at all.

And reaction at publication was strong. Many of the otherwise over-whelmingly positive reviews dedicated more space to speculation on my motivations than on the thesis of the book. Michael Lewis, the talented author of *Liar's Poker*, was representative in this regard. Lewis said the book was "brutally honest and socially valuable" and "the best account [he has] read of how the Internet boom and bust was experienced inside the invest-ment banking department of a big Wall Street firm."[2] Yet he spent far more time deconstructing my imagined unspoken objectives in producing the book. His conclusion was that the book is an effort on my part to achieve what I "really want: a life as an important person in and around Wall Street. (Though not as an investment banker.)" I am still trying to figure out what this job I apparently aspire to is. I am, by the way, still an investment banker.

The book was meant to be provocative and I certainly hoped it would inspire a public dialogue on the role of investment banking. Given my deci-sion to use my own story as a tool to help paint the industry landscape, I also was prepared for a degree of personalization in response, even if not to quite the level I have received. And despite the initial horror I felt when I read Sorkin's article, in retrospect I realize that this initial publicity had an incredible multiplying effect on how many have and will actually read the book.

After all the unexpected publicity and all the unforeseen personal and professional reverberations that have flowed from it, the biggest and most pleasant surprise has been the reaction from within the investment bank-ing community itself. I confess that Sorkin's article and all the subsequent press suggesting how unwelcome I would now be in the community of invest-ment banking professionals had made me—well, a little nervous. Yet time and again, senior managers from the business have gone out of their way to compliment me on the book. Group heads from bulge bracket firms approached me to say that they purchased copies for all of their analysts and associates. A retired éminence grise from the industry sought me out for a quiet lunch through mutual acquaintances. A cynical person might think that such flattery reflects precautionary measures in case I write a sequel. Yet this feedback has been overwhelmingly from individuals I didn't know and would be unlikely to write about. And when I learned that one of the most prominent financial supermarkets was using my book in their new associate ethics training course, it confirmed in my mind that something more might be going on.

And then there are the other many little satisfactions that have made me feel my book has served at least some of the objectives I set out to achieve with it. A young managing director from Morgan Stanley quietly turned up with a stack of books for me to sign with dedications to his clients. I received invitations to speak about the book at law firms, where I enjoyed overflowing internal audiences who were clearly interested in understanding better what their investment banking brethren really do, but also unnerved by the parallels to their own profession. Many investment bankers, both newly minted and well-wizened, told me that they bought second copies for their mothers to help bridge the communication divide; they hoped it would help their mothers understand what they do, and their frustrations over how their profession has changed over the years.

Investment bankers young and old do not like the trends described in this book, in particular the structural obstacles to providing good, unbiased counsel, any more than their clients do. The diminishment of their roles and the roles of their once-great institutions has been demoralizing. My bemoaning the decreasing relevance of investment banking—or at least the part of investment banking that allows bankers to provide independent strategic advice to corporate clients—has been welcomed as a rallying cry against the continuing efforts to relegate this function to an increasingly insignificant portion of the portfolio of products hawked by financial supermarkets.

But let's not get carried away. Not everyone liked the book. A great deal of criticism was directed toward the specific portraits painted of individual people and institutions. Some reviews and even Sorkin's initial "DealBook" treatment have suggested that at least certain aspects of the narrative were "gratuitous" or "score-settling" in nature. Ironically, many of the complaints from actual investment bankers in this regard said I had been too "nice"—and came accompanied with embarrassing "deep background" anecdotes about competing investment bankers or banks for inclusion in a subsequent edition. Did I know which highbrow investment bank had offered a subsequently disgraced research analyst millions to join them? Didn't I hear what happened at that firm's Christmas party? How could I not include the famous antics of this senior banker?

The criticism that certain portraits were incomplete is fair but misses the point. I used real people, situations, and institutions for the narrow purpose of explicating a particular theme or chapter in the history being related. Whether someone ended up being pleased or unhappy about his or her portrayal usually depended on what phenomenon the behavior or incident described was meant to exemplify. I did not mean to suggest that those involved were the only ones "guilty" of the identified conduct. Indeed, in most instances I made it clear that different versions of the same stories were being played out everywhere.

There has been, however, one recurring and disturbing substantive criticism of the book from investment bankers. Some charge that the book is overly sentimental and exaggerates the virtues of the golden era of relationship banking, when choosing your clients was viewed as a serious undertaking by an investment bank, one that created lasting obligations that were not lightly cast aside in favor of more financially attractive opportunities. But the deeper charge lays the blame for the decline of investment banking on the clients themselves. What is a banker to do when dealing with clients who abandon long-standing relationships in favor of bidding out every piece of business to the cheapest investment bank? Beginning in the 1970s but accelerating in the '80s and '90s, client loyalty indeed became more and more of an anachronism. Mercenary clients beget mercenary bankers, the argument goes, and the clients have no standing on which to complain about it.

Although tempting to dismiss as a mere self-fulfilling prophecy by greedy bankers, this is a serious argument and there is more than a grain of truth to it. At some level, there is a chicken-and-the-egg quality to the thesis—did greedy clients produce greedy bankers, or the opposite? But if one believes that investment banking is or should be a profession, then the chicken/egg conundrum becomes, to mix food-related metaphors, something of a red herring.

The very concept of a profession is of a job that owes obligations to society at large. Professor John Coffee, who in his latest book tracked the decline of a number of once-revered professions, says "This ability to do good and do well at the same time entitled the profession to aspire to loftier ambitions . . . and enjoy a higher sense of self-worth than the mere merchant or employee."[3] It is the antithesis of the idea of a profession to argue that the standards to which investment banks once held themselves was simply an attribute of a grand financial bargain between banker and client that is no longer operative. Thus if the defense is valid, investment banking may have won the rhetorical battle but at the cost of its professional soul. Indeed, that this form of self-justification has so much resonance within the industry reflects the fact that many no longer think of investment banking as a professional calling.

Some of the most interesting feedback I have gotten about *The Accidental Investment Banker* has come from professionals in fields entirely outside of investment banking. Whether in medicine or law or accounting, each person spoke of a similar sense of loss of self-worth as various financial and institutional pressures have reduced their once-honorable callings to something more like serving as a "mere merchant or employee." Each profession has its own peculiar facts surrounding the sources of its decline— the growth of consulting profits in accounting, for example, the increasing influence of HMOs, insurance companies, and litigation in medicine.

I cannot help thinking, however, that a more widespread cultural malaise has been a common source of this epidemic of professional distress. Professions came into being as a means for a newly aspirational middle class to gain a social standing previously unavailable to them. Our society's increasing emphasis on celebrity, self-realization and personal wealth over more communal concerns has reduced the social benefits associated with pursuing a higher professional calling—at least one that doesn't make you rich and famous.

I wrote this book because I believe that the industry can do better. I am not so naïve as to think that we can ever go back to an innocent golden age of relationship banking. The structural changes outlined in the pages that follow make that impossible. But the worst lapses described here were not the result of any structural changes, but of individual decisions by individual people who could have decided differently. To the extent that this book has encouraged a more honest dialogue both within firms and between bankers and clients, I believe it can help. But I also believe that, as a culture, in some sense we get the professions we deserve. And until we learn to honor those who pursue higher callings just because they do, our professionals are likely to continue experiencing prolonged identity crises, the ultimate resolutions of which have important implications for all of us.

CONTENTS

INTRODUCTION

THOUSANDS PACKED the pews of the Riverside Church on the Upper West Side of Manhattan that foggy, wet January afternoon for the memorial service for Richard B. Fisher, former leader of Morgan Stanley. Mayor Michael Bloomberg attended, as did David Rockefeller and other dignitaries. So did scores of young bankers who may never have met Fisher, but for whom his name was legendary.

This outpouring of affection was both touching and somewhat unexpected. By the time he died at the age of 68 on December 16, 2004, Fisher had become a marginal figure at the global financial institution with which his name was once synonymous. Fisher joined Morgan Stanley in 1962 and became its president in 1984. By the time he negotiated the fateful merger with Chicago-based Dean Witter, Discover and Co. in 1997—making Dean Witter's Phil Purcell the combined company's CEO and Fisher's protégé John Mack president and chief operating officer—Fisher had been chairman of Morgan Stanley for six years.

Yet well before the recurrence of the prostate cancer that ultimately took his life, Fisher had been drifting, or rather been pushed, further and further away from the investment bank he had once led. Although Fisher became executive committee chairman immediately after the merger, this was downgraded to something called chairman emeritus in 2000 soon after he was nudged from the board. When, in 2001, a frustrated Mack resigned and Fisher asked for the opportunity to address the board, Purcell delivered the painful news: the board did not wish to hear from him. Even Fisher's office had been moved first off the main executive floor and then out of the building altogether, quietly banished to a place known internally as Jurassic Park—where retired senior bankers were given cubicles and secretarial support.

Among the throngs at the service were a distinguished group of seven fellow inhabitants of Jurassic Park, including Fisher's predecessor as chairman, S. Parker Gilbert. Most of these men had grown up with Fisher in the Morgan Stanley of the 1960s. Looking around the crowded church they could not help but ponder just how much had changed since that time.

In the 1960s, Morgan Stanley quite pointedly did not have a securities sales and trading operation, viewing it as a low-class business engaged in by mere, and largely Jewish, traders. In 1971, however, the bank had established its own sales and trading desk, and put Fisher, a young partner at the time, in charge. In recent years, the profits from these operations had come to dwarf those of the traditional gentleman banking in which they had engaged in their heyday. The introduction of sales and trading at Morgan Stanley coincided with the firm's launch of one of the first mergers and acquisitions departments among the major investment banking houses. Prior to that, these firms had often treated advice on mergers and acquisitions as something given away free to longstanding clients of the firm. Within a decade or two, "M&A" would establish itself as the profit engine of traditional finance, with high-profile bankers whose names were often better known than that of either the clients or financial institutions they in theory served.

And, of course, the biggest change of all was that, with its couple of dozen partners and several hundred employees, the Morgan Stanley of the 1960s was the dominant investment bank in the world. In the competitive and labyrinthine world of contemporary finance, such overall consistent preeminence was simply not possible. But even within the relatively narrow realm that had been the core of Morgan Stanley's great franchise —providing quality independent financial advice to the leaders of the world's great corporations—the torch had been passed some time ago to Goldman Sachs.

If the emergence during the 1970s of sales and trading and M&A as the new profit centers planted the early seeds that changed the culture and structure of the investment banking industry and Morgan Stanley's place in it, many other internal and external events played critical roles in bringing the firm to the state in which it found itself in early 2005. Morgan Stanley's own decision in 1986 to sell 20 percent of its shares to the public was dramatic both for its rejection of the private partnership tradition that had prevailed for so long and for the fact that the money was being raised to enable Morgan Stanley to participate more aggressively in the leveraged buyout (or LBO) fad then sweeping the industry. During this era, public companies perceived as undermanaged or undervalued became the target of takeover artists who financed these deals by placing previously unheard of amounts of debt. In these deals, Morgan Stanley might not only place this debt, but invest its own money to consummate a transaction. As controversial as it was for Morgan Stanley to sponsor companies with such a heavy debt burden, a more significant line was crossed when the firm moved from agent to principal and actively pursued these opportunities for its own account, even in competition with clients.

The government's decision a decade later to allow the large commercial banks to aggressively pursue investment banking business put further pressure on the old way of doing things. The Depression-era legislation known as Glass Steagall had long insulated the rarified investment banking partnerships from assault by these better capitalized institutions. Its ultimate repeal in 1999 paved the way not only for radically intensified competition but a wave of mergers that created enormous financial supermarkets with an entirely different ethos.

But at Morgan Stanley, nothing compared with the changes wrought by its combination with Dean Witter Discover. Although billed as a "merger of equals," it soon became clear that the most venerable Wall Street brand of all time had actually sold itself to a decidedly down-market retail brokerage and credit card company. When longtime Morgan Stanley veteran Robert Scott got up to speak at the memorial service, the small clique of Fisher's contemporaries was reminded of just how badly things had gone for the Morgan Stanley side of the once-promising deal. Scott, although ten years younger than Fisher and not precisely of their generation, had been only the latest of a steady stream of senior Morgan Stanley executives who had been ruthlessly dispatched by Purcell once they began to pose a threat or their usefulness to him had expired. Fisher had designated Scott, a former head of investment banking, to lead the merger transition team for Morgan Stanley when the deal was announced in February 1997. But before the month was out and well before the deal closed that May, Scott suffered a heart attack. Purcell's decision to appoint the physically weakened Scott as Mack's replacement as president and COO in 2001 was widely viewed as the least threatening way to throw a sop to the Morgan Stanley side of the house in the face of their heir apparent's departure. Two years later, after Scott's 33 years at Morgan Stanley, Purcell told him that his services were no longer needed. The only other board seat reserved for a company executive was quietly eliminated, leaving Purcell clearly, and solely, in charge.

"Dick's still watching over us," Scott assured the gathering, his voice cracking with emotion.

"We're going to be all right."

Some were not so sure. Within a few weeks after Fisher's funeral, the same seven distinguished group of Fisher's peers that had attended joined with Scott and were at former chairman S. Parker Gilbert's apartment actively plotting to depose Purcell. A number of them had for some time been informally discussing how best to voice their discontent with Purcell, but the emotion of the funeral served as a catalyst to action. Now calling themselves the "grumpy old men," the eight former Morgan Stanley senior executives ultimately hired veteran investment banker Robert Greenhill—who himself had become a Morgan Stanley partner in 1970 as part of the celebrated "irreverent group of six" that included Fisher—to represent them in their efforts. Letters to the board were sent, press releases issued, interviews on CNBC given, and full-page ads taken out in the *Wall Street Journal*. Although Morgan Stanley would attempt to dismiss their complaints as those of out-of-touch former employees, their pedigree made this particular spin a hard sell.

But despite the group's pedigree, or perhaps because of it, there was something strange about the campaign. They had not complained at the time of the merger with Dean Witter and over the years many had agreed to be trotted out at various events to assure the newer generations of Morgan Stanley employees that the best traditions of the past were being upheld. Furthermore, at least initially, they were not asking for a specific change of strategy and had not proposed a particular alternative management team. Beyond asking for Purcell's head, they suggested only a few modest changes to the firm's governance. Finally, although the grumpy old men boasted of owning 11 million shares among them—which on an absolute basis was worth over half a billion dollars—there were now over a billion shares outstanding. The grumpy old men were storming the palace gates with barely 1 percent of the outstanding shares.

At the time of Morgan Stanley's IPO in 1986, Chairman S. Parker Gilbert alone owned almost 4 percent of the shares. When the three other management directors of the newly public Morgan Stanley were added (these were Fisher, Greenhill, and another member of the grumpy old men, Lewis Bernard) their holdings approached 15 percent. But today, taking into account the shares the group itself had sold in the intervening decades and the new shares that had been issued both to employees and in the Dean Witter deal, all the grumpy old men combined would be lucky to creep onto the list of top ten shareholders. And the company had a staggered board closely allied with Purcell that would require three-quarters of its members to remove the CEO.

So even if there were justification for many of the complaints over Purcell's tenure as CEO, the logical course of action would be to sell one's shares and get on with life rather than to hold a press conference. Put another way, it is puzzling why a group of otherwise intelligent financiers, some might say among the most brilliant of their generation, would launch an attack whose only realistic prospect of success as they defined it would come from creating so much turmoil at the institution they claimed to love that the board would be forced to act. And by the time the board did act on June 13, 2005, and Purcell was finally forced to resign, dozens of Morgan Stanley's finest had departed. Some were ousted as part of the final efforts by Purcell to hold on to power. Some took financially attractive long-term contracts elsewhere as competitors exploited the instability at the firm. And some just left in disgust.

The grumpy old men had won. And the prize was a profoundly weakened, initially leaderless institution, with poorer prospects than ever of regaining its earlier glory. Although John Mack would return to take over the helm of Morgan Stanley within a few weeks of Purcell's resignation, as of this writing, none of the senior bankers who left during 2005 have come back. In *Business Week*'s 2005 review of the top 100 global brands, Morgan Stanley had the distinction of having lost more of its brand value (15 percent or almost $2 billion in brand value) than any other U.S.-based peer in any industry. The management turmoil and ouster of Purcell, the magazine said, had "seriously damaged the firm's sterling reputation."[1]

What explains this apparently self-destructive crusade by the scions of Morgan Stanley's halcyon days? Mere dissatisfaction with Purcell's management is not a credible explanation. Some less generous commentators have suggested that "the attempted putsch may represent the final death rattle of a Wall Street era personified by . . . well-born, Ivy League educated investment bankers."[2] In this version, the intensity of the personal animus against Purcell is heightened by the shame over their own complicity in letting the infidels into the temple in the first place. "It was a merger of patricians and plebeians, and the final irony was that the plebeians out-witted the patricians," argued historian Ron Chernow, author of the definitive history of Morgan Stanley.[3]

Although there is more than a grain of truth to this characterization of the struggle between the old guard and the new, it does not tell the whole story. S. Parker Gilbert, stepson of Harold Stanley and son of a legendary J. P. Morgan partner who had run the Treasury Department under Andrew Mellon in his twenties, may fit neatly into the stereotype of a Morgan Stanley partner of yore. But these partners of Fisher's generation or just after were hardly a homogeneous group and both represented and had encouraged a sharp break with that past. Fisher himself was the son of an adhesives salesman and struggled valiantly with the physical constraints imposed on him by childhood polio. Lewis Bernard was in 1963 the first Jewish hire at Morgan Stanley—made only after carefully checking with selected clients, one of whom embarrassingly turned out to *be* Jewish—and an important strategic innovator at the firm. Even Bob Greenhill, also the son of immigrants, was highly controversial as he became the first bona fide celebrity of the early M&A wars of the 1970s. Ironically, Greenhill had been a rival, not a friend, of Fisher's and did not attend his funeral.

As revolutionary as Fisher's generation was at the time, it was not really hypocritical for them to now claim the mantle of Morgan Stanley family values. For all the dramatic changes they produced, they always abided by J. P. Morgan, Jr.'s, simple dictum about the firm only doing "first-class busi-ness in a first-class way." The depth of the anger and frustration voiced by the grumpy old men can only really be explained by the extent to which they had seen this very fundamental value systematically challenged. But the disturbing changes at Morgan Stanley over the past decade were not primarily the result of Phil Purcell's leadership. Rather they, and corre-sponding changes at all the major investment banks, were driven by the unprecedented economic boom and bust that placed extraordinary pres-sures on the values that had once prevailed at these institutions.

Much has already been written about the various economic "bubbles" of the late 1990s—the Internet bubble, the telecom bubble, the technology bubble and the stock market bubble. Much has also been written about the role of investment banks in fueling these ephemeral bubbles. Much less has been written, however, about the investment banks' own bubble. While the investment banks in some ways made possible all the other bubbles—by, for example, legitimizing hundreds of speculative start-up companies for public market investors and opining as to the "fairness" of incredible values placed on these businesses—these institutions themselves were fundamentally transformed by the unprecedented number of deals the forces they unleashed created.

With roots going back over a century, the major investment banking houses largely eschewed publicity and had developed their own idiosyncratic cultures built on notions of exclusivity, integrity, and conservatism. This culture served a valuable self-regulatory function in an era where governmental institutions were not equipped to provide that service. And it provided CEO's finding their way in the newly globalizing consumer society with faithful financial advice about the increasingly complex markets in which they found themselves.

Suddenly these investment bankers found themselves cast as principal players in the free wheeling go-go Internet economy complete with their very own public celebrities. There was a corresponding emergence of the celebrity CEO, who no longer saw loyalty to a financial advisor as in his short-term interest. And in this environment, investment bankers' ability to take market share from their competitors often became a function of their willingness to relax previously held corporate values. The boom accelerated what had already been an emerging shift in the self-conceptions of investment bankers themselves—from discreet trusted advisors to increasingly mercenary deal hounds for whom not just profitability but now publicity became prime objectives. No longer mere agents for their corporate clients, banks and their star bankers now positioned themselves as prime actors in the unfolding economic drama.

Once the bubble burst starting in 2000, these banks were barely recognizable from what they were before. Their efforts to re-establish their former cultures, reputations, and profitability in the face of a shrinking business base and increased regulatory scrutiny once again severely tested the organizations' leadership. And with much of that leadership having ascended to power during and because of the earlier boom, the results were predictably uneven and highly ironic. The "celebrity" bankers of the era had made many enemies—within their own institutions, among regulators, and even in some cases among their formerly loyal corporate clients.

Some were pushed out, some were indicted and some managed to re-invent themselves and survive. The industry that these changes left behind was both less trusted and less profitable.

In 1994, I was a midlevel airline executive. More by accident than by design, I ended up with a front row seat for both the boom and the subsequent bust at the two most prestigious investment banks on Wall Street. This book tells the story of the past decade from that unique vantage point. I use my own experiences first at Goldman Sachs and later at Morgan Stanley as the launching pad to tell the story of the transformation of the industry as a whole. In doing so, I aim to provide candid and accessible descriptions of how these firms operate, what investment bankers actually do and how "deals" are done. More broadly, however, I tell the story of how these firms and the industry responded culturally and structurally first to their unprecedented expansion and then to the devastating retrenchment of the new century.

It is a portrait of how the culture that emerged during the boom undermined the integrity of these institutions in a way that will make it difficult if not impossible for them ever to regain the role they once held. New organizations such as multibillion-dollar hedge funds and LBO firms have begun to step in and play some of the roles once dominated by the investment banks. Whether our financial markets or culture are better off with these new and largely unregulated institutions is very much open to question. As either providers of capital or as providers of a preferred home to our best and brightest graduates, hedge funds and LBO firms raise import-ant issues relating to the transparency and risk profile of our economy as well as the values that economy promotes.

The fundamental shift in investment banking to a more aggressive, oppor-tunistic, and transactional business model from one rooted in long-term client relationships and deeply held business values was not a product of the Internet era in particular. A variety of structural and regulatory changes had incrementally moved the industry in this direction over the previous decades. The boom of the late 1990s simply accelerated the rate of change so that many of these institutions became unrecognizable from their for-mer selves in the space of a few short years.

At one time, the investment banker viewed his interrelated obligations as to the client, the institution, and the markets. The client might have been with the firm for generations. The institution's reputation was viewed as its most important asset. Internal standards went well beyond any regula-tory requirements to protect investors. And investment bankers advanced based largely on their success in simultaneously serving the client, preserving the franchise, and protecting the public.

In place of this ideal a culture of contingency emerged, a sense not only that each day might be your last, but that your value was linked exclusively to how much revenue was generated for the firm on that day—regardless of its source. At the height of the boom in 1999, I had recently left Goldman Sachs for Morgan Stanley. Once white-shoe Morgan was now locked in battle with relative upstart Donaldson, Lufkin and Jenrette to claim the mantle of junk bond king, up for grabs since the final implosion of Michael Milken's Drexel Lambert in 1990. The popularization of junk bonds by Drexel had made the debt markets available to all manner of highly leveraged speculative companies—companies, in short, that were the antithesis of Morgan Stanley's once-pristine client list. Morgan's primary weapon in this war was its willingness to sponsor debt for "emerging" telecom companies that required huge capital investments. This represented a new level of risk because, unlike even most junk issuers up to that point, these companies had generally never generated any cash flow and their business models in some cases were entirely new. Although the same could be said of the Internet start-ups of the period, those companies usually at least had the good sense not to borrow money.

The bankers who pressed these questionable telecom credits at Morgan in their quest for market share, fees, and internal status coined an acronym that could well be a rallying cry for what the entire investment banking industry had become more broadly. "IBG YBG" stood for "I'll Be Gone, You'll Be Gone." When a particularly troubling fact came up in due diligence on one of these companies, a whispered "IBG YBG" among the banking team members would ensure that a way would be found to do the business, even if investors, or Morgan Stanley itself, would pay the price down the road. Don't sweat it, was the implication, we'll all be long gone by then.

In April 2005, Daniel H. Bayly, the former head of investment banking at Merrill Lynch, was sentenced to 30 months in jail for conspiracy and fraud in connection with a now-infamous Enron transaction. Merrill had "purchased" a stake in three Nigerian barges to allow Enron to book a profit in time for its earnings announcement. Enron had secretly agreed to buy the holding back in six months from the investment bank, which hoped to secure future banking business for its trouble. After Bayly and three other ex-Merrill executives were convicted for their role in the transaction, a collective cry arose from the investment banking community. But instead of denouncing the decline in standards in their industry, the complaint was of prosecutorial overreach.[4] Just beneath the surface of these bankers' high-minded policy arguments about the dangers of criminalizing merely aggressive business practices, however, lurked a more visceral sentiment: there but for the grace of God go I.

It is tempting to dismiss the "grumpy old men" as an anachronistic throwback to a reactionary era better left behind. But for these men and their generation, doing "first-class business in a first-class way" actually meant something. It is not excessively romantic to think that on the road from this one-time credo to "IBG YBG," something meaningful was lost. And maybe the true aim of their ultimately successful quest to unseat Phil Purcell was to remind the world of what investment banking once was, and to force ourselves to ask whether there might be some good reasons to want it to be that way again.

A CHICKEN IN EVERY POT

"**H**ILLSDOWN HOLDINGS," the enormous, balding figure who appeared over my desk shouted.

I almost choked on the Cornish pasty I had just brought up for lunch during an otherwise typically calm day in the London offices of Bankers Trust. Andrew Capitman, a senior mergers and acquisitions banker transplanted from New York, glared at me with a satisfied conspiratorial grin. I studied his intimidating figure with my full mouth agape. Capitman clearly expected me to appreciate the profound significance of the two words he had just spat out. After a few moments of frozen silence, his grin disappeared as my ignorance became apparent.

"Chickens," he shouted, even louder, annoyed that this third word was required to explain the magnitude of the situation.

"Oh, yes, great," I stammered weakly, having no real idea what I was getting into.

I never really seriously thought about becoming an investment banker. Business school itself had been something of a lark. I was living in Dublin at Trinity College in 1983–1984, coming to the end of an all-expense-paid party courtesy of the Rotary Foundation, when I realized that I would need to find something to do when it was over. Having loved being a philosophy major but hoping to ultimately put any great ideas I might have to some practical use, I applied to Yale Law School. Then someone told me that Stanford Business School was the Yale Law School of business schools. I didn't know exactly what that meant, but I figured it meant the hard part was getting in. My interest in an MBA was purely philosophical stemming from my youthful skepticism regarding the emergence of the "Professional Manager" as an important contemporary cultural icon. On a less lofty note, I also liked the idea that no one would ever be able to pull rank on me by claiming to know something I didn't by having a fancy MBA.

When I got into both schools, I started working the phones and quickly realized that whatever else the two institutions had in common, they had very different approaches to customer service. Where Yale Law School seemed willing to do almost anything to accommodate a student they had deemed worthy of admittance, Stanford seemed annoyed that you were doing anything but calling to accept. In the end, I figured out that if I deferred my Stanford admittance by a year and spent next year at Yale, I could then double count so many of the classes I took during my subsequent two-year stay at Stanford that I could complete the whole thing in less time than a traditional JD/MBA at a single institution. By doing the bicoastal joint degree I was basically trading in one year of New Haven for just under two years of Palo Alto. I had been to both places and knew this was a good trade. The MBA was an extra door prize for thinking it all up.

My first, and at the time I assumed my last, experience with investment banking was this summer job in 1987 at Bankers Trust in London at which I now found myself being harangued about chickens. Many of my best friends from Trinity had moved to London and I was very much in the market for a lucrative job that would bring me across the Atlantic. Bankers Trust was at the time desperately trying to break into the top tier of investment banking and was noticeably more flexible with respect to summer employment than the actual top tier of investment banking. In addition, the bank had in place incredibly generous expatriate pay packages—presumably designed for commercial bankers assigned to unattractive developing-country outposts—which it inexplicably offered to summer associates working in London. In addition to $1,000/week, I got a beautiful one-bedroom apartment on chic Sloane Street complete with cleaning services and unlimited phone usage, as well as a $50/day tax-free per diem. Life was very good indeed.

Work, on the other hand, was not very interesting. Margaret Thatcher's "big bang" deregulating London's financial markets in 1986 had caused a gold-rush mentality among U.S. institutions seeking to capitalize on the perceived market opportunity. Permitted for the first time to join the London Stock Exchange, most of the big names in U.S. commercial and investment banking either established or dramatically expanded their London operations. In these early days, however, the bang was largely a bust.

Although the new rules allowed foreign institutions to provide a range of financial services to potential U.K. clients, mergers and acquisitions (M&A) was initially viewed as among the most attractive profit opportunities. An M&A advisor represents a company in either selecting and pursuing an acquisition target or selling a subsidiary, line of business, or the entire company for the highest price. Since most companies spend their time running their operations, the notion is that bringing in an expert who knows all the tricks of the M&A trade to effectively execute a transaction is a good investment and avoids management distraction. The M&A advisor typically receives a small percentage of the transaction size as a fee, but this can run into the many millions of dollars, particularly for a large deal. What made this business theoretically attractive for a new entrant in the market was that it really didn't involve many people or much capital. No big trading floor is required and you don't need a big balance sheet. A handful of smooth, well-paid, professional-looking individuals are all that is required to set up shop.

The trouble with this theory was that, culturally, British executives had no tradition of paying for advice in connection with buying and selling companies—and certainly not at the level of fees customary in the U.S. market. And the overwhelming share of advisory fees that were available went to the major U.K. financial houses that had served these local businesses for generations. So the U.S. newcomers had the double challenge of convincing these U.K. companies both that they needed an advisor at all in these situations and that they should jettison their long-established relationships, often cemented by complex social and personal bonds, in favor of the invading Yanks.

Bankers Trust had a tiny piece of the already small share of M&A activity split among the U.S. players. The result was that M&A bankers there spent most of their time thinking up deal ideas, cold calling companies, and occasionally getting the opportunity to formally "pitch" their services, although almost always unsuccessfully. Investment banks "pitching" business usually bring along a prop to assist them in their efforts. This central item in the lives of investment bankers is known as a "pitch book."

Even today, whether in London or elsewhere, the mindless production of fat pitch books is probably the single least attractive aspect of the investment banking job to young analysts and associates. Pitch books typically contain many pages and are for some reason blue (hence the inter-changeable phrase, "blue book"). The guts of the contents include (1) attractive summaries of public information regarding the potential client, its competitors, its industry and any companies they might be encour-aged to buy, (2) current "boiler plate" pages describing any investment banking product they may be willing to purchase—"The Current Merger Environment," "The Current Equity Environment," "Recent Deals We Have Done," etc., and finally, (3) investment banking credentials complete with attractive color logos of companies previously represented and "league tables" that purport to show that whoever is presenting the credentials has num-ber one market share in whatever product is being pitched at the time. Some of the most entertaining reading in any pitch book are the tortured foot-notes to these league tables that allow anybody with a semistraight face to claim they are number one: "includes transactions over $500 closed since January 1, XXXX," "excludes transactions over $500 closed since January 1, XXXX," "league tables are for transactions other than Comcast/AT&T and AOL/Time Warner," and so on. Many an analyst has spent many a sleepless night cutting and recutting the data to come up with the least ridiculous way to demonstrate number one market share. They could be forgiven for their occasional temptation to throw up their hands and sim-ply include an omnibus league table page for all products, for all times that would simply read: WE HAVE 100% MARKET SHARE OF ALL DEALS WE DID.

Oh yeah, I almost forgot. Sometimes, though by no means always, among the reams of paper squashed between the two blue pieces of cardboard, is an actual actionable strategic idea. And very, very occasionally this idea is thoughtful or original. The most precious commodity, of course, is when it is both.

Ironically, client surveys consistently yield an insight that should probably be less surprising than it always seems to be among investment banking management: pitch books are no more fun to read than they are to produce. The reasons clients hate these books are pretty self-evident.

Less obvious is why midlevel and even some more senior bankers con-tinue to insist on producing them. The short answer is simple: stage fright. The psychic experience of showing up to a meeting without a book is akin to the stage actor's experience the first time he performs a piece "off book." It's just you and your mind and the audience and it can be terrify-ing. For the actor, the audience consists of an all-knowing director and peers whose approval he craves. For the banker, the audience is a CEO or other executive who probably forgot more about his own business than the banker can ever pretend to know and who has probably recently sat through multiple presentations by other competing bankers. And a banker's reputation and success "in the market" is ultimately determined in large part by the combined effect of the multiple impressions made on company executives at just such meetings. So it should not be that surprising that the inexperienced and insecure insist on clinging tightly to their fat pitch books or that they surround themselves at meetings in a protective coating of junior acolytes whose specific roles often remain a mystery to the company executive (size of contingent usually closely follows size of pitch books on the list of most frequent client complaints).

Every year or so—usually after commissioning an expensive client survey—investment banks go on the warpath against fat pitch books. Maximum page counts are imposed, spot checks of books by banking bureaucrats are instituted. The results are necessarily as insignificant as they are short lived. Under such a regime the impact on a seven-section, 70-page pitch book is invariably that it becomes a three-section, 30-page pitch book —with four appendices adding 40 pages provided as a "leave behind" for the client.

At the time I was at Bankers Trust in London, I of course did not appreciate all of these nuances. I just knew that producing pitch books was not particularly stimulating. The investment banking group there was run by a slim, handsome, and elegant Brit named Colin Keer. He was always perfectly coiffed and had a detached air of bemused disbelief about the band of noisy American bankers who had descended upon his previously genteel world. Yet he seemed to get the joke, never got ruffled, and displayed surprising flashes of generosity and humanity that to a summer associate were a source of comfort that things would never get too out of control.

Andrew Capitman was Keer's point person for Mergers and Acquisitions, the group to which I had been assigned. I don't remember if Capitman actually always had an unlit cigar in his mouth as he barked out orders, but the caricaturish nature of his personality was such that that is indeed how I remember him. Seeing Keer and Capitman together, which didn't happen that often, had a Laurel-and-Hardy quality.

My personal introduction to pitch books came more or less simultaneously with first hearing the words "Hillsdown Holdings."

"Meeting them next week," Capitman had responded to my unconvincing show of interest. "Put a book together."

"Company on the move," he shouted over his shoulder as he walked away. "Let's get going." He disappeared around a corner.

It turned out that Hillsdown was a very sensible company for an American investment banker to target. In the financially conservative United Kingdom, Hillsdown had been described as "the country's most acquisitive company."[1] Founded in 1975 by a London lawyer and a butcher-turned-investor focused on buying undervalued companies on the cheap, Hillsdown went public a decade later. The broad-based conglomerate purchased well over 100 companies in the next three years.

Although the part of Hillsdown that dealt with chicken, Buxted Poultry Ltd., was not its largest division, Capitman was delighted to have gotten the meeting. And he clearly wanted us to have something important to say when we got there.

Chickens. I didn't know a lot about chickens. It was my favorite meat. I knew that people who preferred white meat were discriminated against at KFC through the imposition of an unfair surcharge. I also vaguely remembered that a great-grandfather in Poland killed chickens for a living and that my grandmother bragged about this to neighbors with fathers who held less lofty positions. The sense she gave me was that chicken killer (in Yiddish a *shoichet*) was just below chief rabbi of Warsaw in terms of holiness and prestige in the Jewish community. But this pretty much exhausted my knowledge of, and indeed, interest in chickens.

Where to begin? I went to the library and immersed myself in all things poultry. It turns out that there were quite a few companies that involved themselves with performing a variety of activities on chicken carcasses. But which company and which activity Hillsdown should target was far from clear to me. Buxted Poultry already appeared to do most things one could think of to dead chickens. But since Buxted seemed to focus on murdering British chickens, it seemed logical to suggest opportunities to do the same back home in America.

I kept reading lots of equity research reports about the publicly traded U.S. chicken killers and noticed that the post-mortem protocols of these companies fell into two main categories—cutting them up in various ways to be sold as chicken parts and performing "processing" procedures that turn unspecified body parts into frozen patties, nuggets, and strips (we'll call this latter activity PNS). The research reports described companies with PNS as "value-added" processors, which apparently justified higher valuations.

By this time, there were only a couple of days to go before our meeting at Buxted, so I went to Capitman's office to give him the results of my research. He leaned back in his chair and listened patiently as I described my recent investigations. When I was finished, a silence filled the room. "That's it?" he cried in disbelief, moving his head and arms threateningly toward me across his desk. I wracked my mind for some incremental "nuggets" of minutia about chickens and the companies that kill them and frantically began to spout them out.

"No, no, no," he cut me off, standing and waving his arms as if to swat away my irrelevant words.

I stopped and we just stared at each other. Then a flash of realization crossed his face and he slumped back in his chair. "Oh my God," his expression seemed to be saying. "The meeting is in two days and I'm dealing with an idiot." Finally, he leaned forward slowly and said, carefully enunciating each one syllable word as if to a child.

"What . . . should . . . they . . . BUY?" The first three words were spoken softly, but the last exploded from his mouth as his head moved a few more inches toward me.

Despite my business school education, I had never really thought about actually valuing a company. I knew a lot about these chicken companies, but really never considered whether any represented a particular bargain from a value perspective.

"Oh sure," I lied. "I'm bringing that tomorrow. I just wanted you to know how I was thinking about the industry."

He sat back in his chair, eyeing me carefully. I was pretty sure the jig was up.

"I wanna see it first thing," he said, waving me away and returning to his *Financial Times*.

I returned to the research reports and desperately focused on the sections headed "Valuation." Almost all the reports for all of the companies had some version of a "buy" recommendation, but none of the reports compared one company favorably or unfavorably to another. The valuation metric for all of these companies seemed to be a "price-earnings ratio" or P/E. The P/E basically told you at the current stock price, how many dollars (or pounds) an investor is paying for every dollar (or pound) of earnings. I had no idea how earnings were actually calculated or what the differences were between different countries' accounting methods, but I did know that a higher P/E meant more expensive and a lower P/E meant less expensive. This, at least, was a start.

I also remembered that analysts said that companies with more PNS deserved to be more expensive. Then it hit me. I might not know anything about valuation or accounting or, if truth be told, chickens. But I had been a math major. (O.K., it was a joint degree along with philosophy and a minor in theater, but I remembered the basics.) And I certainly knew how to put points on a two-dimensional graph. So if you had six chicken companies each with a different P/E (the y axis) and each with a different percentage of revenues (the x axis) coming from PNS, I could certainly chart a graph with six data points. Using the spreadsheet available at the time, Lotus 123, I could print out a very attractive graph with the bold heading: The Price of Poultry.

Then I noticed something wonderful about Lotus 123. If you highlighted the six different (x,y) coordinates on my little graph you could click on an icon called "regression." Regression in this context is a statistical term that enables you to draw a straight line on the graph that best approximates where the six data points are. In other words, it gives you the equation of the straight line that is closer to those six points than any other straight line and tells you on average (at least as far as these six companies are concerned) how much incremental P/E is attributable to every incremental percentage of PNS. The idea was simply to find the mathematical relationship between how a chicken company was valued and how much of its chicken was PNS.

Once Lotus drew my straight line I was home free, even if it was 3:00 AM by the time I figured all this out. We could now claim to have developed the magic formula that connected what the shares of chicken companies were really worth to what they did with those chickens. All the companies with a data point above the line were "expensive"—the price was high for the level of PNS you were getting. And the ones below the line were a bargain! I found the company represented by the point with the greatest distance below the line and declared it the biggest bargain in the global poultry firmament.

Now, of course, I knew this was mostly nonsense. Lots of other factors can impact even a chicken company's P/E other than PNS. Is management good? Is there too much debt? Is there a big lawsuit pending? What accounting method do they use? And objectively "cheap" or not, an entire other set of questions, both operational and financial, affected whether a particular company would make sense for Hillsdown to buy. But the desire to get an hour or two of sleep before presenting my results to Capitman allowed me to convince myself that it was good enough.

The next morning I stopped by Capitman's office with the results of my labors. He looked up from his *Financial Times* warily and said nothing as I approached. I presented my page and took him through the thinking and calculations. As I explained, I saw the tension in his body subside and I even think I saw the beginnings of a smile. He went back to his *Financial Times* without looking up. "I wanna see the whole book before I go home tonight," he said waving me away.

Now as a practical matter, this single page was all we had to say even of arguable importance to the CEO of Buxted, who we were to meet. But the rest of my day was spent bulking up the book with Capitman's biography, laudatory descriptive material about Bankers Trust in general and its previous work in the food industry, several-page overviews of each of the six companies including Hillsdown itself, a selection of relevant research reports on the companies and industry, a summary of how all the six companies traded in the public markets and how their stock prices had performed, and descriptions of previous M&A transactions in the food industry. And voila, a page becomes a full-fledged, 50-plus-page pitch book.

As it turned out, Capitman had never met David Newton, CEO of Buxted, but had cold called him possibly after reading some quote in the *Financial Times* suggesting they were planning to be acquisitive. "We've been doing some very innovative thinking about your industry," I overheard Capitman say to him as he confirmed our meeting, "very proprietary stuff." In general, analysts and associates, and certainly summer associates, are thrilled to have the opportunity to actually attend a meeting at which material they worked on is presented. But frankly, I was afraid Newton might roll over in hysterical fits of laughter. I imagined 101 reasons why the company we had identified as too cheap not to buy might be a complete nonstarter for practical reasons obvious to anyone with even passing familiarity with the industry. I imagined the deadly glance across the table from Capitman that would ensue as a precursor to my permanent exile to some unattractive corner of Bankers Trust for the balance of the summer.

The meeting began as I watched Capitman perform the investment banker's rendition of the old parlor trick perfected by gypsies and fortune tellers. Just as Professor Marvel drew the runaway Dorothy out with stolen glances at the contents of her bag in *The Wizard of Oz,* Capitman drew out the client, using whatever tidbits he could from Newton's banter to feign increasing familiarity with the subject matter, then used that to draw out even more information. The point was to create the sense of intimacy necessary to gather as much information as possible before moving ahead. Once Capitman had learned everything he could from Newton and convinced himself that what we were proposing would not be a complete anathema to what Hillsdown was considering strategically, he dramatically produced a copy of our thick pitch book.

"I think I mentioned on the phone that we have been doing some very serious thinking about your sector," he said conspiratorially, still holding the book closely as if unsure whether to share its valuable contents. "We see a window of opportunity here for those few companies who are in a position to be consolidators," he said as he slowly pushed the precious cargo across the table.

"The question is not whether but who, what, and when," said Capitman with an apparent self-confidence that left me breathless. I wanted to just open the book to The Page and flee the room to await the reaction.

"What we've done here is identified the what. Who and when frankly will be determined by which of you has the vision and the courage to move first. The reason we are here is that we think it should be you and we think it should be soon."

I would later be able to recognize this as a version of what investment bankers call the "Dare to be Great" speech. But at the time I was stunned. He had never met this guy before. And he hadn't even told him the idea yet, which I for one still wasn't sure made any sense at all. Yet, so far anyway, Newton seemed hooked. Capitman began going through the book with remarkable self-assurance, using each page to draw out Newton more. Then we got to The Page. I literally held my breath. Capitman explained. There was a silence.

"Interesting," Newton said thoughtfully. I saw Capitman try to stop himself from smiling, unsuccessfully.

In the cab on the way back to the office, Capitman was almost giddy with joy. He barely acknowledged my presence and appeared to be talking to himself. "That," he said with emphasis to no one in particular, "was a great meeting." He could barely contain himself in the cab and bounded out the moment we arrived back in the city, presumably to relate his success to anyone who would listen. What a strange business, I thought to myself. I am definitely not doing this for a living.

As far as I know, although Hillsdown continued to make acquisitions over the ensuing years, including a number of chicken-related transactions, the company never hired Bankers Trust to advise them. In 1998, Hillsdown would split itself up, spinning off its prepared foods (including the PNS part of Buxted) and homebuilding divisions and selling a number of other operations. And Bankers Trust finally did get payday from Hillsdown. The year after the split-up, Bankers Trust financed Texas-based buyout shop Hicks Muse in its successful billion-dollar takeover of the company after troubles in its remaining chicken operations left it vulnerable. In 2004, Hicks Muse took the company public again, this time under the name Premier Foods, having already sold off or closed the chicken businesses.

Toward the end of the summer there was a fair amount of tension among the summer associates as to how many of us would be given offers for permanent positions. One day, Keer called me into his office.

"I'm sure you know that you have a real aptitude for this," Keer began matter-of-factly. "And of course you would be welcome back should you decide that is what you want to do."

"But," he continued, "I don't think you really have your heart in it. And there is nothing worse than doing something you don't have your heart in." I thought maybe he was speaking from experience.

"Take your time. As I say, you will always be welcome here. And let me know if I can be of any assistance."

That was it. At the time I did not fully appreciate the unusual generosity of Colin's gesture in giving me an offer in this way. Later I would learn investment banks and investment bankers rarely offer anything without asking for something in return. Many banks would insist that summer associates promise to accept an offer should one be proffered. And at every step along the way in one's banking career, with each bonus or promotion, there is an expectation of some explicit act of fealty to the institution as a whole or the individual actually delivering whatever benefit is being bestowed. Although you may think you actually earned it, there seems to be an irresistible urge by the bank to take one more pound of flesh. Maybe it's just the nature of the business—everything in banking is, after all, a negotiation.

Looking back on that summer, I realize that I missed a number of important lessons that I would only appreciate years later. In much the same way

I had pursued an MBA in part to avoid being looked down on by those who had one, I had taken the summer job in part to confirm my preconceptions about the shallowness of investment banking and to be able to say that it was my own choice to pursue a different profession. And I saw what I wanted to see. To be sure, the marketing aspects of all service professions are easy enough to parody. The "spin" involved in any sales job has a comic aspect that takes on an even more absurd quality when the financial stakes are as high as in investment banking—"Take my company, please." "You can't afford not to buy this." Because of Bankers Trust's weak market position in the United Kingdom I observed much more selling than advising. But even the fact that the CEO of Buxted Poultry would take our meeting at all should have tipped me off to the role a well-placed, thoughtful investment banker can play. And that someone as sensitive and intelligent as Keer would have been attracted to the job at all equally should have given me pause.

But this was not something I was ready to seriously consider at the time. In addition to his kindness, Keer had correctly sensed my lack of interest in business generally. I was still much more interested in policy making rather than money making. Even when at Stanford Business School we were encouraged to read the entire *Wall Street Journal*, I couldn't bring myself to do so. I would flip straight to the Politics and Policy page and on Fridays look at Washington Wire, but I found the rest of the paper heavy going. What Keer couldn't appreciate without knowing me better, but I would eventually come to understand, is that investment banking can offer more intellectual fulfillment to the policy wonk than most government jobs. But having accumulated more than enough ammunition to dismiss the profession as intrinsically unworthy, I smugly returned home from my very profitable summer to complete my final year of graduate school, confident that I would never again be an investment banker.

I would later sadly learn that Keer died far too young. But in researching for this book, I discovered that there was a happy ending to his story. Prior to his death, he had done something investment bankers rarely do—quit at the top of their game to pursue their true love. For Keer, this meant starting his own business as a landscape and garden designer in 1992 at the age of 42. As a senior industry headhunter observed at the time, "His quitting came as a shock to the industry. He had the courage to bail out and do something that was likely to be more fun."[2]

· 2 ·

THE ACCIDENTAL
INVESTMENT BANKER

ECAL MATTER in the coffee pots in the first-class galley. A friend over in corporate communications called with this update on the latest innovative negotiating tactic being employed by the unions. Seven years after leaving my little summer job behind, I was working in Chicago as director of International Affairs for United Airlines, having recently left a position as a Washington lobbyist at a firm run by Stuart Eizenstat, President Carter's domestic policy chief. My official role was to direct a staff responsible for securing and protecting United's international route and facility rights. My unofficial role was as aide-de-camp for CEO Stephen Wolf and his longtime consigliere, General Counsel Lawrence Nagin. Although I loved the job, unfortunately, after barely a year we began to negotiate with the unions over the possible sale of the airline in return for a variety of wage and work concessions to make the airline more competitive. By the spring of 1994, these negotiations were reaching a crescendo, as the coffee incident and others like it made clear to me.

My fondness for the job stemmed from the fact that in no other industry did strategy require as thoughtful an understanding of the interplay between law, policy, politics, and finance. Although the industry had been deregulated domestically, internationally it was still subject to a complex web of bilateral international agreements. And at home, the financial impact of deregulation heightened tensions with unions and raised a variety of contentious issues with local airports, constituencies, and politicians.

I wrote speeches, prepared briefing books, and traveled with Wolf all over the world to meet government and industry leaders.

Wolf and his team had long been vilified by the unions. Despite having grown the airline into the premier international carrier by tripling the number of international destinations served on three continents, union leaders never forgave Wolf for his very public stance that the industry status quo was not sustainable. It came as a surprise to no one that any deal would be conditioned on the departure of Wolf and Nagin. Although I was free to remain in my official capacity, the most exciting part of my job—the unofficial one—would be over. Neither Wolf nor Nagin knew what they would do next and I really had no idea what else I might do.

I was still reeling from the latest culinary development from the front lines, when the phone rang again. I braced myself for even more grotesque news, but was pleasantly surprised to find my old law school classmate Kevin Czinger on the line. I had met Kevin ten years earlier on the first day of law school in 1984. We were assigned to the same "small group" section that took all their classes together and became friendly right away. A diminutive former Yale football star, Kevin was legendary for his intensity and after law school had gone to work for Rudy Giuliani when he was a prosecutor. There, he befriended fellow Yale Law School alumnus Arthur Liman while they were on opposite sides of United States vs. GAF Corporation, the first major insider trading case (Liman lost at trial, won on appeal). Liman encouraged Kevin to go into investment banking and arranged introductions to then co-chiefs of Goldman Sachs, Steve Friedman (former Cornell wrestling star) and Robert Rubin. Kevin was then referred to John Thornton, a controversial young partner who was building Goldman's European investment banking business out of London.

By the time Kevin called me, he had been at Goldman for two years, and had been working in London directly for Thornton for 18 months following a six-month training program in New York. We had talked about investment banking before and Kevin knew I was not really interested. Two things had changed. On my side, I knew life for those loyal to the former regime at United would be unpleasant once we handed the keys to the kingdom over to the coming dictatorship of the proletariat. On Kevin's side, Thornton had now asked him to help build the European media effort by hiring a handful of smart, hungry, young professionals from the outside. And once given a task, Kevin did not like to fail. Thornton specifically wanted individuals who would not have been tainted by indoctrination into Goldman's insular culture, whose epicenter was New York, so I fit the bill.

"Kevin, I could have become a banker when I left school six years ago. I tried it, I didn't like it, I'm doing other things. Why would I start over now doing something I never wanted to do in the first place?"

"This is different," Kevin insisted.

"Admit it. That shit is B-O-R-I-N-G," I protested.

"I'm telling you, this guy is the real thing. It's media. We've got an open playing field. We'll do it together. It'll be fun." He rattled off the logic, hitting a different hot button with every sentence.

Media was certainly more interesting than chickens. I was a theater and movie addict and a frustrated actor, having put my thespian aspirations to one side after I failed to get into Yale Drama School after college. Although I loved Kevin, the idea of working with him every day was a little, well, scary.

"But Kevin, Goldman? You know I'll never fit in." I knew enough about the Goldman culture from my business school days. Rigid, hierarchical, homogeneous. It attracted lots of ex-military, jocks, and Catholics (Kevin was all three) who were used to keeping their head down and following orders. Taking it for the team and all that stuff. Endless rounds of interviews where everyone you meet has a veto. This was not me. This was not going to happen.

"You don't understand, man," Kevin pressed, "this guy Thornton thinks all that's bullshit. He really wants to build something cool here. He owns this office. He'll protect you. They won't be able to touch you. We can do our own thing and just go for it. We'll give you credit for some of your other experience so you won't be starting over. I'm telling you, it will be fun.

"Just take a goddamn meeting with the guy," he shouted.

"Fine," I shouted back. What did I have to lose? It was looking less and less likely that Steve and Larry would have something lined up by the time we actually turned the company over to the unions. I liked media. I liked London. I had no particular other prospects. What the hell.

When I arrived in London on the appointed day, Kevin was in Hong Kong, so there were no familiar faces at Goldman's elegant modern offices. These sit on Fleet Street, discreetly hidden behind the façade of the former headquarters of a now-defunct newspaper. The actual address is known as Peterborough Court, and it is said that the Goldman taxi rank there is the busiest in London after Heathrow. The date on which

Goldman switched its taxi account is still referred to as "Black Tuesday" by the company that lost the business.

I was brought to a large conference room on the ninth floor, which was the top floor and served as a conference centre for meetings with outsiders. The meeting was scheduled for 6:00 PM, but Thornton did not arrive until after 7:00 PM. When he finally bounded in and shook my hand I was struck by his youth and intensity. Thornton was only 40 at the time and his entire body literally twitched with raw energy. He was a handsome man, with a slight paunch and roundish, bulbous nose that was vaguely reminiscent of W. C. Fields. When he spoke, his words were clipped as if he were annoyed that communication had to be slowed down by the convention of speech. He had a slightly comical involuntary tic, almost Rodney Dangerfield–like, of continuously readjusting his collar and pushing back the flop of brown hair that drooped over the right side of his forehead.

At close to 9:00 PM Thornton left as suddenly as he had entered, quickly shaking my hand and mentioning that Kevin would be back to me with the terms of the offer in the next few days. I sat back in my chair in the empty conference room and looked out over the darkened London skyline.

"Offer?" I thought to myself, "What about the other interviews? What exactly is this job, anyway?"

I certainly didn't learn anything about the job from my two hours with Thornton. We didn't discuss anything about investment banking, so I wasn't reduced to trotting out my chicken story. It was a rat-a-tat of questions going back to high school and what I studied at college. If he stumbled on a thread that interested him, he pulled on it until there was no more. As soon as a topic did not hold him, he was on to the next with no polite segue. In the end, it seemed that his decision-making was concise and simple: "I'm looking for smart guys who get it. Steve Wolf and Stuart Eizenstat are smart guys who get it and probably want smart guys who get it to work for them. You worked for them and they seemed satisfied. So let's get started." The rest of the conversation seemed to have less to do with me or the job, but rather seemed designed for him to soak up information about a variety of topics he found interesting.

As promised, Kevin faxed me a contract a few days later back in Chicago. At the time, I did not know what machinations were required to get Goldman's Human Resources department to allow the letter to be sent.[1] Kevin wanted me to experience a bureaucracy-free institution. The terms were generous enough. Through the end of the fiscal year, which ended

November 30, I would be paid a prorated portion of $225,000. This was more than double my current salary. After that it was up to me, but Kevin suggested salaries go up about $100,000 each year. The contract said they did not need to consider me for promotion from associate to vice president until 1996, which I took to mean I was being given two years of credit for my time as a lobbyist and airline executive. Frankly, it was so much more money than I ever thought about making, I didn't even try to negotiate. I just signed.

Steve and Larry seemed a little peeved that I had not waited to see what they were going to do before committing myself. And when I explained the job, they seemed as surprised as I was that it had been offered. A few weeks later, as the bittersweet July 12 shareholder meeting where we formally turned the company over approached, Larry told me that Steve wanted me to meet his car in the basement of the Chicago Fairmont Hotel and take him up to the meeting. I knew that meant I was forgiven.

The shareholder meeting was on a Thursday and I was to start at Goldman in London on Monday. After saying goodbye at the hotel, I went back out to headquarters to clean out my desk. As I walked past the executive suite, the scene looked like something out of the French Revolution. The glass walls separating the suite from the outside had been taken down and union members roamed freely through the offices. I walked by Steve's office and saw a mechanic taking a stapler as others went through his desk drawers. It was not an auspicious beginning.

Later, I got a call from a *New York Times* reporter who was writing an article on the new era of employee ownership and participation in American industry and wanted to use the United deal as the centerpiece. I gently tried to suggest that the unique airline industry history and entrenched animosity not only between management and employees but among employee groups made it a poor case study. He cut the conversation short and the *Times* ran a multipart series lauding employee ownership as the ultimate panacea to both competitive and industrial relations challenges facing the business world. United's subsequent bankruptcy suggests that the issues facing the industry are somewhat more complex.

Flying over the Atlantic, I was glad to get away from the tension surrounding the last weeks leading up to the transfer of power at United. And I was looking forward to starting a new life in London, seeing old friends, and learning about the media industry. But I really had no idea what to expect from Goldman Sachs or what they really expected of me. On Monday morning, I would begin to find out.

· 3 ·

AN EMPIRE OF ITS OWN

WHAT INVESTMENT BANKERS do has been the source of much continuing confusion. This confusion has been exacerbated over time by a variety of factors: the shifting lines between commercial and investment banking, the changing roles and importance of various functions and divisions within investment banks and the overall secrecy of these institutions. That said, a few basics are more or less intact. Investment banks are broadly divided between "corporate finance" and "sales and trading" operations.

The corporate finance function is what most people think of when they close their eyes and imagine an investment banker who interacts with corporate executives. It is also the focus of this book and the world that I was immersed in when I arrived in London in 1994. Corporate finance bankers assist corporations in two ways. They raise money, which is known as "financing." They provide advice on "deals," which generally falls under the rubric of mergers and acquisitions. Sometimes investment bankers do both at the same time, as when advice is provided on an acquisition and financing is arranged to complete the deal.

The money raised comes from third parties—rich individuals, mutual funds, insurance companies, pension funds—and can come from the sale of anything from an initial public offering of equity to junk bonds. The process by which an investment bank represents a company in finding investors to whom it can sell a particular securities offering at a particular price is called "underwriting." Although the term "underwriting" may suggest that, if the investment bank fails to find buyers, it would be obliged to take up the slack and buy the securities itself, this is rarely the case. An underwriting investment bank is generally only required to make its "best efforts" to find a home for the securities. The M&A advice can be on an acquisition, as we were attempting to get hired to do for Hillsdown, a divestiture or a sale or merger of an entire company.

The sales and trading function, of which much less will be said here, is focused on buying and selling the securities in the companies covered by the corporate finance function. The clients, however, are not these corporations but institutional investors and rich individuals seeking an attractive return on their holdings. Part of the tension of operating both sales and trading and corporate finance businesses is that the respective customers often have structurally inconsistent objectives—investors want the highest possible returns and issuers want the cheapest possible capital. The recent prosecutions of investment banks over their use of equity research were based on the theory that issuers were being favored over investors and that the Corporate Finance Divisions were manipulating the supposedly objective advice being distributed through the Sales and Trading Divisions.

Whether working in sales and trading or corporate finance, investment bankers are primarily middlemen between parties on two sides of a transaction. This is equally true whether an equity trader is facilitating a trade in securities between two institutional investors, a sales person is marketing a new equity offering or an M&A banker is managing the sale of a corporate subsidiary. In each case, they serve as "agents" rather than "principals" in these deals.

Many of the other investment banking controversies of recent years have stemmed from the decision by most investment banks to cross the line from agent to principal to a greater or lesser degree. The use of proprietary trading strategies, where the investment bank puts its own capital at risk, usually developed in windowless rooms by rocket scientists of various stripe, has resulted in sales and trading accounting for the majority of the profits of some investment banks during certain periods. Although there is nothing wrong with this per se, it has raised questions as to whether these profits come at the expense of other investors. And those who analyze the public securities of investment banks are loath to value these profits in the same way as business that is more predictable and recurring in nature. On the corporate finance side, the decision by most firms to raise principal equity funds that would directly compete with both corporate clients and other funds in making acquisitions for their own account has raised questions of client loyalty, confidentiality, and conflicts of interest. In recent years, a number of large investment banks, including Morgan Stanley and Credit Suisse First Boston, have announced plans to spin off their principal equity funds into independent entities to address these concerns.

The mere "agency" function of an investment bank does not mean that these institutions do not take any financial risk. While disclaimers on the prospectuses issued in connection with a debt or equity offering may say otherwise, an investment bank implicitly endorses a company's prospects when they market its securities.

Similarly, although to a lesser extent, boards and managements rely on investment banks' advice before agreeing to an M&A transaction. On occasion, unhappy investors and corporate clients have successfully sued— or the SEC successfully pursued enforcement actions against—investment banks for failing to have adequately protected those investors' interests. The most recent examples are the massive $1.5 billion judgment Ron Perelman won against Morgan Stanley for failing to provide adequate disclosure in its sale of Sunbeam, and Citigroup agreeing to pay $2.65 billion to settle claims by purchasers of stock and bonds issued by the now-defunct WorldCom. And, even in the absence of private or government lawsuits, if a particular investment bank is too often associated with situations that go bad soon after its involvement, it makes getting hired next time more difficult.

As my discussion of pitch books earlier suggested, the pecking order among investment banks is in part driven by "league tables." Several third-party sources put these rankings together and they show which firm was involved with the most transactions of a particular kind during a particular period. Although this sounds objective enough, they are easy enough to manipulate to find some basis upon which any of a dozen firms might claim they are in the top three. For instance within the M&A league tables, you can count the number of transactions or the total size of transactions, you can focus on domestic or all global deals or just deals above a certain size or in certain industries. And of course you can pick the time period to suit your particular need. But the firms themselves know full well who the leaders are for particular products. And the overall market leaders are those who consistently appear at the top of the league tables for the most profitable products.

The two most profitable investment banking products are M&A advice and leading (IPOs—initial public offerings, or the first sale of stock to the investing public by a private company). The profitability of M&A comes from how little overhead is required to provide such services. The profitability of IPOs comes from the fact that investment banks can charge as much as 7 percent of the money raised in return for finding institutional investors with whom to place the offering. (This percentage that the banks keep is known as the "spread" in financing transactions.) It remains a mystery to many—including the Justice Department, which has investigated whether there is collusion among investment banks—how underwriters have been able to maintain this fee scale for IPOs even as spreads have tightened considerably for many other products, including all forms of debt securities and even follow-on equity offerings, as a result of competitive pressure.

When I arrived in London in 1994, investment banks were just finding their sea legs again after emerging from a recession in 1990–1991 that had produced widespread layoffs. Morgan Stanley and Goldman Sachs were the overall market leaders, although Goldman appeared to be in the ascendant, as Morgan was weakened not only by the recent downturn but also by the loss of many of its most productive partners after its own IPO in 1986. The cultures of these two firms were also quite different at this point.

Probably just behind these two market leaders was Merrill Lynch. Merrill was the only major investment bank to have built a large institutional business from roots in the retail brokerage business. As a result, it was sometimes looked down on by its peers. But by the early 1990s Merrill was consistently the biggest overall underwriter of securities. Unfortunately, regulatory and market developments that had begun to squeeze industry margins were particularly hard on Merrill given its market positioning. Prior to 1975, brokerage firms benefited from fat government-established commission rates on all trades. When, in 1975, the Security Exchange Commission (SEC) eliminated fixed commissions on stock trades, it had the result of squeezing out the smaller players and allowing market leaders like Merrill to consolidate their market position. But it also put pressure on the profit margins of underwriting and trading operations. Other rules subsequently enacted by the SEC also made it easier, and cheaper, for certain companies to sell securities directly to institutions without the expensive help of an investment bank.

With its bread-and-butter business under margin pressure, Merrill focused on building more profitable businesses like M&A. When in 1988, the firm appointed 35-year-old Jack Levy head of its M&A effort, competitors were not particularly concerned. Merrill's core financing franchise put its bankers in touch with corporate treasurers and CFOs, not the CEOs that make strategic M&A decisions. But after luring a number of bankers away from his competitors, the dapper 6'2" Levy began to make progress. In 1996 Merrill would finally take the top spot in the U.S. M&A league tables, although its weakness internationally would never allow it to challenge Goldman or Morgan for the top global position. So euphoric was Levy over this long-in-coming milestone that he produced a year-end video for the troops starring himself doing a creditable Jerry Maguire imitation screaming "Show me the money!"[1]

The rest of the investment banking landscape of the early 1990s was occupied by a number of other firms either on their way up or down, or who managed to distinguish themselves as consistent leading "niche" players in a particular product. Among niche product leaders, two notable examples were First Boston in M&A and Donaldson Lufkin and Jenrette (DLJ) in "junk bonds."

Although already a full-service investment bank, during the buyout boom of the 1980s, the team of Bruce Wasserstein and Joe Perella established First Boston as a viable alternative to Morgan Stanley or Goldman Sachs for strategic M&A advice. The short, ill-kempt, and egomaniacal Wasserstein was perhaps the most well-known banker of that era. But the two left to start their own boutique advisory firm, Wasserstein, Perella in 1988, precipitating the decision by First Boston's European affiliate, Credit Suisse, to merge the firms (CSFB)—and consolidate decision-making power in Switzerland. Despite the departure of the founders of that franchise, the rechristened CSFB would occasionally still break into the top three of global M&A advisors through the early 1990s.

DLJ was founded by its named partners in 1959 and focused primarily on underwriting smaller, less-established companies with greater growth prospects than the blue chip corporations the more established investment banks served. As late as the 1980s, DLJ was still a relatively modest firm, although it had made a successful early push into the controversial areas of establishing principal equity funds with its own capital. But after the bankruptcy of Michael Milken's Drexel Burnham in 1990, DLJ would emerge by the mid-1990s to take the mantle of leading junk bond house.

Junk bonds are issued by companies that are too small, too young, too leveraged, or otherwise seen as too risky to attract more traditional and less expensive forms of financing. Junk bonds are defined as those that receive a rating from Moody's or S&P that designates them as "speculative" credits as contrasted to the "investment grade" ratings earned by larger, less leveraged, more established companies. In addition to carrying a higher interest rate, junk bond issuers pay a higher "spread" to the investment bank that places the bonds, making this the most profitable part of the debt finance business. Lending to blue chip "investment grade" companies, by contrast, has become a commodity business with very narrow spreads. But, despite the intrinsic profitability of junk, the investment banking leaders liked to be associated with names like Ford and AT&T rather than the cash-strapped Chrysler or the start-up McCaw Cellular. This conflicted attitude created an opening for a niche player to take the leading position in this attractive business.

What sends an investment banking firm into decline is typically a major scandal, a capital crisis, a mass exodus of productive partners or, usually, some combination of the three. Salomon Brothers, using street smarts and creative structuring particularly in the fixed income markets, had clawed its way to the top of the overall financing league tables in the 1980s. The downside of its out-of-control trading culture would be well documented in Michael Lewis' *Liar's Poker*, in which the author wrote about his experience as a young bond salesman in the years leading up to the crash of 1987. But by the late 1980s cracks in Salomon's armor began to show. Lew Ranieri, the brilliant architect of Salomon's once highly profitable mortgage-backed trading operations, left in 1987. The firm then suffered a major reversal after a 1991 treasury-market scandal. Although the firm received a reprieve in the form of an investment from Warren Buffet (not one of his better deals), by the late 1990s Salomon would be combined first with Sandy Weill's Smith Barney brokerage and then subsumed into the massive Citigroup. Citigroup recently dropped all reference to the Salomon name.

What can send an investment banking firm into ascent is typically a series of high-profile transactions, an infusion of cash from an outside investor or well-heeled corporate parent or, occasionally, a favorable regulatory change. In the early 1990s, major commercial banks like J. P. Morgan and Bankers Trust were still operating under the restrictions placed on them by the Banking Act of 1933, the aforementioned Glass Steagall, which barred commercial banks from securities underwriting. Even with one arm tied behind their backs, these institutions had been investing heavily for at least a decade in expanding their investment banking activities in anticipation of the rule's ultimate repeal. They hired high-profile bankers, pressed various loopholes in the existing rules, exploited their balance sheets and strength in all aspects of the debt markets by virtue of their massive commercial loan portfolios. And J. P. Morgan in particular had managed to leverage its historic international lending relationships into a prominent position as an M&A advisor outside the United States.

1994 "League Tables"

Global M&A	U.S. Junk Bonds	U.S. IPOs
1. Goldman Sachs	Donaldson Lutkin & Jenrette	Merrill Lynch
2. Morgan Stanley	Merrill Lynch	Goldman Sachs
3. Merrill Lynch	Salomon Brothers	Morgan Stanley
4. Lehman Brothers	Morgan Stanley	Lehman Brothers
5. Salomon Brothers	Goldman Sachs	Donaldson Lufkin & Jenrette

Source: Thomson Financial

J. P. Morgan's relative success overseas was the exception, not the rule. Although international financing and deal volumes exceeded those in the United States, most of the U.S. investment banks' global operations were still relatively young in the early 1990s. The cultural and legal barriers, as well as the existence of entrenched local competitors, are major challenges to successfully establishing overseas operations. Domestic U.S. league table position may still provide bragging rights, but it translates into surprisingly little practical benefit in these very distinct markets. And although there is something sexy about working overseas, it is often a graveyard for more seasoned bankers: a high-risk posting with little upside. When a press release goes out saying that a banker is being transferred to supervise certain international operations, the explanation given is invariably the growing importance of the particular markets involved. The reality, more often than not, is that the banker lost out in some internal struggle. No matter how globally integrated these institutions like to portray themselves, the corporate decision-making remains at headquarters in New York.

This picture was certainly consistent with what I found at Goldman Sachs' London operations when I arrived in July 1994. The office seemed to operate in its separate little world, the only evidence of New York being the occasional banker who would pass through for a meeting or on his way somewhere else. Goldman may have been a leader in IPOs in the United States, but it had been largely absent from the IPO market in the U.K. market. At this point, I had never worked on any kind of financing transaction and, although I had a dim memory of what it was like to pitch an M&A deal, had absolutely no idea of what actually executing an M&A transaction would involve either. Within a few weeks, however, I would become the point person for Goldman as it led the highest profile U.K. IPO of the decade.

Although I had a dotted line to Thornton, I was formally placed in Goldman Sachs' Communications, Media, and Technology Group, known as CMT, in London. This group was run by a short, balding, nerdy former lawyer named Scott Mead. Mead was very friendly and did not seem bothered by the fact that he had not been granted the courtesy of an interview before being saddled with me. He was a little shy and self-conscious and nothing like what I imagined a senior investment banker, particularly one serving the media industry, would be like. What I would quickly learn was that Mead had next to nothing to do with the media practice. The European communications practice of that era involved filling out detailed RFPs (literally a "request for proposal") issued by foreign governments looking to privatize their national phone companies. Once selected, an investment bank would reposition the bureaucratic government-run agency as a dynamic public company and sell its stock to the public. The myriad legal and regulatory issues involved in managing that transition made nerdy former lawyers particularly well suited to practice in this very specialized area of finance. Mead also had lived near Thornton on campus at Harvard University and could be counted on to let John pursue his media banking strategy in any way he wished.

Mead would ultimately make a name for himself internally for bringing in huge fees associated with first Deutsche Telecom and later Vodafone. His 15 minutes of fame would come in 2002 when, to the delight of the London tabloids, his secretary was arrested for stealing more than $5 million from him without his noticing for some time. This episode and the subsequent trial, replete with surprising revelations of a personal nature, even became the subject of a made-for-TV movie in the United Kingdom. In 1994, however, Mead was not well known internally or externally, having come to London in 1988 after only two years in New York.

Even if Mead was not intimidating, I was still self-conscious about the fact that, beyond a vague memory of my experience studying the poultry industry seven years earlier, I didn't know much about investment banking and even less about the media industry. All I had going for me is that I had basic research skills from my time as a lawyer, could draft cogent and concise bullet points from my time as a lobbyist, and had some math from college. My plan was to try to make myself useful by getting every last inch of mileage out of these modest skill sets while I figured out what the job really entailed.

And it helped that I had no shame. Many bankers, and indeed professionals in general, are afraid to show any weaknesses to their peers. It already was pretty obvious, however, that the former airline executive who had been designated a senior associate in the CMT group was clueless. So there was little downside to stapling myself to the smartest, most seasoned young analysts I could find until I learned the basics. Although they weren't always happy about serving as a tutor to some American ten years older than they, these young Brits pretty much saved my life during my first year as a real investment banker.

My first awkward weeks were filled mostly with preparing pitch books. This was not unlike my experience seven years earlier at Bankers Trust, but with one major difference. The extent to which the business had been institutionalized was striking. Where Capitman had been reduced to cold calling companies he read about in the *Financial Times* that morning, by 1994 Goldman had a well-organized European calling effort, with geographic coverage officers assigned to every major local corporation. Although Goldman had had an office in London since 1969, it was primarily focused on selling U.S. equities to European institutions and secondarily on serving the needs of its U.S.-based clients. It wasn't until the mid-1980s that a concerted focus had been placed on investment banking. Thornton was assigned to run M&A there simultaneously with this enhanced but still fledgling effort. In the intervening decade, Goldman had hit a number of potholes along the road to success—most notably the hugely embarrassing and ultimately expensive association with Robert Maxwell, the British entrepreneur, media mogul, and crook. In 1991, Maxwell died in mysterious circumstances off his yacht in the Canary Islands, leaving Goldman and many others holding the bag. Goldman would ultimately pay over $250 million to settle charges related to Maxwell's looting of his employees' pensions. But by the time I had arrived, Goldman was established as a serious U.K. presence, particularly in the lucrative area of M&A.

Equally striking for me was the institutionalization of the "production process" involved in all aspects of investment banking. Though this was the pre-Internet era, our computer screens seamlessly integrated key third-party information on any company—everything from current news and public filings to deal databases that showed what deals the company had done and who had advised them—with proprietary internal Goldman Sachs information such as the history of the relationship, key contacts at the company, and deal team members within different parts of the firm. This software utilized dedicated lines to proprietary databases and customized programs developed in-house. Other sophisticated software applications had been developed to analyze potential mergers and leveraged buyouts based on providing simple inputs. Updated standard exhibits were catalogued by topic and easily retrieved. And a culture of communication within the firm allowed you to quickly collect whatever institutional knowledge already existed about the people, company, or situation with which you were involved.

But one key aspect of being an investment banker had not changed meaningfully since my experience at Bankers Trust. And it was an aspect that seemed all the more incredible to me having spent four of the intervening years working at a law firm where young associates can slave for weeks producing draft after draft of a legal memorandum before it is deemed by the partner in charge of the account ready to be shared with even an assistant general counsel. At an investment bank, with a couple of days' notice, you are expected to be able to slap together a book that should be the basis for a serious strategic discussion of the key issues facing a company with its senior-most management.

And the books themselves, just as before, rather than containing thoughtful detailed analyses of strategic options, are mostly filled with pages containing concise but ambiguous bullet points (to allow for plausible deniability if the client clearly disagrees with the point you meant to make) and cheesy graphical representations (boxes, arrows, simple charts, standard drawings of objects—a newspaper, a radio tower, a TV set—meant to represent the businesses being discussed). The banker's work product bore a closer resemblance to a comic book than a legal memorandum. The new technology and infrastructure described had made the production of the books easier than ever—something more than the touch of a button, but something well short of a fully baked idea. This is not to suggest that investment bankers couldn't or didn't provide thoughtful, serious analysis for actual clients. But the tools used by overworked bankers in full pitch mode are realistically designed more to provoke and engage rather than genuinely enlighten.

All of this leaves unanswered the obvious question of why otherwise intelligent senior executives put up with it. Why take meetings with these people at all? The answer to this is complicated. Most obviously, the subject matter of the meetings—raising capital, going private, major acquisitions or divestitures—is central to the future of the company and the executives involved. Hence, even if the chances of an original idea being presented at any given meeting are low, an executive could calculate that if enough are attended, something of interest should eventually emerge. And if such an idea does come up, bankers do know a lot (although sometimes much less than they let on) about the practical market feasibility of executing a particular transaction.

Less obvious, and maybe more important, is that bankers sometimes have access to critical information about the thinking of both competitors and investors that would not otherwise be available to executives. Most bankers focus on one industry, and thus accumulate a good deal of industry-specific knowledge. A banker who is "in the flow" is likely to obtain a more nuanced view of the strategic approach and perspective from key competitors or potential acquisition targets than those executives would likely be comfortable sharing with each other. In addition, by tapping the intelligence gleaned from his or her firm's Sales and Trading Division, the banker can obtain important candid assessments of investors regarding the company.

This business model is reminiscent of that of the Corporate Executive Board (CEB), the wildly successful brainchild of entrepreneur David Bradley. While still a law student at Georgetown, Bradley identified an exciting business opportunity in the deep interest of corporate executives to know how their counterparts at other corporations perform the same function as they did. The business model he developed to exploit this opportunity was remarkably simple. Executives pay a substantial subscription fee for the right to provide CEB with proprietary information relating to their own business practices. CEB then tabulates this information from all major industry participants and effectively sells it back to them in aggregated form. By participating, corporate marketing chiefs, CFOs, general counsels and the like can all sleep well at night knowing that they are unlikely to be fired because the CEO discovered that their peers at other major corporations are performing the same job smarter or better.

Similarly, corporate executives are likely to provide a more honest perspective on their strategic aspirations and views of competitors to an investment banker than to those competitors. And investors are more likely to tell a trader, salesman, or research analyst what they really think about management than they are likely to tell management to its face. The investment banker, therefore, can be the conduit for this information. And information, maybe more than ideas, is the coin of the realm in investment banking.

This description of what bankers do highlights the sensitive issues of conflicts and confidentiality that necessarily arise all the time and colors much of the interaction between bankers and their clients and potential clients. A CEO who wants to know when certain kinds of acquisition targets arise needs to share a fair amount about his own strategy if he is to expect a banker to present truly appropriate situations. But he will be reticent to share very much if he fears that this information will be quickly shared with his competitors. And corporate executives themselves are a little schizophrenic about what they want from their investment bankers— on the one hand they may long for a simpler time when a particular banker was their exclusive "trusted adviser," but on the other hand they want access to market intelligence that is less likely to be made available to a banker too closely associated with a single industry participant.

But the very best investment bankers manage to be much more than mere traffickers in industry or market gossip. They address a fundamental need that derives from the surprising fact that the CEO job in particular is a painfully lonely one. The CEO is surrounded by multiple internal and external constituencies each with their own axe to grind, product to sell, or position to protect. Like a Hollywood ingénue with a battalion of new "best friends" following the successful opening of her debut film, the CEO must find a way to sort through the cacophony of self-serving requests, biased advice, and unrelenting flattery. Finding an advisor who can honorably provide both a fair synthesis of the relevant information and demonstrate consistently sound judgment regarding its strategic implications is an extraordinary service and relief to a CEO.

Another reason why companies and CEOs are nervous nonetheless about being too open with any particular advisor is the rapidity with which investment bankers moved from firm to firm by the early 1990s. A confidence given to one firm, even if kept, became highly vulnerable if any team member left for another firm. At one time, it was not unusual for a banker to pass his entire career within the confines of a single financial institution. But with the growth of the industry, the surge of new entrants and mergers of existing ones, the cycles of layoffs and hectic hiring binges and the split-off of celebrity bankers into boutiques like Greenhill, Gleacher and Wasserstein, Perella, this had become the exception rather than the rule.

The one institutional exception to this rule was still Goldman Sachs. Very few people left Goldman, except to retire or do something altogether different. And, conversely, Goldman was not given to "lateral" hires—people who had worked elsewhere and who were hired to fill positions higher than entry level. Part of the effectiveness of the internal communications described derived from the fact that the overwhelming majority of bankers had never worked anywhere else and shared much the same training and many of the same experiences. As a former Management Committee member told one writer, in his view "lateral hires are like foreign bodies, . . . [t]hey do not speak the language."[2]

Despite Mead's graciousness toward me, it was not surprising that my welcome at Goldman was a little cool. I was after all not just a lateral hire, but one with no real banking experience. People didn't really understand how I got there or what I was supposed to be doing. At the time I didn't fully appreciate the historical significance of the suspicion with which outsiders were greeted. Goldman's first big experiment with a lateral partner, Waddill Catchings, hired in 1918 after having worked as a lawyer at Sullivan and Cromwell and then a banker at J. P. Morgan, had literally almost destroyed the firm in the 1920s. The Goldmans and Sachses were just two of the nineteenth-century German-Jewish immigrant families who, with little financial capital and only modest experience extending credit, would transcend their garment-peddling origins after the Civil War. These original "rags to riches" stories would ultimately challenge the supremacy of the established banking houses, known generally as the "Yankee" houses because of their predominantly New England pedigree, that were made up of partners from families on the Social Register.[3]

This success was owed in part to the ability of family members to rely on each other in a sometimes hostile financial world. And they understandably resisted inviting outsiders into their partnerships until it was absolute necessity to permit further expansion. At Goldman Sachs, it was 50 years before someone without the last name of either Goldman or Sachs became a partner. This was quicker than at Lehman Brothers, another Jewish firm with which it would collaborate for decades.[4] Goldman did not become a full-fledged investment bank until 1906 when, along with, Lehman Brothers, it underwrote an offering for a small mail-order house owned by a distant relative of the Sachs family. That little company was Sears and its took three months to find buyers for the modest $10 million offering. But that first transaction "put Goldman Sachs on the threshold of a new era."[5]

Much as the Jews who were excluded from the theater industry created "an empire of their own" in the form of the early film industry, these Jews aggressively developed investment banking through a tight web of family relations in part because they were not welcome in the established commercial banking industry.[6] Using a combination of financial creativity, willingness to provide banking services to smaller businesses (particularly in the retailing and light industrial sectors) and family connections to the large European financial houses, which then provided a critical outlet for distributing U.S. securities, these once-fringe players changed the landscape of global financial markets. Ultimately even J. P. Morgan, the most traditional of Yankee bankers, would need to work with the German Jewish banking houses to ensure proper distribution of major securities offerings. Morgan complained bitterly about their growing influence and by the turn of the century claimed, inaccurately, that his was one of only two firms in New York still "composed of white men."[7]

With no obvious family member to fill the void left by the departure of Henry Goldman in 1917, Waddill Catchings must have seemed an inspired choice.[8] The charming southerner was a natural salesman and already a well-known author. Never mind that the thrust of his best-selling, *The Road to Plenty*, which aggressively proselytized the notion that the economy could continue growing indefinitely, was at odds with the fundamentally conservative Goldman financial ethos. Catchings had befriended the Sachs boys at Harvard, making all these differences in style and disposition seem complementary rather than threatening.

Unfortunately for Goldman, Catchings convinced the firm to package and market the type of investment trusts popularized during this period and reflective of Catchings' own economic credo. Units in the investment trusts were sold to the public on the promise of untold compounding riches as more and more participated. The collapse of the Goldman Sachs Trading Corp. in 1929 may not have been the most spectacular example of the dangers of these pyramid schemes. But Goldman Sachs nevertheless attracted disproportionate attention because of Catchings' high profile, its bad decision to use the Goldman name in marketing the investment trust[9] to the public, and having the misfortune of selling units to Eddie Cantor, one of the most famous entertainers of the era. Cantor not only sued the firm, as many others did, but worked the scandal into his popular comedy act and books.

It is probably unfair to blame Catchings for the difficult treatment of laterals at Goldman. The insularity of the firm in this regard certainly predated him. Better to say that their experience with Catchings merely confirmed a predisposition to deal exclusively with homegrown talent. And over 60 years later that predisposition was still alive and well.

Nonetheless, I had been hired by John Thornton, and at least in this little outpost of Goldman Sachs, he was basically the boss. At this point, with well over 1,000 employees, the London office was actually not even that little, at least by the standards of the transplant operations of the other major U.S. investment banks. So my new colleagues were generally polite and helpful, if a bit wary. At least until they found out what Thornton had in mind for me.

One day late that summer, while he was briefly back from some Thornton mission in Germany or Australia, my old friend who had gotten me into this, Kevin Czinger, came by my desk.

"Thornton wants us to go out to Isleworth," he said.

"What's an Is-el worth anyway?" I asked.

"Very funny," he said, "we can talk in the cab."

Isleworth, it turns out, is a not terribly attractive suburb of London, a little more than halfway to Heathrow from downtown, which houses the studios of BSkyB. BSkyB was the only satellite TV operator and, since cable was really in its infancy in the United Kingdom, for most Brits pretty much the only way to escape the BBC sisters or ITV. Owned by a consortium of Rupert Murdoch, Pearson, Granada, and Chargeurs, BSkyB was an incredible business. In addition to national distribution, BSkyB had tied up all—literally all—the pay-TV rights to first-run films from the major studios. It had done so on a staggered basis, so that in any given year only one studio contract would come up. Unfortunately, as any potential competing bidder would know, you need the output from at least two movie studios to create a credible pay-TV movie channel. So, for a cable provider—or even a consortium of cable providers, all of whom were losing buckets of money—to attempt to outbid BSkyB for a major studio contract was folly. Any cable operators who wanted to offer a premium movie tier had to buy it "wholesale" from, you guessed it, their main competitor, BSkyB. And BSkyB could set prices to the cable providers at a level that made it, shall we say, challenging for them to be competitive with BSkyB's offerings.

Ditto for sports broadcast rights, the only other area (not counting pornography), for which the public has demonstrated an almost unlimited willingness to pay incremental dollars to receive "exclusive" programming. At the time, Sky Sports had the next three years' live broadcast rights to the Premier League, the country's top soccer league, the equivalent to owning the rights to all NFL games, and pretty much the only thing that really mattered in the U.K. market. And on the basic service tier, Sky redistributed a dozen third-party channels (many of which had been convinced to give BSkyB an equity position) and four wholly owned channels. The four Sky Channels included the 24-hour Sky News and the flagship, Sky One, which transmitted *The Simpsons*, *Beverly Hills 90210*, and other popular fare that the BBC mandarins considered beneath them.

And all this was supported by a state-of-the-art customer service (something of an oxymoron in the British Isles) facility in Scotland where a free call was quickly answered to instantaneously deal with any billing or service issue.

Talk about a license to print money.

But it wasn't always so. At one time, the losses associated with Rupert Murdoch's Sky satellite TV operations had almost brought down his News Corporation Empire. The fierce battle for dominance between Sky and competitor British Satellite Broadcasting (BSB) has been the subject of other books.[10] The major studios laughed all the way to the bank as each satellite platform tried to outbid the other for pay-TV movie rights. Once an armistice was reached—and BSkyB was created—Murdoch immediately sent his CEO, Sam Chisholm, to Hollywood for some "friendly" renegotiations. When the smoke cleared, Chisholm, a profane, hard-drinking, chain-smoking, bulldog of a man, stood atop a business that is akin to what DirectTV could be in the United States—if Echostar didn't exist, cable were a minor competitor, and it owned all of ESPN, HBO, Showtime, Cinemax, and STARZ. "Top of the world, ma," Jimmy Cagney's character shouts at the end of the classic film, White Heat. You could be forgiven for confusing Sam Chisholm with a kind of Kiwi Cagney, a comparison some executives reportedly made.

Chisholm, in addition to running BSkyB, was on the board of News Corp. and responsible for Murdoch's pay-TV strategy in Asia. Czinger had met Chisholm and his team when Thornton had sold a majority stake in Star TV—the largest satellite TV platform in Asia—to Murdoch for Richard Li, Hong Kong mogul Li Ka-shing's 27-year-old son. It was a testament to Thornton's skill that although he had gotten an enormous price from Murdoch for Star (and the asset was something less than advertised) he had endeared himself to the News Corp. team for delivering them the deal while at the same time securing the devotion of his own client, Richard Li.

During the car ride to BSkyB headquarters, I learned from Kevin that there was to be an IPO for BSkyB. Since the business had turned around, Murdoch had already begun pulling cash out of BSkyB to repay his substantial loans to the company. The IPO would allow Murdoch in one fell swoop to accelerate the repayment of another £600 million in loans, potentially buy out annoying minority partners, and provide a highly valued currency to make further European acquisitions without diluting his ownership in News Corp. itself. Kevin, who would not have any continuing day-to-day involvement on the project, was to introduce me at this meeting to the BSkyB finance team as Thornton's point person in the CMT Group on this assignment. And it was clear that this was an assignment, not a pitch. Thornton had already used his relationship with Murdoch and Chisholm to establish Goldman as the key strategic advisor to BSkyB, and they had asked him to lead this project, as far as I know, without any formal pitch at all. I also learned that none of Murdoch's "partners" were to know of this plan until the very last possible moment, when they would have little choice but to accede to it.

From Goldman's perspective, the secrecy had very particular competitive appeal. Although already established as a credible player in U.K. mergers and acquisitions, Goldman was a minor participant in the equity markets there. Goldman had undertaken a very high profile block trade for British Petroleum in 1987 (block trading, in which the investment bank purchases a large position directly based on its ability to quickly resell it to multiple institutional accounts at a profit, was a well-established Goldman specialty) and in 1988 Thornton himself had used creative takeover defense work for Racal to secure Goldman the lead position on the IPO of the company's Vodafone subsidiary. But Goldman had never been the primary global "book runner" for a major IPO of a stand-alone U.K. company. The book runner was the bank actually responsible at the end of the day for placing the securities—in other words, finding the buyers who would actually take the stock at the price offered. And this was not just any IPO. This would be the deal of the decade. Goldman knew that once the prospect of an IPO was public, there would be enormous pressure for a U.K. broker to lead the deal, because of the historic relationships in the British market.

In addition, once the "partners" knew, there would be no way to keep the well-established U.K. house of Lazard Brothers from being a major participant (and irritant) in the deal. Lazard Brothers was partially owned by Pearson PLC, the second largest shareholder in BSkyB. And there were parallel but interrelated tensions between Pearson and News Corp. on the one hand and Lazard and Goldman on the other. Pearson CEO Frank Barlow, represented by Lazard as usual, had been the primary other suitor for Star TV the previous year. And there was some lingering sense from their side that Thornton had somehow favored News Corp. in the process, leaving Barlow with egg on his face. Barlow would soon enough be humiliated for a second time.

BSkyB's CFO, the genial, unassuming Richard Brooke, was one of the few remaining employees who had originally worked at BSB. His shy, elfin assistant Roger Blundell had short, bright red hair and boyish, bright red cheeks to match. I was expecting something a little more intimidating, based on what I had heard about Chisholm, but would soon learn that Brooke was not part of the inner circle at BSkyB and was viewed as a processor to deal with annoying regulatory requirements. We discussed timing of an organizational meeting, who would be in the know, what our cover story was for why we would be engaging in "due diligence" and, as in every confidential investment banking project, our secret project name. At the time, I had only a very general sense of the meaning of "due diligence," which I came to understand was a term of art used to describe the investigation undertaken by an underwriter to ensure ultimate buyers of shares that the business is as advertised. Just in case anyone wasn't sure about just how secret these proceedings were, the BSkyB IPO would be called Project Hush.

What I really didn't understand was, why me? Notwithstanding Thornton's involvement in the Vodaphone offering six years earlier, as a practical matter Thornton, Czinger, and I together could barely spell IPO. Why position someone so clearly out of his depths this prominently on a deal as important to the overall franchise? Kevin explained that within the insular Goldman culture, there were any number of strong and even more insular subcultures. Equity Capital Markets (ECM)—the part of the firm responsible for distributing equity securities—was ruled with an iron fist out of New York by another bulldog of a man, Eric Dobkin. The diminutive, cigar chomping Dobkin's ECM franchise had consistently been number one in IPOs, along with M&A the highest margin business in investment banking, and his word was law. He was a legendary figure both within Goldman and on the Street, as the investment banking community referred to itself (in London, "the street" was called "the city"). Although he had hired most of the London ECM team himself, Thornton seemed to want someone on the ground with absolutely no allegiances to anyone but Thornton.

At our first internal team meeting shortly thereafter, temperatures associated with my generally cool initial reception at Goldman quickly plummeted to arctic levels. These people were not pleased. When I spoke, it was as if I hadn't said anything. I was invisible. Everyone in the room, from the two young analysts Ulrika Lindgren and Jean Marc Huet to the head of ECM in London, Michael Evans (a former Olympic rower for Canada) had worked together before and exuded self-confidence. This was clearly the "A" team, carefully selected to work on the most important deal the office had ever done. Which was precisely why they were so annoyed not only that they had to baby-sit me but that I was being given the opportunity to participate in a project for which I clearly had not paid my dues.

Also on the team was a senior corporate finance banker who had spent a considerable amount of time in ECM himself, Tim Bunting. Bunting was slightly overweight with bad teeth and often looked as if he had slept on a park bench. With short, unkempt blond hair and pin striped suits that frequently were torn at the pockets or the seams, Bunting had the air of a disorganized professor. But he had consistently stellar strategic judgment and a far better understanding than any of us of what we were undertaking.

Finally, the team included a shy, solid, well-liked senior associate named Fergal O'Driscoll. Fergal had clearly been put on the team by Mike and Tim as the price for taking me. At least Fergal had been at Trinity, although long after me, so we had that in common to talk about. But it would be some time before my interaction with any of my "team" would be anything but awkwardly formal.

I said pretty much nothing at the meeting, which seemed to be appreciated. There was almost no eye contact from anybody there, even when I did speak if just to clarify something. I did at least begin to get a sense of what "due diligence" would entail. Essentially we would be spending the next several months interviewing the key BSkyB executives about their businesses and then sitting down with the lawyers to draft a prospectus describing the organization, the operations, the financials, and the offering.

Even if I had had the first clue about what I was doing, the following weeks would have been difficult. The analysts would accidentally neglect to let me know about meetings at BSkyB. I somehow seemed to get only about every other team voice mail update. I tried charm, without result. I tried confrontation, they played dumb. I refused to be reduced to whining to Thornton, so I just soldiered on trying my best to absorb as much as I could and look like I knew what I was doing.

The good news was that this due diligence stuff is made for the naturally curious and extroverted like me. Just asking people about how their businesses work, the key drivers and risks, fascinates me. And I find that people like to talk about their own businesses and are flattered when outsiders take an interest in what they do. So while others dozed at sessions where group heads talked about their businesses—signing up sports rights, selling advertising against the entrenched incumbents, dealing with regulators, managing the call center or the satellite uplink—I listened closely. And rather than rushing back to the office to attend to more pressing matters with my colleagues, I would stick around and ask a few more questions. As a result, by the time we started writing I knew more about the businesses than my colleagues, so it wasn't hard to make it look like I was contributing at the endless prospectus drafting sessions.

But what really saved me, despite all the obvious strikes against me, was that I really liked and got along with the people at BSkyB. The BSkyB culture, and the Murdoch culture generally, is incredibly results oriented, with a certain populist disdain for pomp and pretense. Fancy degrees and self-important attitudes are just not the currency for dealing with the people who made Homer Simpson a household name around the world. Although my politics couldn't be further from the right-wing views systematically and effectively espoused by the Murdoch empire, I developed a deep empathy for the antiestablishment ethos of the place. Over time, the relationships I built there seemed to pay off, at least in terms of my credibility with the client if not my Goldman teammates.

Although I didn't complain to Thornton about the shunning I took from my colleagues, I had talked about it with Czinger. One day he came by my desk and said "Thornton wants you to do the Analysts' Presentation." I soon found out that in the United Kingdom, before going on the road show, making dozens of 45-minute presentations to investors to sell stock, management makes a full-day presentation to the research analysts. These presentations allow the analysts, who investors turn to for the intellectual support for the valuation being sought for the new stock, to prepare their financial models and have their written research reports ready for the IPO. When the team was informed that this would be my responsibility, there was for the first time palpable anger instead of feigned indifference.

"Fine," Fergal said abruptly and stormed from the room on being informed that he would not be involved.

Among the team, this anger soon seemed to mellow into a kind of quiet satisfaction that came from knowing that I would make a fool of myself. But turning a complicated legal document (in this case, the offering prospectus) into a simple story told in bullet points was actually one of the few things I did know how to do. My four years as a lawyer-lobbyist would finally come to my rescue when I most needed the help.

When we presented the final product, David Chance, Chisholm's handsome, unflappable deputy, responsible for day-to-day operations, seemed startled and asked who had prepared it. I meekly raised my hand. Maybe I just imagined the disappointment on the rest of the Goldman team's faces when he said "This is damn good!"

Shortening the Analysts Presentation into a Road Show Presentation was pretty straightforward. I assumed we were all set when Tim asked me to come down to Mike Evans' office for a conference call with New York about the road show. What he didn't say until I arrived is that "New York" was code for Eric Dobkin. Everyone apparently understood that the personality combination of Chisholm and Dobkin would be explosive and disastrous and we had avoided interacting with New York altogether. But at Goldman, Dobkin approved all road shows. I was asked to take him through the management presentation.

Dobkin didn't talk, he screamed. At the time I did not appreciate either the fear or influence Dobkin wielded within ECM, so I was just a bit bemused by this character. Thornton tried to run London as an independent outpost and I was having a hard enough time navigating that little world. Although I had by this point done a reasonable job of mapping out the political landscape within Goldman London, I had no real exposure to the broader firm context. I had not even been to the New York offices beyond a few days of perfunctory training.

As we flipped pages Dobkin would yell an observation and I would respond respectfully. We reached the end, Dobkin said, "We need to put in more about growth from new products and interactivity and all that stuff." In general it makes sense to highlight prospective growth opportunities, even if a little speculative, because investors will pay more for current earnings when they believe there is much more around the corner. But BSkyB had so much built-in growth, it seemed crazy to me to spend any time at all on anything else.

At this point I was a little tired and didn't know exactly why I had to explain myself to this guy. Besides, if we changed anything at this point, Chisholm would eat me alive.

Anyway I said, "We have a core business that has a rock-solid growth trajectory, no credible competition, and no meaningful business risks. We can easily justify the valuation we are seeking just on this business. As you suggest, there are some services that we may provide in the future, but they have technological and competitive risks and basic questions about whether people will pay for them at all. Now we can focus our presentation on the foolproof business or we can focus on the speculative business." At this point Mike and Tim were almost apoplectic, making wild hand signals suggesting I should shut up. No one talked to Dobkin that way. I stopped talking. There was silence as everyone in London stood frozen staring at the speaker phone.

"O.K." Dobkin yelled. Everyone started to breathe again, Dobkin moved onto another topic.

As anticipated, before the prospectus was finalized, Pearson's Barlow complained loudly about both Chisholm's competing responsibilities at News Corporation, where he was a director and still served as the chief strategist for all their cable and satellite interests outside of the United States, and the size of the bonus scheme for Chisholm's team, which by U.K. standards of the time was quite generous. Although Barlow did manage to get the bonuses scaled back somewhat, his harping alienated the rest of the major shareholders who were more focused on the high values attributed to their stakes so soon after being at the brink of bankruptcy. And Sam had the last laugh as usual. Prior to the first board meeting after the IPO, Murdoch and Granada CEO Gerry Robinson pulled Barlow aside in an adjacent conference room and gave him a stark choice: resign as chairman or be kicked out. "I've got the votes, Frank," Murdoch explained to him. Barlow resigned that day.[11]

During a road show, the lead banks chaperone management through an exhausting series of group and one-on-one meetings with prospective investors, relentlessly hopscotching around the globe for several weeks. Sam didn't like to deal with strangers and I was asked to travel with him as Goldman's representative for almost the entire road show. Despite my lack of experience, I bet that the road show came as more of a shock to investors, particularly in the United Kingdom, than it did to me. Sam didn't particularly like the Brits. To say that U.K. fund managers, more used to being fawned over than anything else, were surprised to hear those sentiments from someone trying to sell them stock, would be an understatement. If a fund manager in a large gathering asked a question that Sam took to be provocative, Chisholm might go on a riff about how phony the British are: pretending to read the *Times* when all they want to do is see the Page Three girl in the *Sun*, acting as if the drivel on the BBC interests them when they really want to be watching *The Simpsons*. What he was offering to the British people was choice for the very first time. These fund managers could think whatever they wanted about whether it would make a difference in viewing habits, as far as Chisholm was concerned. But, he suggested, just watch the ratings and the subscriber numbers.

In more intimate settings with fund managers, Chisholm could be even more withering. At a lunch with five prospective investors, one had the temerity to ask Sam whether he thought the government would block him from purchasing any more sports rights. Sam looked up from his lunch at the man with undisguised disdain.

"Block me?!" Chisholm barked at the man, who was visibly shaken. "What do you think we are, in fecking boarding school? Nobody's going to block me!"

And it was true that Sam could be cruel to those he did not consider one of his guys. During one investor presentation, BSkyB CFO Richard Brooke took it on himself to answer a question that Sam thought properly his. While Richard answered, Sam got up and walked behind him staring with a quizzical grin. When Richard finished, Sam patted him on his head, as if his dog had somehow managed to bark a tune. But for all Sam's personal failings, if he trusted you, he was incredibly kind and generous and one of the funniest people I have ever met.

The quality of the business allowed us to "sell through" our unconventional marketing efforts, and the offering was a huge success—we raised $1.4 billion at a valuation that established BSkyB as one of the 50 largest publicly traded U.K. companies. Needless to say, however, we sold a lot more stock in the United States than in the United Kingdom—65 percent in North America for a company whose only customers were in the United Kingdom. By the time things came to an end, I had actually developed reasonable working relationships with all of my Goldman teammates. No one had any illusions about the depth of my investment banking skill set, but I had tried to use my relationships with both the company and Thornton to facilitate those aspects of the transaction for which they were responsible. Eventually my name seemed to have been added to most everyone's team distribution list. And occasionally I would be asked to join them at the pub.

Having survived my immersion course in investment banking and gotten engaged, 1994 was surely a momentous year for me personally. But as the year came to an end, it became clear that it was possibly even more momentous for Goldman. And not in a good way.

"LET'S ASK SIDNEY WEINBERG"

CONGRESS HAD ENACTED Glass Steagall in 1933 in large part to reduce the power and influence of J. P. Morgan. The forced separation from the J. P. Morgan bank of the newly created Morgan Stanley investment bank in 1935 planted the seeds for the inevitable rivalry between Morgan Stanley and Goldman Sachs that continues to this day—although at the time Goldman was still recovering from the Trading Corp. scandal and hardly viewed as being in the same league. But Glass Steagall also had another equally significant but unintended consequence—protecting the pure investment banking houses from competition from J. P. Morgan or any other well-capitalized commercial bank, current or future, that had a mind to compete for securities underwriting business. This was well understood for generations to come at the investment banks. As Lisa Endlich, author of a kind of semiofficial history of Goldman Sachs, writes, "One [Goldman Sachs] partner remembers that at his first partners' meeting in 1981 two large portraits of old men with long beards were held up. The audience was told that these were two of the most important men to the firm's business and was challenged to guess who they were. After the names Goldman, Sachs and Weinberg had been discarded, the answer was revealed: The portraits were of Senator Carter Glass and Representative Henry Steagall."[1]

The investment banking partnerships, both Yankee and Jewish, that had survived the Depression entered a golden age of relationship investment banking. The values of this era had been established beforehand as the best of these firms began to develop corporate identities associated with loyalty, exclusivity, and giving first-rate independent advice. What had changed, however, was that after Glass Steagall, the partnerships could practice this genteel form of relationship investment banking in relative safety, protected from undue competition from commercial banks with deep pockets and established relationships.

The single figure who best epitomizes this era is Sidney Weinberg, leader of Goldman Sachs from 1930 until his death in 1969. Weinberg's ascent within Goldman was a highly unlikely one. Not only was he neither a Goldman or a Sachs, his background could not exactly be called distinguished. Weinberg, whose formal schooling ended after eighth grade, began at Goldman as an assistant porter in 1907 at the age of 15. He would be made partner 20 years later, and soon thereafter be given responsibility for cleaning up the Goldman Sachs Trading Corp. scandal.

Weinberg had been an acolyte of Catchings', as well as the treasurer of the investment trust that had almost ruined the firm, which made him in some ways an unlikely choice to lead the firm once Catchings stepped down in 1930. But Weinberg quickly took charge and established credibility by ensuring that the firm never sold a share—at a personal cost to the partners of around $12 million, which would be more like $130 million in today's dollars—and successfully liquidating the trust by selling it to Floyd Odlum's Atlas Corp.[2] It would be five years before Goldman led another offering. But as John Kenneth Galbraith would write 25 years later in his seminal review of the crash and its aftermath, "Goldman, Sachs and Company rescued its firm name from its delinquent offspring and returned to an earlier role of strict rectitude and stern conservatism."[3] This was thanks largely to Weinberg's leadership.

Of equally long-term significance, Weinberg assumed most of the corporate board seats once held by Catchings. Weinberg would ultimately sit on as many as 31 boards simultaneously and earn the moniker of "the Director's Director." Although by the standards both of today and then, 31 directorships seems excessive, Weinberg viewed his board responsibilities as a form of "semipublic" service. "Directors should look at it that way," Weinberg wrote, "or not serve."[4] He viewed this role as a sort of halfway house between the two other main responsibilities he took up during his career—leading Goldman Sachs and serving the nation. And to a remarkable degree Weinberg was successful at using his board positions and reputation both to serve these specific companies wisely and help reform corporate governance more broadly.

Well over 50 years ago, Weinberg was pressing for outsiders to make up a majority of public board members and other revolutionary modernizations. His pithy 1933 "Memorandum Re The Responsibilities of Directors and an Outline of the Program Suggested as The Basis of Cooperation Between Officers and Directors of a Corporation" is still available on the Goldman Web site today. And his reputation for preparation for board meetings, with the help of young bankers back at the office, was unprecedented at the time. Rather than scaring off CEOs, "[a]s word of these conscientious practices got around, the presence of Weinberg on the board became a point of pride with many companies," as *Fortune* observed in the 1950s.[5]

Weinberg did allow himself to be stretched too thin, as the 1938 scandal surrounding McKesson & Robbins demonstrated. There, company president F. D. Coster was ultimately revealed to be a con artist named Philip Musica who had fabricated millions in "assets" through a dummy corporation. When the board met to formally discharge Musica, word came that he had already committed suicide.

"Well come on gentlemen," Weinberg was reported to have said in breaking the stunned silence, "let's fire him for his sins anyway."[6]

No single episode reflects the complex intermingling of the public and private in the highly personal form of relationship banking practiced by Sidney Weinberg than the 1956 initial public offering for Ford Motor Company. This transaction did more than anything else to establish the reputation of both Weinberg and Goldman Sachs as undisputed industry leaders. In 1933, Weinberg had organized a Business Advisory Council to the Department of Commerce, composed of various captains of industry, designed to give the administration "a businessman's slant on how things are going."[7] Weinberg would meet Henry Ford II when he joined this group in 1947. In October 1953, Ford asked Weinberg if he could help the family figure out how to sell some of the Ford Foundation's shares in the automaker to the public. This was complicated by the fact that although the foundation owned 88 percent of the equity, the family's 10 percent held all the voting power. Weinberg spent half of his time over the next two years presenting 50-odd different reorganization plans dealing with the sensitive legal, tax, and governance issues, before getting approval from all parties. In addition to being one of the managers of the offering in November 1956, Weinberg was placed on the board.

Three aspects of this transaction reflect the high-minded form of investment banking perfected, if not invented, by Weinberg.

First, Weinberg represented the family rather than the Foundation offering the stock. Although the Foundation's chief financial officer had sought to get Weinberg to represent them, Weinberg worked for the family. Since it was the Foundation that would be selling the stock, this assignment could have been more lucrative. Ultimately, the Foundation appointed Blythe & Co. to chair a group of seven co-managers of which Goldman was just one. When Ford had asked Weinberg early on what he would charge for the advice, Weinberg refused to set a fee "saying that he would just as soon work for a dollar a year and then, when everything was over, let the members of the Ford family decide what they felt his efforts were worth."[8]

Second, although from the perspective of today, Weinberg's interweaving of public and private roles might seem a cynical and self-serving business-development strategy, it was something much more than that. Weinberg provided a service of quality and loyalty that is simply not available to CEOs today. If Sidney Weinberg was on your board, this meant not simply that Goldman would not do business with a competitor. As a National Dairy Products board member, for instance, he would take it on himself to berate the dining car steward on the Twentieth Century Limited for not carrying Kraft cheese slices.[9] Today the notion of agreeing not to do business with client competitors at all is viewed as quaint and unrealistic. In its stead, clients hear double-talk about Chinese Walls and compartmentalization. And the idea that the senior partner of a major firm would spend half of his own time over two years on a single account and leave the fee to the clients' good judgment once it was all over is unthinkable.

To point to the potential conflicts of board members who provide services to a company is simply to highlight the shift in perspective during the intervening decades from a relationship orientation to a transactional one. These conflicts only seem insurmountable today because they are, and they are insurmountable only because the nature of the institutions these bankers serve has changed so fundamentally. It is not fair to project the decline in standards that is the subject of much of the rest of this book onto poor Sidney Weinberg.

Third, the transaction that secured Weinberg's place as an iconic adviser and Goldman's place as the premier Jewish banking house, was reflective of changes in the industry and society at large. Henry Ford's deep and well-documented anti-Semitism makes it highly unlikely that he would have invited a Jew into the inner family sanctum. Henry Ford II, however, was committed to erasing his grandfather's legacy of bigotry. He would later publicly refuse to join the Arab boycott of Israel, at significant cost to the company.[10]

And Sidney Weinberg wasn't just a Jewish banker, he looked and sounded like one. At 5′ 4″, Weinberg looked "less like an elder statesman than like a kewpie doll."[11]

Weinberg never converted, changed his name, or lost his thick Brooklyn accent, unlike many aspiring financiers before and after him. The nineteenth century's most influential banker, August Schonberg, became one by reinventing himself as some kind of European royalty with the name August Belmont. Even Clarence Dillon, patriarch of one of the most white-shoe Yankee houses of the twentieth century, Dillon, Read, was actually a Polish Jew born Clarence Lapowski.

In fact, the automotive business had been initially snubbed by the Yankee houses as an upstart industry unlikely to achieve meaningful scale. For this reason, J. P. Morgan had refused even to meet with Henry Ford and gave up the first General Motors financings to J. and W. Seligman and Company, the first major Jewish firm. The core of Morgan Stanley's franchise was servicing those established clients bequeathed by its predecessor firm. As newer industries came into their own, Morgan Stanley, though still the leading Yankee house, no longer had the lock on the Fortune 500 that it once did. And Weinberg's ability to secure a high-profile account like Ford for Goldman anticipated even greater changes in the established order to come.

The values Weinberg represented—loyalty, humility, independence, public service, and humor—are today frequently invoked, but rarely followed. Some of the specific rules that flowed from these values seemed hopelessly old-fashioned long after they were still in place. It has been suggested by competitors that both the values and the rules were a kind of posturing designed to burnish the Goldman brand. But many of these rules could only have been justified based on a deep belief in them, and a deep belief in a responsibility to the overall financial system and the public, rather than simply competitive positioning. Upholding these values cost the firm many millions of dollars in foregone income. Goldman would not back gambling companies, for example, because they were thought to provide no benefit to society. Nor would it sell shares in advertising companies because, in Weinberg's view, they should be privately owned. Goldman would not underwrite nonvoting shares because of belief in the principle of the shareholder's right to vote. Most famously, the firm refused to act as a dealer-manager in unfriendly takeover bids; it held to this principle through the late 1980s, while every other major bank—some with more scruples than others—happily and profitably pursued such business.[12]

The death of Sidney Weinberg in 1969 roughly coincided with the end of the golden era of relationship banking. The corporate values just mentioned are still articulated at Goldman, but each of the particular manifestations noted above have, one by one, fallen by the wayside. In hindsight, we can see the emergence of two phenomena, both of which will be explored in more detail shortly, that fundamentally undermined the paradigm of relationship banking. First, the emergence of the publicly held financial supermarkets to replace the private partnerships that had dominated corporate finance for the previous century. Second, the emergence of the pure M&A professional as the new iconic figure in investment banking, displacing the relationship banker as the industry representative of the new era.

Still, 25 years later in 1994, Goldman had managed to avoid most of the major pitfalls that by then had forced other private investment banking partnerships to sell out, shut down, or go public. Discord between the banking and trading sides of the house had torn a number of the old partnerships asunder. But Goldman had grown up as a commercial paper operation. Marcus Goldman started by literally walking the streets stuffing IOUs from merchants into his hat and trading them to a bank at day's end. So the tensions between banking and fixed income trading never reached the fever pitch it had elsewhere. Leadership also moved from banker (Sidney Weinberg) to trader (Gus Levy) to partnerships that typically included one of each (Robert Rubin/Steve Friedman) demonstrating an institutional respect for both. Furthermore, at least since the departure of Catchings in the 30s, the strength of Goldman's leadership and thoughtfulness of the succession planning had kept the culture strong and smoothed any divisions. Finally, the modern Goldman had never experienced a serious "run on the bank," in which a significant portion of the partners retired at once and removed their precious capital from the firm.

In 1994, all those factors that had helped hold Goldman together, seemingly effortlessly, evaporated. Substantial fixed income trading loses—worse than experienced by peers—meant that despite a stellar year in banking, stated profits would be negligible for the year. And for the first time in over 50 years, the partnership capital declined by 10 percent. Since Robert Rubin had left to join the Clinton administration in 1992, his co-chair Steve Friedman had been running the firm himself. Friedman suddenly announced his retirement in September, citing exhaustion.

Former Chairman John Weinberg was so furious with Friedman that when he visited London he invited the younger bankers for a meeting to share his views. The stunned vice presidents listened quietly as this Goldman icon called the departing chairman a "yellow-bellied coward" and graphically and unfavorably contrasted Friedman's behavior with that of his comrades during the Korean War.

Fixed income head Jon Corzine, whom many blamed for the trading losses, was appointed sole chairman, with Chicago-based banker Hank Paulson as his deputy. Among their early official acts was to announce layoffs for the first time in recent Goldman memory, and to do so barely a month before bankers would be entitled to their annual bonuses (which represented the vast bulk of annual compensation). They apologized for the timing and manner of the layoffs but promised they would never do it again. When they then announced another round in January 1995, many at the firm felt betrayed.

More disturbing, in 1994 partners representing fully a third of the existing capital base of the firm announced they would be retiring, immediately triggering the process by which they would withdraw their capital. Maybe most ominously, for the first time in the firm's history a banker invited to join the partnership at its biannual election politely declined. And to top it off, the Maxwell pension trustees picked 1994 to sue the firm in U.S. court for fraud (Goldman would ultimately pay a quarter-billion dollars in 1995 to settle all the outstanding cases).

Although markets recovered and the crisis of 1994 was eventually averted, the fragility of the social and financial compact that allowed Goldman to operate so seamlessly had been revealed. Although the idea of an IPO would be definitively rejected in 1996 as it had been before in 1986, 1991, and 1993, it now felt more like a question of market timing than one of principle. And Corzine, by so publicly associating himself with the forces favoring an IPO, reinforced the view that his weak leadership was at least partially responsible for the need to tap the public markets. In so doing, he would create a surprising opening for Thornton and sow the seeds of his own downfall.

THE MORE I worked with Thornton, the more aware I became of how antithetical his approach was to aspects of the Goldman way—and how despised and resented he was by many of the key establishment partners because of it. This was really brought home to me at the annual internal investment banking conference held in New York each winter, where Thornton was invited to speak about his approach to banking and the success of Goldman's London office. Thornton had already been in London for almost a decade so many of the younger bankers did not know him or even what he looked like. As he got up to speak in front of 2,000 bankers at the Grand Hyatt you could feel the anticipation from the crowd, most of whom only knew of him by reputation. And that reputation was largely of a self-promoting wild man who flouted Goldman rules and culture but was humored because of his relationships and the business he had built in Britain. With him safely across the ocean you could treat Thornton like the crazy cousin in the attic who you just didn't talk about. But now he was in New York about to speak to the assembled troops.

Usually, such talks involve PowerPoint presentations that look very much like the pitch books we produce for clients. But Thornton got up without notes and walked over to an ordinary white board and uncapped a black felt pen.

"These are the important people in the world," said Thornton, as he put apparently random black dots around the board. "I don't know exactly how many there are," he added, "but there are not that many."

"Now this is these people's orbits," he said drawing large circles, many overlapping with each other, around the dozen or so black dots. A big, crazy Venn diagram with dots.

"Inside these circles are the people they know, the deals they do, the ideas they are thinking about. Pretty much everything important that happens in the world, happens in these circles."

"This" he said pointing to what appeared to be the point in the diagram where the most circles overlap, "is where I want to be. That is our strategy. Thank you."

As Thornton sat down and took questions, I looked around the room to see if my colleagues appreciated just how fundamentally subversive what Thornton had said is to everything that is the Goldman way. Emphasizing the importance of relationships with important people was not in itself subversive. But the notion that only a handful of these relationships—and the handful of bankers responsible for them—were really important to the

franchise, very much was. The entire Goldman ethos was built on the idea
that no one was a star, that the whole was greater than the sum of the parts
and that every faceless contributor was in some metaphysical sense equally
responsible for the firm's success. There were 2,000 bankers in the room
that day in New York. It didn't take a rocket scientist to know that most
of them had nothing to do with any of the nameless dots on the white board.
But in Thornton's world these guys were just a waste of space. I was reminded
of this presentation recently when current Goldman CEO Hank Paulson
publicly declared that only 15 to 20 percent of the bankers were responsible for 80 percent of the firm's value.[13] Although Paulson was later forced
to apologize for the remark, at that moment I knew that the Thornton ethos
had taken over.

Thornton thought of himself as epitomizing the best traditions of
Goldman relationship banking. When in the late 1980s he was given
responsibility beyond M&A in London, he broadly distributed both E. J.
Kahn's 1956 *New Yorker* profile of Sidney Weinberg and Former Chairman
John Whitehead's ten commandments of effective client coverage—neither
of which many of the bankers had ever seen. Indeed, many of Thornton's
more controversial "counter-cultural" behaviors—or even something as
trivial as putting me on the BSkyB deal—could be generously interpreted
as designed to definitively ensure that the client relationship would be
protected.

Even accepting this explanation, a subtle but important perceived distinction between the Thornton approach to relationship banking and the
traditional Goldman one related to whom Thornton chose to pursue and
the lengths to which he would go to cement the relationship. In 1994,
Thornton thought Richard Li was one of those dots. He had $525 million
from selling the Star TV stake to Murdoch. And as the son of one of the
richest men in the world, he wanted to show that he could build something on his own with the proceeds. Li had asked Thornton to help him
raise money in a "private placement" for his newest venture, something
called Pacific Century Telecom (PCT). Thornton had told me to get on a
plane and go to Hong Kong, meet with Li, write an offering memorandum, and get it done. Thornton didn't really seem to care what the venture was. He just wanted to be in the circle.

Beyond telling me to show up at Goldman's offices and ask for Mark
Evans (the brother of the London ECM Evans, also a Canadian Olympic
rower) to give me an office, Thornton had not given me a lot of details. It

did seem odd to be sending a London banker to execute a private place-ment in Hong Kong when there were many professionals based there who should have been perfectly capable. I didn't realize how odd until I bumped into the banker with day-to-day client responsibility for Richard Li. His name was Peter Wheeler and Thornton had not mentioned his exist-ence. When I told the stunned Wheeler what I was doing in Hong Kong, he was first speechless. Then he said simply, "We turned down that pro-ject weeks ago."

I explained that I had my orders and asked for directions to Li's offices.

Upon arriving at PCT, I was ushered into a large circular conference room with huge screen hanging overhead. Two attractive and very serious middle-aged Asian women greeted me introducing themselves as the gen-eral counsel and CFO, respectively.

"Richard is sorry he could not be here in person. He will be joining from Singapore momentarily," one of the women said.

Sure enough within a few moments the screen illuminated and a larger-than-life version of a very small young man, still in his twenties, appeared. After initial pleasantries, Li launched into a slightly messianic description of the ambitions of PCT and the potential for something called VSAT technology to bring China quickly into the twenty-first cen-tury. I felt like a minor character in a James Bond movie and hoped to turn the conversation to some practical issues raised both by the business plan and his plan to fund it. But such discussions were apparently not for the Supreme Leader, who vanished from the screen as quickly as he appeared.

I spent the next days writing and trying to understand the business con-cept in meetings with the two women I had already met, plus a hapless former U.S. telecom executive who had been recruited to be at least the nominal CEO and a befuddled young American who apparently thought he had been Richard's best friend at Stanford (where both had attended college for a time) and somehow had gotten tricked into the thankless job of being his gopher.

In brief, VSAT technology, which stands for Very Small Aperture Terminal, can in theory enable large corporations to efficiently bypass inefficient phone systems by renting bandwidth on a satellite that can relay signals between VSAT dishes installed at various corporate locations. Now I was no telecom expert, but it seemed pretty clear to me that the concept of wiring China's businesses (where the bulk of the projected revenues came from) by circumventing the state phone monopoly using VSAT dishes raised myriad regulatory, technological, economic, and practical questions, none of which I received a terribly satisfactory answer to. I took the information I needed to complete my sales memorandum and returned to London to report on my progress to Thornton.

When I relayed my concerns about the viability of the project to Thornton, he would hear none of it. We are trying to raise money from large phone companies in the United States and Europe, he said. Disclose the risks and let them make their judgments. It's not like selling stock to widows and orphans, these are big boys. But, I pointed out, they want us to prepare a valuation with the Goldman imprimatur to help market the placement to these companies—that can't be good for our reputation given the layers of uncertainty around this project. Now Thornton was getting impatient.

"Just build a model assuming it gets regulatory approval, assuming whatever technological issues get resolved, assuming whatever the hell else you need to assume. People can discount it all they want."

Thornton then directed me to go see Robert Morris, the head of European Research and former telecom analyst, to test the assumptions and just get it done. I was dismissed but there was one other topic we needed to cover.

"I was told that because this is a private placement of equity, we need to have the project approved by the Commitments Committee."

"That's crap," Thornton said, waving me away, "I've never been to Commitments Committee in my life. Call Kevin Kennedy in New York and take care of it." We were done.

The Commitments Committee was the ultimate arbiter of what people and companies the firm would do business with. Although you didn't need to go before them to undertake an M&A assignment, if the firm was going to underwrite securities you did. And in theory a private placement involved offering equity securities, even if we were not literally underwriting them. Goldman took its reputation and the role of the Commitments Committee seriously. They even had a guy named David Lawrence on staff to do background checks before they took on certain assignments. A banker would dial Lawrence's extension, give the name of the prospective client, and within a few days get a call back with the verdict as to whether he or she met Goldman's standards. The Committee included only very senior bankers, people like Dobkin and Kevin Kennedy, one of the heads of Corporate Finance.

"You can tell John Thornton if he thinks he is too good to come to a Commitments Committee meeting he can go fuck himself." The call with Kennedy was not going well. He eventually relented when he learned of Morris' involvement, but it was the first time that I appreciated the depth of the animosity in New York toward Thornton.

I was happy to hand the project off to others with relationships with the phone companies once I completed the information memorandum and valuation work early in 1995. I read later that year that Richard sold the business to his dad at Hutchinson Whampoa for cost, allegedly to avoid a conflict of interest. The renamed Li investment vehicle, Pacific Century Cyberworks (PCCW), bought the business back from his father's company for stock in 2001 after PCCW's stock collapsed along with rest of the cyber sector. At the time, the *Economist Intelligence Unit* reported that "[t]he 'sale' reflects PCCW's dire financial situation. . . . There is no business case for Hutchison to accept PCCW shares in exchange for the [unit]." In 2000, the business still had revenues of under $40 million.

With the exception of a break for my marriage and honeymoon in February, I spent most of the early 1995 shuttling between London, Hong Kong, Delhi, and Bombay as we tried, unsuccessfully, to replicate our success with the BSkyB offering in India. At the time, Murdoch had a joint venture with Indian media mogul Sabash Chandra. The business was called Zee, which encompassed a number of popular satellite and pay channels as well as a network of cable operations called CitiCable. The sensitive disclosure issues that arose in the Indian context made anything we dealt with on Sky seem tame. Zee had written proof of its exclusive rights to a large number of films. Unfortunately, we discovered that it is an Indian tradition to sell exclusive rights multiple times so that the number of exclusive rights claimed by the various pay-TV competitors added up to a significant multiple of the number of films actually made. CitiCable had even bigger potential disclosure issues. Let's just say that to describe some of the standard subscriber acquisition techniques utilized in India as "aggressive" would be a significant understatement. At the end of the day it was disagreements between Murdoch and Chandra that forced us to abandon the offering.

During one of my trips back to London over this time (I ended up banking more than 100,000 flight miles in the first five months of 1995) someone told me that Joe Zimmel, co-head of the New York Communications, Media and Telecommunications (CMT) effort, was interested in seeing if

I would be interested in moving back to the United States and would be calling. My new wife, whom I had met at United, was ready to leave but we were undecided between New York and London. I knew that Joe and his co-head Pete Kiernan resented Thornton for his refusal to share any of his media relationships. Thornton for his part just thought these guys were useless—not close to any of the relevant circles. Joe in particular seemed to get under his skin. They had grown up together in the tight M&A sub-culture and Joe seemed to symbolize for John the kind of rote, plodding execution skills that the firm trains bankers for. These skills are perfectly useful for the specific tasks for which they were designed. But the notion that Joe could lead a group, much less the CMT Group, was laughable on its face to John.

So Joe and I started trading calls. When we finally connected, he started by saying, "Are you calling me or am I calling you?" I soon surmised that Joe was worried that he not be seen as poaching people from Thornton. For as much as Joe disliked Thornton, he clearly feared him.

For my part, I had been thinking that at some point, if I were to have a future at Goldman Sachs, I would need to develop other relationships and, more important, learn the Goldman way (even if only to disregard it later as Thornton had done). Neither would be easy to achieve in London given Thornton's relentless demands and the understandable perception by other partners that I was his guy.

I had put myself on a major assignment unrelated to Thornton for the Anglo-Dutch publisher Reed Elsevier, but found that I was frequently forced to fly to Bombay at awkward moments in the project. I was enormously thankful for Thornton's willingness to give me assignments for which I clearly was unprepared and had learned in under a year more than I could have any other way. But I did feel like I had begun to burn out. I did not know how many more months I could take of urgent private voice mails (in response to some pathetic plea of mine for clarification or guidance) telling me to "just fucking do it."

And I had the sense that Thornton was a great guy to have worked for. I had already stumbled upon the informal secret society of former Thornton acolytes, and they were generally well regarded and well placed. They had all the benefits of association with Thornton without the down-side of the day-to-day grind of actually dealing with him. And I now had a wife I could blame it on so there was less risk he would resent me for abandoning him for Zimmel.

Kevin Czinger, who was still my only real friend in investment banking, had left to be the number two executive at Bertelsman's Music Group back in New York. He had departed shortly after writing Thornton a memo arguing that the management of CMT in New York and London, given its focus on the highly regulated communications business, was ill suited to attack the more entrepreneurial media business opportunity. Thornton, who didn't disagree, promptly shared the memo with Scott Mead (as well as Zimmel and Kiernan), and then wondered why Kevin and Scott couldn't seem to get along. My only other friend at the firm was Josh Bolten, a former general counsel to the U.S. trade representative, who worked in the legal department as a kind of "control" for a network of former (and sometimes current) European government officials who helped Goldman get business in their home countries. Bolten was incredibly kind, but ultimately could provide no cover or guidance for me within investment banking.

Finally, although I do not believe it affected my decision to return to the United States, by the spring of 1995 I did begin to wonder how long Thornton would survive at Goldman. Aggravating the powers that be in New York was one thing, as long as he did not rub their noses in it. But in April, Thornton was actually quoted in the *New York Times* as saying he would consider going to competitor Lazard Freres, but "only for the top job." It had long been an unspoken rule for bankers that being quoted in the press—even on mundane matters, much less publicly negotiating for a promotion—was grounds for dismissal. This was part of the antistar, proteam culture that Goldman sought to epitomize. To my surprise, however, nothing seemed to happen. No apparent repercussions—no one even spoke about it. As I prepared to notify Thornton of my planned move to New York, I had a feeling that more must be going on behind the scenes.

The meeting with John where I broke the news of my decision was brief and to the point, like all meetings with John. The wife explanation did the trick. He did not fight battles he couldn't win. Thornton warned me that I would learn nothing important from either Zimmel or Kiernan but said I would learn a lot about the Goldman culture and the basic blocking and tackling of investment banking. He thanked me for my help, wished me luck, and told me to keep in touch.

WHAT INVESTMENT
BANKERS REALLY DO

THE TELECOM AND TECHNOLOGY BOOM is often remembered as having come upon us suddenly in the late 1990s and disappeared just as quickly early in the new century. Neither recollection is accurate. Even those who date the birth of that euphoric era to the Netscape IPO of August 1995 understate the extent to which the underlying assumptions that drove the boom were already securely in place by that time. An unspoken belief in the inevitability of growth had already taken hold. By 1995, when I came to Goldman in New York, the industry, the economy, and markets had experienced solid and largely steady growth since the end of the recession in 1991. Although Goldman had experienced significant trading losses in 1994 and the stock market appeared to pause, investment banking business was up substantially just as it had been the previous year and the one before that.

It seemed to me as if there were almost an entitlement mentality both around perceptions of the inexorability of growth and compensation generally. My 1994 salary had already been set by contract at the pro rata portion of $225,000. Not only was this more than double my base salary at United Airlines, but the generous expatriate package probably cost Goldman double that again. Even the arrangements that were made for my move from Chicago left me breathless. My furniture was largely cheap, second-hand stuff, with the exception of a couch I had bought new for $199.99 at a discount store called Marlo's in Washington, DC several years earlier. When I had moved to Chicago I remember wondering whether it was even worth dragging the already badly stained item across the country in my rented truck.

Goldman's international movers treated it, along with every other item that came across, as if it were being shipped from Tiffany's. When the bulky couch could not fit through the door of my rented Soho flat, I suggested putting a match to it. The shipping company, however, got a permit to close down the street one weekend, brought in a crane and managed to get it into the apartment via the roof through an internal patio in the apartment. Such treatment could go to a person's head.

I still had no idea what to expect for a bonus in 1995. At United in the early 1990s the range of annual increase for nonunion employees was usually somewhere within a range of 0 to 4 percent. And this was on a very low base. Indeed, in a company of 80,000 employees, outside of several thousand pilots who *averaged* over $100,000 annually, only 30 employees (including the CEO and his senior management team) made more than that. Already being in a range well beyond my expectations or intrinsic worth, I would have been thrilled with $250,000 or, maybe in my wildest dreams, $300,000.

Shortly after I arrived in New York I asked a senior colleague how I should think about compensation at Goldman. He explained, matter-of-factly, that salaries are set by "class" (this refers to the year you graduated from business school and started at Goldman) with 90 percent of every class paid within a very narrow range. Each year, he told me, I should expect my "number" (this is what the modest base salary plus annual bonus is called) to go up by about $100,000 year, except for a couple of years (like moving from first to second year vice president), which should be a little more.

Putting aside my effort not to give away my glee and incredulity that I could be making a half-million dollars in a couple of years, there was an aspect to this salary scale that I found even more shocking than the mind-boggling absolute numbers involved. Both at Goldman and more broadly even at business school, the basic persona of investment bankers or aspiring bankers is wholly inconsistent with this compensation structure. One cannot spend even a few minutes talking with an investment banker without getting a palpable sense that they view themselves as defined by— and see the extraordinary salaries they make as being justified by—their aggressive, entrepreneurial, risk-taking approach to life and business. But the lockstep compensation scheme described was clearly designed for exactly the opposite type of person.

The key to successfully managing large numbers of highly competitive, ambitious people, it seems, is to feed their most unrealistic illusions about themselves. And the best way to keep them is to instill a subconscious belief that those illusions will be shattered when exposed to the light of the outside world. I remember particularly a leadership training course that I went to with a dozen other young vice presidents at Goldman at which we were all asked to put our heads down on the table. The facilitator asked those who believed they were in the top 1 percent of their peer group to raise their hand. The bar was then lowered to top 3 percent and then 5 percent. When we sat up I discovered that I was the only member of the group who had not raised his hand. It takes a very special kind of skill to keep more than 90 percent of the bankers believing they are in the top 5 percent of their class.

EVERYTHING ABOUT Goldman Sachs' headquarters in New York was intimidating. The 30-story building, a nondescript brownish color taking up the full block between Water and Pine on Broad Street, looked like a prison. And I quickly realized that my experience in London would be of only marginal assistance in understanding the business and culture of Goldman Sachs, New York.

In London, Goldman was an aggressive, hungry, upstart competitor. Sure, it had enjoyed some success, particularly in transplanting U.S.-style M&A tactics, but on the ground, day-to-day, it was on the outside looking in. Pitching long shots, making cold calls, building a franchise in a market still dominated by the traditional U.K. banking houses.

In New York, Goldman was the Establishment. By the mid-90s Goldman had left its commercial paper roots and was the clear leader in the two most profitable investment banking businesses—initial public offerings and mergers and acquisitions. And leadership in each of these businesses fed continued leadership in the other: newly public companies flush with cash frequently turn to their lead underwriter for advice on their first big acquisition and the advisor on that last deal that made you big enough to go public often gets the nod to manage the offering. And despite the turmoil of 1994, on a relative basis Goldman was still the rock of Wall Street, internally and externally. Internally, its systems, processes, and databases were second to none and fortified by a combination of strong, centralized management and an unparalleled culture of teamwork and communication. Externally, Goldman experienced a fraction of the banker turnover that others did, and it was not unusual that a client coverage team could trace its roots to the days of Sidney Weinberg.

My first Monday morning CMT New York group meeting came as a bit of a shock. As people went around the conference table, I felt like I had been invited to dinner by a foreign family. I could make out the occasional word or impute meaning by interpreting a particular gesture. But mostly, I had no idea what they were talking about. Sometimes it was because they were talking about a technology I had never heard of. Sometimes it was a financial instrument I had never worked on. Sometimes it was companies, or people, that meant nothing to me. I sat quietly, shaking my head and smiling now and again to give the impression that I knew what was going on.

It struck me almost immediately that my job in London had been less that of investment banker and more that of "special assistant" to Thornton. And probably my success was largely due to the experience I already had as a kind of special assistant to demanding bosses like Steve Wolf at United and Stuart Eizenstat before that. But there was no such job at Goldman in New York. I was supposed to be a general purpose, plug-and-play Goldman banker available for any assignment that might come up within the CMT universe. In short, I was screwed.

Although I seemed to have earned the equivalent of investment banking "street cred" for having worked on the BSkyB IPO, my colleagues once again eyed me warily. And Zimmel and Kiernan did not seem to make any special effort to integrate me into the group. For what would not be the last time during my stay at Goldman in New York, I simply could not figure out what Zimmel had had in mind. Why had he recruited me? Did he just need people and hear that I was good and potentially available? Did he hope to transplant my relationships with the Murdoch crew to New York? Did he realize the group's overall weakness on the media side and hope to bolster it through me? Or did he just want to annoy Thornton? I really had, and to this day have, no idea.

Joe Zimmel and Pete Kiernan were as unlikely a pair as one could imagine. Zimmel was tall, slightly overweight, and both physically and interpersonally awkward. He wore thick glasses and spoke very deliberately and quietly, and seemed to be trying just a little too hard to appear unflustered and unflusterable. His strength was an encyclopedic knowledge of M&A execution practices and Goldman standards and procedures on everything from conflicts to fees. His weakness was any kind of creative thinking. Zimmel thrived in a rule-based environment, which is why he had naturally gravitated toward the highly regulated telecommunications sector but seemed to flail in the media environment. Zimmel trying to tell a joke or propose an out-of-the-box idea was always sure to elicit a collective embarrassed cringe. For all of his limitations, Zimmel was generally well liked both in the group, where he was viewed as fair and approachable, and outside, where he was seen as a reliable team player.

Tales of Zimmel's interpersonal cluelessness were affectionately and regularly shared by bankers. My personal favorite relates to the time that Zimmel discovered that another banker in the group was having trouble conceiving a baby. Zimmel unselfconsciously shared his own travails in this area to anyone who would listen, and his secretary complained that Zimmel would inform her when he was calling from "that little room" where he would produce his sperm sample. Zimmel called the banker in, raised the topic and asked the banker his sperm count. As these stories were passed around, they of course became embellished. The last time I heard this story, the encounter with the banker supposedly took place in a crowded elevator and Zimmel was carrying a paper bag containing a sperm deposit he was on his way to make at the clinic.

Despite his popularity, I always had mixed feelings about Zimmel. Part of this may have stemmed from his difficult relationship with Thornton. But I always sensed a dark side to his persona. This would manifest itself in an almost Nurse Ratchet–like passive-aggressiveness. Indeed, it seemed to me that the feeling of power over the bidding parties that Zimmel got from running an M&A process was what drew him to this line of work in the first place.

Pete Kiernan, on the other hand, could have been a news anchor or, better yet, a televangelist. He was always impeccably dressed and coiffed. Kiernan's polished and funny annual presentation during Goldman's orientation sessions for its incoming associate class gave him a certain iconic status among the troops at large. Smart, and good with clients, Kiernan should have been a superstar at Goldman. But he wasn't.

It is hard to pinpoint where Kiernan went wrong. Within the group, he loved to give inspirational speeches about how well we were doing. But particularly among bankers whose job it was, like Kiernan, to call on companies for business ("coverage officers") he was viewed suspiciously at best. Kiernan would list himself as the "senior" coverage officer for almost every major media and telecom client, far more companies than anyone could effectively "cover." Whoever was responsible for the day-to-day calling effort below Kiernan knew they were being set up: if a deal was missed, Kiernan would blame them, but on any successes he would swoop in for the close and take credit.

All of this would not have been so bad had Kiernan actually become seriously engaged with the ongoing coverage effort on even a few of these accounts. One of the great mysteries was why he did not. Given his natural banking skills, the conventional wisdom was that if Kiernan spent half the time he devoted to office politics on calling CEOs instead, he could have been a great success. My only conclusion is that he must have been far more insecure and have a much deeper fear of failure than his suave exterior betrayed. By staying above the fray he could maintain plausible deniability. If he had become too closely associated with any particular account he would have to risk public failure.

I realized, having seen Kiernan in action over the years, that one of his problems was that he had not actually done that many deals. Although a master at spinning even tangentially related experiences into an effective pitch, at times he was reduced to drawing on material well beyond even the tangentially related. Short meetings were always fine. Kiernan had a great 15 minutes. As the meeting got longer, however, the situation became more unpredictable. For instance, Kiernan apparently had a close personal relationship with inspirational speaker Tony Robbins. If a meeting went over an hour, there was a high probability that Kiernan would bring this up, regardless of the company or the situation (e.g., "You should talk to Tony about doing a video," "Have you ever considered doing a magazine with Tony," etc.).

My sense was that the powers that be viewed Kiernan as a banker with great potential, but too much out for himself—a quality deplored at the Goldman Sachs of the time. Being partnered with Zimmel to build a media business was his opportunity to prove he was something more. By the time I arrived in the group, it seemed clear to everyone except Kiernan that he had not stepped up to the challenge.

My own relationship with both Kiernan and Zimmel was always clumsy. Kiernan's back-slapping, good-old-boy style and preoccupation with appearances naturally clashed with my own indifference to social and stylistic mores. I didn't follow sports, dressed haphazardly at best, and was a euphoric newlywed, eliminating most obvious topics of "guy" small talk that might bring us closer. And Zimmel, for whatever reason, decided that he should try to turn me into a more acceptable version of a Goldman Company Man. Whether scolding me for coming into the office in overalls on the weekend, suggesting that certain office wall hangings might reflect badly on the group (specifically a costume I wore at Carnival in Brazil with a caricature of now president, but then Socialist Workers' Party candidate, Lula) or calmly explaining the virtues of keeping a tidy office, Zimmel always seemed oblivious to the futility of his overall objective. To be fair, my office was an abomination, attracting sightseers from other floors. At one group Halloween party, a creative co-worker collected refuse from around my workspace and, with the help of some glue, string, and rubber bands, came as Jonathan's Office.

I was still young and naïve enough to think that if I just worked hard and exceeded expectations, I would be able to compensate for the lack of personal connection with my group heads. To pull this off, however, I knew that I would need to carve out some domain that was of no particular interest to anyone but that I could turn into a real business. This is easier said than done. Just as I was becoming disheartened as to the feasibility of such a strategy, a project I had been working on in London offered an extremely fortuitous opportunity.

Reed Elsevier is one of the largest publishing companies in the world. At the time, it owned everything from consumer magazines and books to legal and scientific journals. After an exhaustive review of the portfolio, we had advised the British CEO, Ian Irvine, to dispose of consumer publishing and redeploy its assets to establish itself as the clear global leader in business and professional publishing. The CEO agreed. But there was a problem.

Created through a complex merger, Reed Elsevier is an operating company whose shares are held by two separately traded public companies, one British (Reed International plc) and one Dutch (Elsevier NV). The board of the operating company was half British, half Dutch. And each side hated the other. What one wanted, the other opposed on principle. Bob Krakoff, the sole American board member at the time, describes the board dynamic of that era, "Whatever the Dutch thought was black the British thought was white and vice versa. There was complete paralysis."

Unfortunately, Irvine had not adequately prepared us for the intensity of the personal vitriol and the depth of the mistrust. At the premeeting where we went through our proposed board presentation with him, Irvine seemed very satisfied and suggested few changes. At the board meeting itself

—with the dour Dutch directors lined up on one side of the table and the dour British directors on the other—we had barely begun our presentation when Irvine began screaming. He challenged basic assumptions. He taunted us with small technical errors. Other directors jumped in. They were enjoying this. At the time I was mortified. Only later did I realize that if Irvine was seen as having put us up to the proposed strategy, there would be no way to convince the Dutch to accept it.

It would be many months and many more ugly board meetings before we gained consensus. We tried everything. At one point we enlisted a Dutch Goldman banker, David Meerschwam, who was a former Harvard Business School professor. Although considered technically brilliant, Meerschwam was extremely arrogant and generally not thought of as "client friendly." The idea was, however, that he might speak the same language as this collection of other arrogant Dutchmen. It was a failure. The Dutch found Meerschwam as unbearable as the rest of us. "Shut up and sit down," said one Dutch board member shortly after Meerschwam had begun his highly technical presentation. That was the end of Meerschwam's brief sojourn on the Reed team.

By the time final decisions on what was going and what was staying were made, I had already been in New York for several months. One of the things that definitely was going to be sold was a small collection of consumer magazine assets that the company owned in the United States. The group was called Cahners Consumer Magazines and included *American Baby*, *Modern Bride*, *Sail*, and *Power and Motoryacht*. As I was the only person in New York who knew anything about these assets or anybody at the company, I argued strongly (despite my having never sold anything before) that I should execute the transaction. I also saw an opening to establish an area of specialty I could call my own—I would be King of Publishing. That both gambits worked was a function of the deal and the sector.

The deal was small by Goldman standards and, if it had not been part of the larger Reed assignment, might have been considered more trouble than it was worth. With a total value less than $200 million, the best buyers for each of the individual titles might be different, making the sale process sure to be relatively complex and time consuming. We would need to offer the assets both as a group and separately to create the most competition and get the highest price. No serious banker wanted to get drawn into an extended sale process where you could end up having to negotiate multiple different deals for tiny assets.

It is axiomatic in the industry that the smaller the deal, the more painful (meaning time consuming and exasperating) the execution. This sounds counterintuitive, but small deals typically involve less sophisticated parties and advisors. The sale process ends up being as much an education process as a negotiation process. Furthermore, items that might have an impact on the purchase price of a few hundred thousand dollars end up being negotiated intensely, whereas in larger transactions their relative unimportance in the overall deal allows for easier broad compromises.

Equally important, bankers gain stature within the organization and in the community at large by being associated with large, important transactions. You don't become a "Big Swinging Dick," in the phrase immortalized in *Liar's Poker*, by working on crummy little deals. Size in this context refers both to the value paid and the fee collected. The former is relevant for the all-important league tables discussed earlier and bragging rights in general. The latter obviously is relevant to the bottom line. Most investment banks (although not Goldman, which centrally manages fee negotiations based on its own historic fee database) use a variation on the old Lehman Brothers "fee scale" to establish where they want fees to end up. On this basis, deals from $100 to 200 million merit a fee of around 1 percent (translating to a $1 to 2 million fee), which scales down to about .5 percent at $1 billion (for a $5 million fee) and finally bottoms out at .2 percent at $10 billion (for a $20 million fee). Actual fees are all over the place, ranging from flat dollar amounts to flat percentages to more complicated fees with incentive triggers above certain prices. How low an I-bank is willing to go in a particular circumstance will be a function of how many resources the deal will consume, how busy it is at the time, how high-profile or otherwise strategic the transaction is, whether it is for an important client and whether there is likely follow-on business. On a more personal level, Big Swinging Dicks don't like to work on deals that yield less than $5 million and prefer deals that net more than $10 million.

I, of course, did not appreciate any of these nuances at the time. I just wanted something I could call my own. They assigned a relatively senior general M&A banker to "supervise" the project, but for obvious reasons, he wanted as little to do with it as possible and was quite happy giving me general guidance by return voice mail from wherever he was at the time working on a more substantial deal.

With respect to being "King of Publishing"—this was ultimately down-graded to publishing sector head—Kiernan and Zimmel were undoubtedly chuckling to themselves when I asked for this responsibility. Publishing at the time was an area of almost no significant activity in either the merger or financing area. Most publishing businesses were either a small part of larger businesses or just not that big. In the U.S. public markets, newspaper companies were the predominant publishing subsector, and these were almost uniformly midsized, notoriously conservative, family-dominated companies. The exception was Gannett—large, independent, and acquisitive— but they never used a banker. On the financing side, publishing is such a high-cash-flow, low-capital-expenditure business that, in the absence of much strategic acquisition activity, there wasn't going to be much financing activity either. Once every so many years a family business would decide to go public, but this, like everything else in the sector, was irregular and unpredictable.

In short, being made King of Publishing was like being made King of Anyplace Where Nothing Important Much Ever Happens. None of us predicted the unprecedented wave of consolidation that would follow.

The actual sale of Cahners Consumer Magazines was very much like the dozens of similar sales of various shapes and sizes I would execute in the subsequent years. The first discussion with the client is always about what kind of sale process to undertake. The options range from a one-on-one negotiated sale to a broad publicly announced auction. Bankers almost always prefer the latter for four reasons.

First, you are mostly likely to get the highest price, which usually means the highest fee. You never know who a more selective approach might overlook. And if there is even a small probability that some unexpected idiosyncratic buyer with money to burn might show up, the banker's perspective is—why not?

Second, a broad auction more often than not takes less time than a negotiated deal. The only thing that forces a buyer to hurry up is competition. In a negotiated deal your only threat is pulling it off the market or starting over with someone else, which is not terribly compelling leverage.

Third, the worst outcome for a banker is for no deal to happen—fees are almost always entirely "success" based. And success is almost always defined as money changing hands. Once a client has publicly committed to selling, it becomes very difficult to reverse course if there is any halfway legitimate offer.

Fourth, investment banks' most important clients are leveraged buyout (LBO) firms, known as "private equity firms" or "financial sponsors" within the industry.[1] These funds have amassed billions of dollars of equity from pension funds, insurance companies, and the like and are in the sole business of buying companies and then, several years later, monetizing their investments through a sale, a public offering, or recapitalization (i.e., borrowing more money to buy themselves out or pay themselves a dividend). As recently as 1990, only a handful of funds had raised more than $1 billion in capital, all with well-known names like KKR, Forstmann Little, and Morgan Stanley. Today there are over 250 such funds, so many in fact that even seasoned bankers don't know them all. These firms are deal machines: all they do is buy, sell, and finance, all of which are the core fee generators of the investment banking business.

Understandably, keeping financial sponsors happy is a very high priority. Financial sponsors view many of the services investment bankers provide as commodities. What they constantly demand and need to survive is deal flow—access to transactions that can allow them to put their capital to use. As a result, bankers whose job is to manage relationships with financial sponsors comb their firms looking for deals that can be shown to their clients—then actively encourage merger bankers to coax their selling clients to offer the potential deal to the broadest possible universe.

So unless it is absolutely clear that there is only one (or better two or three, for at least some competition) "best" owner(s) of the business, a banker will more often than not argue for a broad auction.

Clients, however, often do not like the idea of a "broad" auction. They are concerned about the impact of publicity on the business and employees. They dislike the idea that anyone with arguable financial ability and even mild interest can take a look at the business. They are concerned about competitive issues. Bankers typically compromise by using calming phrases like "controlled" or "selective" auction, suggesting a hybrid process somewhere in between a negotiated deal and a broad auction. They then usually proceed to run a broad auction. To maintain deniability, bankers highlight for clients the inevitable calls from inappropriate buyers who they would have dismissed even in a broad auction context to demonstrate the discriminating nature of the process. This was more or less what was done in the Cahners' Consumer sale process.

The first order of business once the process is agreed upon is to prepare a "book": marketing materials that begin with "Investment Considerations" or "Selling Points" and contain the basic descriptive and financial materials potential buyers will need to give some reasonable indication of how much they are willing to pay. Here the banker has three main objectives.

First, he wishes to ensure the numbers are as aggressive as possible while being at least theoretically defensible. One-time adjustments, excess overhead, start-up costs, and the like are all identified and backed out to create the highest base cash flow number that you might convince someone to pay for (in publishing businesses cash flow is usually approximated by something called EBITDA—earnings before interest, taxes, depreciation, and amortization). The reader is usually directed toward a number identified by a tongue-twisting appellation like "Adjusted Pro Forma Run Rate EBITDA." The hope is that if a buyer applies some kind of cash flow multiple to arrive at a purchase price he or she can be convinced to apply it to this grossed-up number.

Second, he needs to make sure the numbers, particularly near-term projections, are believable. If too high (shortsighted sellers sometimes think this is smart), there is a risk that a deal falls apart late as a buyer tries to renegotiate when the actual results come in. If too low (managers who plan to stick around still try to sandbag numbers so they will look good when the actual results exceed their projections), there is money being left on the table.

Third, he wants to get the company to write as much of the book as possible.

The production of the book can take two to six weeks depending on how complicated the story is and how much you can get the company to do for you—particularly if there is usable off-the-shelf marketing or financial material already prepared for some other purpose. Meanwhile confidentiality agreements—basically rules for playing the game such as not using the information improperly, or not stealing your client's employees—are negotiated with prospective book recipients. Given that in a truly no-holds-barred broad auction it is not unheard of to invite over 100 parties to participate, negotiating confidentiality agreements can also be time consuming—and again an opportunity to try to get the company or the company's counsel to do it for you. Once this task is completed, book recipients are given two to four weeks to review the materials.

A "Preliminary Bid Letter" is sent setting a submission date for non-binding indications of what the buyers think they would be willing to pay. In the weeks leading up to this date, bankers work with the company on a kind of show where the management team effectively acts out a dramatization of the substance of the book. This live performance will be offered—along with access to a data room and management—to those whose preliminary bids make them appear serious enough to merit the additional investment of time. To be safe, you probably want to invite at least three parties to management presentations, but I have run processes that have involved over a dozen or as few as one (in the latter case, every effort is made to create the illusion of multiple continuing parties). Depending on the number, the management presentation stage is another two to four weeks. Once completed, a final bid letter is provided along with a contract setting a date about a month out for final binding proposals to be submitted.

The process described is usually referred to as a two-step auction, with the first step being the solicitation of preliminary bids and the second step being final bids. From beginning to end—the end being signing up a definitive sale agreement—the entire undertaking usually lasts three to five months. The exciting bit happens once definitive proposals are submitted. A final deal could be signed 48 hours later, or could drag on for weeks. Every situation is different, but the one common element is that the key to a successful outcome for a seller is competition or, just as effective, the perception of competition.

ABOUT A MONTH after I had begun work on the Cahners transaction, Goldman Sachs got a call that in retrospect made my choice of the publishing sector seem very fortuitous indeed. The call came from a midsized St. Louis–based brokerage named A. G. Edwards with which Goldman Sachs had a particularly good relationship. Because Goldman did not own a retail brokerage network, it relied in part on its relationships with independent brokers to distribute its securities. It turned out Edwards had a broker on the West Coast whose father was founder and chairman and whose brother was CEO of a private publishing company based in Minnesota. When the company looked to Edwards for help, Edwards seemed to think the proposed transaction, a sale, might be a little big for them to handle alone and called Goldman. The Company was called West and when we sold it to Thomson the following year for $3.4 billion, it would be the biggest U.S. publishing deal in history and one of the ten biggest U.S. M&A deals for 1996 overall.

Although West was founded by John B. West in 1872, the modern incarnation was the product of its brilliant and secretive chairman and CEO,

Dwight Opperman, who joined the company as an editor in 1951. Opperman had taken what at first glance was a rather mundane business—making state and federal court decisions and statutes easily available to practitioners—and turned it into a franchise almost as strong and defensible as BSkyB. Given that laws and court decisions are available to anyone who wants them for free, the question of how to build a defensible business model that would survive into the digital age was by no means obvious.

Opperman had help. In 1890 the company began developing a proprietary indexing system for organizing legal holdings, now known as the West Key Number System. In a common-law legal system like ours, which relies on precedent to reach decisions, the ability to go to the relevant West Key number and find every holding that deals with the topic is hugely valuable. So, when West published a court decision, it did more than check for typos and technical inconsistencies. It hired a legion of lawyers both to summarize the cases and organize those summaries into the relevant index sections. A single case could have aspects that were cross-referenced into dozens of different Key subheadings. In addition, for each referenced legal issue in a case, West summarizes the specific legal holdings into convenient paragraphs known as "headnotes." West editors produce something close to half a million headnotes each year. And when it comes to statutes, rather than cases, it didn't hurt that in 1925 the federal government had requested West to organize and publish the nation's laws. The resulting United States Code is helpfully annotated to allow easy cross-referencing—by West Key Number of course—to court decisions interpreting the relevant statute.

The sheer magnitude of the accumulated intellectual property represented by the literally millions of summarized cases going back over a century represents a significant barrier to entry. Today, the catalogue that simply holds the topic headings for all the different Key Number entries itself runs to several volumes. As we will see, although the then newly emerging world of digital distribution posed some challenges to this franchise, it offered almost as many new opportunities.

As a highly profitable private company, with no need for outside financing, West bred right-wing conspiracy theories, particularly given the politics and secretive nature of its founder. The local newspaper, the *Minneapolis Star Tribune*, was owned by the liberal Cowles family and ran a series of exposés about extravagant West-financed retreats attended by judges (including Supreme Court justices) around the country.[2] The implication was that West was improperly lobbying the judiciary to promote not only its intellectual property claims against competitors but, more darkly, a broader right-wing agenda. Feeding these theories was the fact that, as West grew, it added subterranean floors to its headquarters on the banks of the Mississippi River in St. Paul.

When we arrived at the airport in Minneapolis, we were met by a spry, well-kept, elderly Lebanese man dressed in a custom-tailored white suit with matching white leather shoes and a bright tailored red shirt. By this time, West had moved to an elaborate campus in Eagan, Minnesota. As we drove there it became clear that our driver was actually a senior West executive rather than a chauffeur. His name was John M. Nasseff and he had the title, VP—facilities and engineering. Now, in general, facilities are not a particularly important part of publishing businesses. I would learn soon enough, however, that Dwight had generously shared the equity of West with many of his friends like Nasseff from the early days of the business— indeed, the 71-year-old Nasseff had preceded Dwight at West by five years. In fact, the top ten executives (including Dwight and his son) owned about 50 percent of the equity, with the rest having been shared with the employees at large. Many of the top executives, with similar lofty titles to our driver's, had long ago stopped participating meaningfully in the day-to-day operations of the company. Their main preoccupation since finding out that Dwight was planning to sell had been establishing residency in a state with a lower tax rate than Minnesota. Given the money at stake, it was an understandable preoccupation.

When we arrived at the headquarters, I at least knew that Nasseff had not been idle in his capacity as director of facilities. Although West was a large company, the facility was appropriate for a much larger business. In addition to thousands of square feet of fully built out but unoccupied office space, the campus included elaborate multicolor printing operations (except for newspapers, which must publish and distribute product daily, almost no publishers in the United States still do their own printing), which were used for their modest college textbook business, and massive duplicate data-storage facilities designed to withstand most natural disasters. When I asked why they had overbuilt so dramatically, Nasseff gave a whispered reply about the continuous need to come up with legitimate business uses for the overwhelming quantities of cash generated to avoid the excess profits tax.

The decision to sell had come after Dwight's wife passed away. He had built her an elaborate wheelchair-accessible garden at their estate to ease her burden while she battled the extended illness that ultimately took her life. With her gone, Dwight seemed to lose the fire in his belly that had driven his remarkable business success. Dwight had two sons. In addition to the one who was a broker at A. G. Edwards, he had another, named Vance, who had recently been named as one of the nation's ten top litigators. Dwight soon turned the business over to Vance, making him CEO, but remaining as chairman.

Vance had the same natural generosity as his father, but in other ways was his opposite. Where Dwight was deeply conservative politically and reserved personally, Vance was unabashedly liberal politically and avuncular personally. And while Dwight was a brilliant businessman, Vance was a brilliant litigator. The company had let an Ohio paper company called Mead beat it to market with an on-line legal information product called Lexis-Nexis, but now split the market after the introduction of their own on-line Westlaw product. Still, West faced a number of important strategic questions that would require it to move beyond the insular world-view that had served it so well for so long. It would need outside capital at a minimum, and probably need to be sold.

To say that preparing West for management presentations was a cultural shock is an understatement. The culture of secrecy was so pervasive that many management members seemed to be learning basic facts about the business for themselves for the first time during our rehearsals. I will never forget arriving at CFO Grant Nelson's office for our first discussion about the company financials. He dramatically got up from behind his desk and walked to a safe from which he withdrew a large old-fashioned ledger book of the sort that Ebenezer Scrooge would make entries in. This was how the financials of the company were still kept, by hand. Grant became our guide to the inner world of West and helped us translate their sometimes arcane ways into a presentation that would be comprehensible to the outside world.

Many were understandably torn by the decision to sell and Grant played a critical role in holding the team together during the process. A profoundly religious and honorable man, Grant was visibly disgusted by the senior executives who were busy researching residency requirements and prespending their anticipated sale proceeds. But more than anything else, he felt that Dwight had more than earned the right to choose the legacy of the company he had built. And Grant was going to make sure it happened in the best way possible.

Despite being held in the dead of one the coldest Minneapolis winters on record, the auction attracted a wide range of high-quality players from

Henry Kravis to the Thomson Corporation. At one point I saw a dogsled calmly make its way past the window during the Thomson management presentation. Thomson had lost out to Reed Elsevier the previous year when Goldman had auctioned off Lexis-Nexis for Mead. At the time, no one thought West would ever be available, allowing competition to drive the price to $1.5 billion. West was far more valuable, but its gigantic size (more than twice as big as Lexis-Nexis) narrowed the range of parties that could seriously participate. Thomson had the financial capacity, and was certainly acquisitive, but had never done a deal of this magnitude. At the time, the company was highly decentralized and representatives from every Thomson unit that was implicated by a potential West transaction flew in to Minneapolis. Ultimately, I had to rent a large tour bus to bring the assembled group of over 50 people from their downtown hotel to headquarters. So much for confidentiality.

During the course of the process, Dwight became convinced that Thomson was the right home for West. It was as if the Eagan facility had been built in anticipation of consolidating all of the scattered related Thomson businesses under a West banner as a Thomson subsidiary. He also grew comfortable with the Thomson management team that would be managing the business. In his mind, before the first bid came in, he had made a decision.

But there was a problem. In most closely held private companies, the owners can do whatever they want. Much of the fun of working for private companies as an investment banker is designing a customized process to achieve whatever idiosyncratic objectives the owner may have. In the category of "no good deed goes unpunished," because Dwight had given stock to many employees, the lawyers told him that to be safe we should act as if it were a public company. A famous legal case called "Revlon" holds that once a public company has been put up for auction, the shareholders have a right to get the highest price. So the only way that Dwight would get his wish was for Thomson to bid the highest price.

On the final bid date we held our breath and hoped that Thomson would be the high bid. It wasn't. Incredibly, a company called Harcourt General came in at $3.3 billion, just $50 million dollars above Thomson's bid of $3.25 billion. Controlled by the Smith family in Boston, Harcourt was part of a conglomerate that included Neiman Marcus. Their CEO at the time, Bob Tarr, was a former nuclear submarine commander who simply refused to break a smile. Because Vance thrived on audience reaction, his presentation to Harcourt got increasingly shrill and over-the-top as he tried to elicit any kind of reaction from the assembled group. Stone silence. At the end of the day, Vance pulled me aside and said, "that's the last we'll hear from them." Apparently not.

We quickly agreed with the lawyers that if we could get an attractive contract and convince Thomson to pay $3.35 billion, we would be safe from a legal perspective.

Thomson agreed and we moved swiftly to finalize the paperwork. The M&A banker I was working with, Ken Leet, and I knew this was the right outcome and avoided taking any of the increasingly frantic calls that were coming in from Harcourt and their bankers at Lazard. We were worried that they might try to contact Zimmel, who although uninvolved with the day-to-day of the deal, was the official Goldman partner assigned to the transaction. Ken and I left numerous messages for Zimmel telling him not to get involved and not to take any calls.

Zimmel, unfortunately could not control himself, although he claimed to have "inadvertently" answered his cell phone. Within a few minutes, a fax arrived at the Wachtell, Lipton law offices in which we were finalizing the deal. Harcourt had bumped their bid to $3.4 billion. Dwight was almost in tears. He had promised Thomson that if they paid $3.35 billion they would own West. He could not go back on his word. But the lawyers warned him against this. We finalized the contract and Dwight insisted that he speak with the Thomson team alone. Thomson agreed to quickly sign up the deal at $3.45 billion.

Although there was no real "harm" done here—after all, Dwight sold the company to his preferred buyer and got more money—this episode highlights an important and inherent conflict between banker and client in sales processes. After a successful transaction, the client disappears and any future business will come from the universe of suitors. This creates a sometimes irresistible incentive to provide, or give the appearance of providing, some form of subtle preferential treatment to those most likely to offer something in return at a later date.

In this case, the strategy backfired as Thomson was convinced that we had done something that cost them an extra $100 million. And although Ken and I had not, Zimmel, it could be argued, indeed had. In any case, Thomson smelled a rat and refused to do business with Goldman for quite some time. But the transaction was one of those rare deals that was good for all constituencies, not only buyer and seller, but employees and community as well. For Thomson, the deal represented a critical turning point, providing the catalyst for the successful transformation from a somewhat random collection of consumer and professional businesses to the global leader in professional information. For the Oppermans and the other shareholders, the deal provided both an enormous payday and the means to expand and secure the West brand and legacy. Thomson's financial strength and strategic focus on "integrated information solutions" allowed it to expand the West footprint well beyond the scope that would have been possible under a go-it-alone strategy. Vance even joined the Thomson Board of Directors. Thomson employees from their other legal publishing subsidiaries soon filled the space that Nasseff had built for them long in advance, making Thomson one of the top employers in the greater Minneapolis area.

The unsuccessful Smith family was to play another important role in the life of the Oppermans. Dwight ultimately remarried his late wife's former Neiman Marcus personal shopper.

For me, the transaction was a professional watershed for a very different reason. When I came to the end of the West process, I felt a totally unexpected emotion: pride. For all my continuing cynicism about certain aspects of investment banking, this was the first time I saw the unique value entailed in providing a client honest, objective advice combined with professional, diligent execution. West's owners achieved their honorable but nuanced set of objectives, but this was not a forgone conclusion. I could see clearly how any number of different paths, suggested at various points by various different parties with their own agendas, would have resulted in a very different outcome.

Many Goldman competitors complain that the firm, just because of its brand, gets more than its fair share of business without really "deserving" it. And the case of the fortuitous West transaction, awarded to us without any competition, would suggest that there is at least a grain of truth to this charge. A look at the flood of publishing deals that quickly followed as part of the broader merger boom that would continue through the end of the decade suggests a more complex picture reflecting a mix of luck, skill, and the power of the continuity of relationships sown over literally decades.

For instance, winning the mandate to sell mapmaker Rand McNally was clearly earned fair and square in a traditional "bake-off" against several competitors, and over some pretty significant obstacles, as Morgan Stanley partner Barton Biggs was on Rand McNally's board. And Goldman's recent experience selling Cahners to Primedia was key to convincing Bob

Petersen to let our group sell Petersen Publishing, his consumer magazine empire. But the right to sell newspaper and business magazine publisher Cowles Media Company to McClatchy Newspapers was earned through the relationship Sidney's son John L. Weinberg had developed years earlier with the Cowles patriarch. For literally decades, Weinberg and then his successor on the account patiently advised the company and the family about the market and its options. I was just lucky that the decision to sell came at this time. Similarly, Weinberg had been on the board of Knight Ridder since 1969 (and only stepped down at age 78 in 2003) and the company never gave any other firm a significant piece of banking business—until 2005 when dissident shareholders forced the company to put itself up for sale and Goldman's cozy relationship with management was viewed as requiring a second advisor. So when the board hired Goldman to sell Knight Ridder Financial while I was there, it was clearly something much deeper than Goldman just trading off its "brand."

As a result of these and other deals, by the end of 1996, I had been involved with sale of just about every kind of publishing asset. And there are quite a few different publishing market segments, each with its own operating characteristics and (sometimes overlapping) buyer universe. In addition to consumer magazines and legal publishing, there is financial information, educational publishing, scientific and technical publishing, market research, business magazines and trade shows, consumer books, and newspapers. And within each of these segments there are usually numerous market subsegments with highly differentiated attributes. So, within the educational segment for instance, there is basal (K–12 textbooks), higher (college textbooks), supplemental (assorted materials to "supplement" the text books), corporate (professional development), and continuing (now called "lifelong learning") as well as a variety of businesses that actually provide educational services rather than simply publish materials.

Working on the "sell-side" rather than the "buy-side" of a transaction has certain obvious and not-so-obvious benefits. As to the obvious, on a probability-weighted basis, representing one of many potential buyers is less attractive than representing the single seller, particularly given that buy-side success fees are on average actually lower than sell-side fees. The only mitigating factor is that there is typically a financing opportunity associated with the buy-side transaction. But even adjusted for incremental financing fees, it is rarely possible to make a rational case for taking a buy-side assignment over a sell-side assignment.

I would nonetheless later often hear the financing side of the house at Morgan Stanley make just such arguments. Calling these "arguments" is being generous. The first time at Morgan I made what I thought was the noncontroversial statement that it is always preferable to be on the sell-side, the head of high yield financing said to me, "Whenever I hear a banker say that, I want to rip his throat out."

But I never heard such remarks at Goldman. The team-oriented culture and reward system made it possible for the institution to focus on the greatest revenue opportunity for the firm overall. Indeed, I grew up there feeling that working on the buy-side simply highlighted that you had failed to secure the sell-side. By the time I left Goldman in 1998, dozens of deals later, I had never worked on the buy-side of a transaction.

On the less obvious side, selling a company gives you an excuse to talk to people. Although bankers hate to admit it, particularly at Goldman where mere "sales" is often viewed as beneath them, investment banking, at bottom, is a sales job. And the hardest part of sales is picking up the phone and making a call, particularly to someone you don't know. Having an asset of even arguable strategic relevance in your inventory is a great excuse to call someone. If you play it correctly, you can use this to learn an enormous amount about a company. If they say they aren't interested, just asking why will likely give you significant insight into the company's thinking. "And maybe we should get together for lunch so we can better understand where you are trying to take Company X?" And if the business is strategic to the company, then even better. Executives have every interest in being solicitous of you if you are selling an asset they want. And if you treat them fairly, keep them informed, and build an understanding of who they are, you will be doing both yourself and your client a service. I initiated most of what were to become my best client relationships through trying—sometimes successfully and sometimes not—to sell someone something. So the real personal benefit of having sold about every kind of publishing asset was that after only a couple of years of working in the sector, I now knew more senior publishing executives on a first-name basis than all but a handful of people on the planet.

THE CULTURE OF M&A

GIVEN HOW MUCH of my day-to-day existence now involved the relentless flogging of one publishing company after another, I kind of assumed that M&A was the guts of what New York investment bankers did and had always done from time immemorial. In fact, it was only after the huge number of mindless transactions during the 1960s binge of conglomerate build-ups that investment banks focused on the potential of M&A as an attractive line of business in its own right.

The value of M&A was evident from the success of Lazard Frères that, under the leadership of Andre Meyer, established itself as the leading pure "merger house" during this period.[1] Although Goldman was involved in over 100 deals in the late 1960s, it was still careful to insist that it saw "its role in these transactions as an extension of its financing services."[2] It was Goldman's deep knowledge of its clients, a spokesman said, that allowed the firm to make a useful contribution on these deals. Its closest peer, Morgan Stanley, similarly objected to marketing M&A "as a discrete service" divorced from the "total advisory relationship with clients."[3]

Up until roughly the time of Sidney Weinberg's death, investment banks viewed advising on M&A transactions as an ancillary service to support long-term relationships whose object was primarily growth financing. As Bruce Wasserstein has said, the established firms "tended to view the M&A practice as a tool to maintain underwriting relationships [as] a loss leader."[4] This conception of investment banking was so ingrained that at many firms of the era, the investment banking division was still actually called the "Buying Department" because a coverage officer's job was primarily to "buy," that is underwrite, securities.

By the early 70s, however, banks began to appreciate the scope of the potential advisory fees associated with this line of work—especially as the margin pressure on some of their more traditional business increased. This was a pure agency business without any of the overhead costs or capital requirements of underwriting. Unlike financings, M&A did not require an expensive trading infrastructure and did not require that the firm put its own balance sheet at risk. All you were doing was giving advice on buying or selling something and if the deal closed you got paid. If the deal didn't close you might still get paid, though not as much, and at worst at least your expenses were covered.

Goldman's M&A group started with just five bankers focused on selling family businesses.[5] Morgan Stanley began a similarly sized effort. This shift toward a transactional focus intensified in the mid-1970s when Morgan Stanley advised on its first major "hostile takeover." An attempt to acquire a controlling interest in a company is described as "hostile" if the bid is made despite the contrary wishes of that company's board and management. Hostile transactions were commonplace in the robber-baron era of the nineteenth century, but the first modern-day "hostile" deal is usually identified as Pennzoil's 1965 acquisition of United Gas.

As hostile deals came back into vogue, Goldman Sachs naturally moved to establish itself as the "defense" advisor of choice for targets of unwanted corporate advances by refusing to represent any hostile bidder. In the short term, a Morgan Stanley banker conceded, this made clients see "Goldman as less mercenary and more trustworthy than Morgan Stanley."[6] In the longer term, even Goldman was not immune from the gun-for-hire ethos that the growth of M&A as a major independent profit center implied. In the late 1980s Goldman dropped its long-held policy and began representing selected hostile bidders, although it still insisted it would do so "rarely and reluctantly." In 1999, after it had advised a half-dozen clients on hostile bids in just the first six months of the year, capturing the leading market share for such services, the firm continued to claim that its policy was to engage in such behavior only "reluctantly, cautiously [and] selectively."[7]

By the late 1970s, all the major firms were building up large M&A capabilities and the enormous profitability of this practice engendered a particularly arrogant culture within an industry already famous for its arrogance. The growing importance of M&A within investment banks accelerated further during the 1980s as the emergence of junk bond fin-ancing and large private equity funds made previously unthinkable deals possible. All the major investment banks raised their own private equity funds, which fed their in-house M&A groups but also competed with clients for transactions. By the time I joined Goldman Sachs in 1994, their global M&A department had well over a hundred professionals and Steve Friedman, who had built the group, had risen to become the firm's sole chairman.

The emergence of the dedicated M&A professional as the quintessential investment banker—a mercenary gun for hire, usually without industry expertise, whose goal was to buy and sell as many companies as possible—had an impact on the overall culture of investment banking throughout Wall Street. "Relationship" banking began to be seen as stodgy and old-fashioned, and M&A professionals were increasingly taking senior roles at major firms. Within most banks, including Goldman and Morgan, M&A bankers were first among equals when it came to both pay and promotion.

This cultural shift likely played a role in the way the firms responded to the Internet boom that was to come in the late 1990s. By that time, the seeds of a full-fledged celebrity culture had been planted. As Ron Chernow has pointed out, "Publicity accompanied transactional banking as natur-ally as secrecy did relationship banking."[8] It is not a coincidence that at Morgan, the M&A group's first head, Bob Greenhill, was one of the few Morgan bankers that had "emerge[d] as a distinct personality in the pub-lic mind."[9] Nor is it surprising, that two of the early leaders of Morgan's M&A efforts, Greenhill and Eric Gleacher, would ultimately open independent firms under their own now well-known names.

After the recession of the early 1990s, there had been some talk of the emergence of a "new generation" of "low-profile" M&A bankers who, in contrast to Wasserstein, Greenhill, and Gleacher, toiled in "relative obscur-ity."[10] Although some of the excesses of the 1980s and the industry down-turn did have some temporary humbling effect, it is a mistake to confuse these minor stylistic adjustments with structural change. The celebrity cul-ture was like a cancer that went into brief remission. When it came back with the boom, it would infect the entire corpus of investment banking, not just M&A where the malignancy initially lodged.

During the downturn that followed in the new century, many firms, including Goldman, disbanded their M&A groups and dispersed the pro-fessionals into the various client-focused industry specialty groups. In so doing, they were implicitly acknowledging that something important had been lost in the glorification of M&A.

By then, such symbolic gestures would be much too little, much too late. So many choices had been made that were fundamentally at odds with the ethos of Sidney Weinberg and relationship banking that dramatic action would be needed to regain credibility with both employees and clients. Such action, however, would be made even more difficult by other structural changes imposed on the industry by regulators, competitors, and the marketplace.

I had no real sense of this history at the time. I was just glad that I had got the knack of selling companies pretty quickly. Selling one company to another draws on many of the same tools as selling the securities of a company to investors. The same lobbying skills that help write an effective investor presentation assist in the production of an effective sales book. And the frustrated actor in me enjoyed the process of scripting and directing the management presentations to convince bidders to pay the highest possible price. Although just selling publishing companies might have gotten old sooner rather than later, I had two other unofficial roles within the group that managed to keep my interest.

The first was to execute any U.S. media transactions that John Thornton brought in. As he was barely on speaking terms with Kiernan and Zimmel, Thornton would simply call and assign me transactions, sometimes remembering to leave my bosses a voice mail on the development. The most memorable of these was the sale of All American Communications. Run by former B-movie actor and small-time record executive Tony Scotti (Scotti Brothers Records is unfortunately responsible for Weird Al Yankovic), All American was famous for owning the rights to the TV series *Baywatch*. By the time I got involved, *Baywatch* was already on its last legs and not a particularly important part of the company. The jewel of All American was the rights to the old Goodson-Todman library of game-show formats. Any time anyone anywhere in the world wanted to have a local version of, say, *The Price is Right*, they had to deal with All American. When we sold it to Pearson (publisher of the *Financial Times*) for $450 million, David Hasselhoff sent the distinguished CEO and former publisher of the *Economist*, Marjorie Scardino, a *Baywatch* bikini. She was reportedly not amused.

The second unofficial role was to deal with people who . . . were not Goldman's sort of people. Like Bob Sillerman. I met Bob when selling Liberty

Broadcasting, a radio station group, to one of several radio companies he controlled. Sillerman may be the smartest business man I have met, but like many executives who grew up in the hardscrabble world of radio broadcasting, he had some rough edges. So, for example, Bob owned a private company with a benign-sounding name—Sillerman Communications Management Corporation—that had long-term contracts with each of three public companies he controlled to provide certain "advisory services." Any time any of these public companies raised money or bought or sold a radio station—even to each other—Bob got a fee, an arrangement with evident conflicts of interest. Now, as much as I liked Bob and respected his business acumen, Goldman Sachs could not underwrite such a company.

So we came up with a creative solution: merge the companies together and contribute the company getting advisory fees to the new larger entity so Bob's interests would be aligned with that of the shareholders. I was responsible for the somewhat surreal negotiations that ensued between Bob and the Special Board Committee over just how much the company would have to pay Bob to stop taking fees from them on deals they did. The first broad organizational meeting on the merger and related financings filled an enormous conference room as both the individual merging companies and their special Board Committees had separate teams of legal and financial advisors. After keeping the assembled throng waiting, Bob arrived and called the meeting to order.

"I like to start a meeting with a joke," he said. Some side conversations quietly continued. Only a minority of those present had worked with Bob before and had any idea what to expect. Many in the room were newly minted associates or analysts at law firms or investment banks.

"A guy goes to a doctor and says 'D-d-d-d-d-octor you have to help me.' The doctor says, 'What seems to be the problem?' The guy says, 'I g-g-g-g-g-ot a st-t-t-t-tutter.'" Bob began, harmlessly enough.

After examining his patient, Bob continued, the doctor explains that there is nothing practical he can do. The reason? "Your cock is so big it pulls down on the vocal chords. Unless you want me to remove the entire center section, you're just going to have to live with it." At this point, all sidebar conversations stopped.

The stunned audience then listened in silence as Bob explained how the patient first elected to have the radical operation performed but later came to regret it. The patient returned to the doctor's office to beg him to reverse the procedure. After Bob provided a graphic but compelling list of reasons that the patient sought relief, he explained that the doctor was unmoved. And for the punch line, Bob shared an important business lesson with potentially broader implications. In the words of the doctor to his unhappy patient, "A d-d-d-d-eal is a d-d-d-d-eal," concluded Bob.

Between publishing acquisitions, Thornton referrals, and situations no one else wanted to be associated with, I was kept quite busy during my first couple of years in New York. But although I did learn something new with each deal, after a while the lessons became fewer and farther between. The things that transactions had in common had begun to so overwhelm the things that were different that I became both pretty good at the job and pretty bored with it. Which got me thinking about what I might do next if I were to stay in investment banking.

Goldman organized its investment banking business slightly differently from its peers. Most banks were organized into tightly defined industry groups that were responsible for covering all of the companies in that sector. These groups together make up the corporate finance function, which is responsible for managing client relationships and executing financing or merger transactions. When executing such transactions, the Corporate Finance groups will call to a greater or lesser extent on other departments for additional resources. On a debt financing, for instance, personnel from debt capital markets will get involved. On a sale or acquisition transaction, depending on how the bank is organized, bankers within the industry group may be supported by general M&A professionals. Although the extent to which industry groups actually incorporate their own product specialists rather than relying on generalist product groups—such as in mergers or capital markets—varies from bank to bank and from time to time, this basic model is the overwhelming norm.

The Goldman model was fundamentally different. First, Goldman had many fewer industry groups, and relied much more on a large generalist pool of pure "execution" bankers, poised to execute any deal in any industry. Second, and more radically, Goldman had created a totally separate department of Uber-bankers called IBS, which stands for the blandly named Investment Banking Services and has no real counterpart at any other investment bank. This cadre of IBS bankers is ultimately responsible for all client relationships. It is made up exclusively of senior bankers whose job it is to get hired and deliver to the client the full resources of the firm. IBS bankers, then, are essentially very high-powered sales reps, their product being Goldman itself. Historically IBS bankers had no particular industry expertise but were viewed as appropriate representatives of the Goldman way of banking.

The brilliance of the IBS model—if you can pull it off, which Goldman did for many years (and to some extent still does)—is undeniable. Where other banks were vulnerable to losing business and banking relationships whenever any given corporate finance banker decides to switch firms, Goldman can simply replace one execution banker with another. It is the firm that the IBS officer delivers to the client, the firm being something greater than the sum of the execution bankers that make up the team. Of course, Goldman was exposed to losing IBS bankers, but in practice they rarely did. And since the IBS banker was often not the industry expert himself, but rather a senior person of judgment who coordinated the services provided by various execution bankers, it was not self-evident that even he (IBS bankers were almost all men, and as highlighted shortly, men of a very particular racial, ethnic, and stylistic type) could take clients with him were he to move to another firm.

The concept of IBS was created by John Whitehead in 1967, over the initial objections of Sidney Weinberg. Weinberg thought the idea of establishing a sales department within an investment bank was "crazy," but Whitehead realized the importance of institutionalizing the marketing function, particularly with the firm's number one marketer was then over 70 years old. As Lisa Endlich describes it in her history of Goldman: "Modeling itself on a manufacturing, rather than a service, industry, Goldman Sachs would build a sales department that would do nothing but sell. Taking a radically different approach from that of its competitors, the members of IBS would fan out and cultivate business, then turn over its execution to specialists."[11]

Whitehead's recent autobiography highlighted the importance of the IBS to Goldman's subsequent success. Having developed the premier distribution system, Goldman no longer needed to invest nearly as much in new financial product innovations. Better to let others make the investment and later exploit the superior distribution network to beat them at their own game. As Whitehead noted, "If it worked and there was a market for it, we had a marketing organization (IBS) that could introduce the idea to a hundred companies in a week. If the product was good, nobody would remember who came out with it first."[12]

Over time, Goldman has sprouted more industry groups and some, but by no means all, of the IBS force has been incorporated into these industry groups. But the basic ethos of IBS still survives, if in a somewhat watered-down version.

What this meant for me as an execution banker in the CMT group was that, although I was King of Publishing, I did not have formal coverage responsibility for any companies in that industry. Sure, if expertise to prepare for a meeting or a pitch were required, I would get a call. Ditto if an execution banker were required for a financing or M&A deal in the sector. But the "relationships" formally belonged to whichever IBS representative had been assigned the particular company involved.

Because most publishing companies are of modest size and, at the time at least, were not terribly transactionally oriented, they usually resided at the bottom of an IBS banker's priority list. So, although in theory I should not have called any of these companies without checking in first with their IBS representative, as often as not the IBS representative had never even called on that company. The obvious solution, from my perspective, was to strip out the publishing names from the various IBS bankers' lists and consolidate them with me. For all that this approach appealed to me personally, I came to understand that there was no possibility of its practical application at Goldman.

I knew my days were numbered at Goldman Sachs when I saw the look of stunned bemusement on Pete Kiernan's face after I first suggested becoming an IBS banker like him. My annual reviews tended to begin with a grudging acknowledgement of what I had done with the publishing franchise and my work with profitable special situations and clients outside of the mainstream and end with a lecture from Zimmel on cleaning up my office and not being quite so vocally candid. I somehow managed to ignore the condescending tone of these sessions and naively thought that if I just continued to outproduce everyone else, the institution would be forced to let me ascend. Kiernan and Zimmel paid me just enough to allow me to nurse this illusion—$400,000 in my first year in New York (promoting me early to vice president) and around $600,000 the next. Although on an absolute basis, this seemed to me like an obscene amount of money, I would learn that these sums never placed me in the top quartile of the banker class to which I was being compared.

Although this probably should have been obvious to me at the time, one of the reasons I was selected to work with clients that were not Goldman's kind of people was that I was not Goldman's kind of people. Goldman Sachs's reputation as a "Jewish" firm is certainly justified by the origins of the firm already described. Politician and provocateur Pat Buchanan's none-too-subtle demagogic use of the name "Goldman Sachs" (pronounced slowly in a sneering tone) is a testament to the continuing symbolic resonance of the name as effectively interchangeable with the phrase "Jewish bankers." And to be sure, Goldman Sachs had its fair share of Jews working there. But interestingly, although this has changed more since the IPO, almost none of them were IBS bankers. There were exceptions to this rule, most notably one-time IBS head Bob Hurst, but the image of the square-jawed, blond, blue-eyed Goldman banker reflects the demographic make-up of this sales force. Indeed, one could be forgiven for confusing a photograph from an IBS retreat in the mid-1990s with that of a German Olympic swimming team.

One might be disinclined to believe that a firm run by Weinbergs for most of its recent history—and one that to this day has a Weinberg in charge of its IBS force—could countenance a model in which the relationship role is reserved for Waspy bankers who call back to the office for those clever "ethnics" to actually execute the deals. But all of the Weinbergs who have worked at Goldman Sachs since Sidney have either not been practicing Jews or actually have become Episcopalian. It has been said that Sidney Weinberg's funeral at Temple Emanuel was about the only time he set foot in a Jewish house of worship. The fact that Sidney Weinberg named his first born Sidney Weinberg, Jr., (who nonetheless went by "Jimmy") is indicative of the fact that, although he never converted, he did have a distinct lack of connection to Judaic traditions. It is highly unusual for Jewish parents to name a child after any living relative, but particularly themselves. Jimmy raised all six of his children Episcopalian.[13]

John Whitehead, the patrician Episcopalian protégé of Weinberg who invented IBS, conceded that he used himself rather than Sidney as the model for the new sales force. "They were picked to be good sales types to make a good impression on the potential client," said Whitehead, who idolized Weinberg, but could not see how his unique style could be replicated. "You couldn't make a good salesman out of people who looked like Sidney."

As 1996 drew to a close, although pleasantly surprised by how long I had lasted and how far I had progressed at Goldman, I thought I had gotten as much as I would out of the experience. Although there were many very intelligent people, with varied backgrounds, at the firm, the overwhelming demands of the job combined with the intensity of the culture had a homogenizing effect on the bankers who worked there. Goldman Sachs, it seemed, was filled with talented people who used to be interesting. And my status as consummate outsider made me a source of curiosity but did not suggest a particularly promising career path. It also did not lend itself to many close friendships.

Yet I had found the people and situations investment bankers deal with a lot more fascinating than I ever had expected. I was intrigued enough by the industry that I thought if I could get a job at another firm actually being responsible for covering clients it might be worthwhile doing it for a few more years. To be the relationship guy myself and try to build a business serving those industry relationships I had developed at Goldman: that could be interesting.

In fact, I had a dangerously naïve perspective on what being a relationship guy at another firm would really entail. This was due both to the narrowness of my experience at Goldman and my lack of significant exposure to any other investment banking culture. And changes that would rock the industry over the next few years would make those merely naïve presuppositions completely unrealistic.

Nonetheless, I quickly got an offer from Donaldson, Lufkin and Jenrette (DLJ), to do just that. DLJ probably had the strongest culture on "the Street" next to Goldman, but it was in some ways the anti-Goldman. Where Goldman sought to be *the* banking choice for the largest, most established companies in the world, DLJ targeted emerging growth companies and industries, emphasizing the highest margin businesses. The result was a wildly profitable freewheeling entrepreneurial culture with the leading share in junk bonds, a strong position in IPOs, and a focus on M&A of midsized companies. DLJ also agreed to move me up an additional year toward being a managing director and pay me accordingly.

Another advantage of DLJ for me was that it had the top-ranked research analyst in the publishing sector. As I had spent most of my time at Goldman on M&A rather than financing, I had not focused until relatively recently on the business opportunities a top-ranked research analyst presented to an enterprising banker. Although research analysts theoretically exist to provide impartial advice to investors—and, indeed, the most important rankings of analysts were based on votes cast by institutional investors—they were a critical tool for bankers in securing financing business. Companies want to be "sponsored" by the research analysts with the greatest credibility with investors and, in this era before New York attorney general Elliot Spitzer launched his high-profile investigations, analysts and bankers collaborated closely on pitches.

Goldman had lost its publishing analyst altogether a year previously and I had been unable to convince Kiernan and Zimmel to replace him. Publishing had little financing activity historically, so they preferred to expend their limited equity research budget on the telecom sector. My view was that given how many of these companies I was selling were being purchased by LBO players, there was going to be an eventual explosion of IPOs in the sector as the private equity investors sought liquidity, but this argument had not swayed my bosses.

I went to tell Thornton the news that I planned to leave. John by this time was on the Executive Committee, but I knew there was only so much he could do. There had been rumors that pressure was being put on Kiernan and Zimmel to move on to other roles within the firm—Zimmel back to general M&A and Kiernan to Private Client Services. The rumors had the ring of truth, given that it was obvious to everyone that these were the roles that made the highest and best use of each person's skills: Zimmel relentlessly processing merger deals and Kiernan smoothly hawking stock to wealthy retirees. John asked me to be patient, and said that things were moving in the right direction. Peter Weinberg, he told me, was being brought in and Kiernan and Zimmel would nominally keep their titles as co-heads of U.S. CME (technology banking had grown to a point that it now had its own group and CMT had become Communications, Media, and Entertainment or CME). But they would now report to "global" CME head Peter.

The notion that adding another level of bureaucracy to the group was a solution to the issues we faced did not seem intuitively obvious to me. But this was Goldman, after all, and everything happened in its time. At any public investment bank, "partners" were employee managing directors, and individuals in Kiernan and Zimmel's situation would be lucky to be offered an option other than the door. But it was part of Goldman's old-world charm—and indeed part of the attraction of that ultimate brass ring of membership in the last great private investment banking club—that being a partner provided a kind of tenure unheard of anywhere else. Although the partnership could certainly force a member to retire, it was rarely done, or done with a level of diplomacy and sensitivity unknown outside of the cultural cocoon of the Goldman partnership.

I agreed to meet with Peter Weinberg, one of Sidney's grandsons and now the head of IBS like his father "Jimmy" Weinberg before him. I took him through my frustrations in the group—the need for publishing research, the lack of focus on media, the lack of leadership—and explained my offer from DLJ. I agreed to give him a year to address my concerns and said I realized it was a long shot but that there should be no hard feelings if it didn't work out. On that basis we moved forward.

For me, things actually did get better under Weinberg, with whom I enjoyed working. But the bigger issues did not get resolved satisfactorily. In the fall, Zimmel came into my office with a nice young man who looked like he was still in his teens. He had been an assistant to the food-processing industry research analyst. Could I help get him up the curve so he could become the publishing research analyst? I knew even with luck it would be several years before he could become competitive with the established players in the industry. And I had already been approached by another firm, Morgan Stanley, to play precisely the role I wanted to try if I were to continue in the industry for a while longer—something that was still inconceivable at Goldman.

Bankers have a nominal base salary and are paid at the end of the fiscal year, which for both Goldman and Morgan is November 30. Each banker is told his number—that is, the total gross salary for the year—by mid-December, but the money does not get wired until early January. People planning to quit wait until the check clears. By the time Weinberg met with me to give me my number—I was actually paid at the very top of my class for the first time—I had pretty much made up mind to leave. I thanked him but reminded him of the other structural issues we had discussed a year earlier that were unchanged. I told him I needed to think about it over the holidays.

There are a number of reasons why so few people leave Goldman voluntarily. First, if investment banking is what you want to do, there is probably no stronger overall franchise. Despite the popular perception that bankers care only about money, many care as much or more about social recognition. At year end, bankers obsess about their relative compensation, not just their absolute compensation. To be sure, the elusive but extraordinarily lucrative Goldman partnership represented a potential pot of gold that no one else could match. Many at Goldman knew, however, that this would never be theirs. At least as important as the money, being at Goldman bestowed a kind of credibility that no other institution could match. Any move, even in many cases a move from being just a vice president at Goldman to being a partner somewhere else—which might well include a multi-year contract providing for guaranteed compensation above what could conceivably be secured at Goldman—usually represented a step down in the social pecking order.

Furthermore, the Goldman culture also simultaneously bred hubris and insecurity in a way that discouraged departure. On the one hand, bankers were convinced that they were part of the premier firm in the business, but on the other hand came to believe that their value as professionals stemmed from their ability to bring that institution to bear on situations. It was their relationships with others inside Goldman, rather than with clients, from which they derived their worth. This again was the brilliance of the Goldman business model.

As I had neither grown up in the Goldman culture nor even grew up dreaming of being an investment banker, none of these factors weighed particularly heavily on me. But I had grown to appreciate the value of the Goldman brand. I understood that a young wiseacre like me, with little experience and a lot of opinions, could be quickly dismissed as an oddball if I were from a lesser institution. But the Goldman business card gave me a huge benefit of the doubt with clients. Whereas a CEO might have thought, "he's got to be kidding" after submitting himself to one of my performances if I were from say, Bear Stearns, as it was I more often got a bemused look that said "Well, he's from Goldman so there must be *something* here."

But from a brand perspective, Morgan Stanley was a reasonably close second. And Morgan was offering me a chance to try to actually go out and build a business as a real live relationship officer, the only job left in investment banking that I was interested in trying. It wasn't that hard a decision. The worst that could happen would be that I would fail.

Although I didn't appreciate it at the time, in the year since I had turned down the offer to go to DLJ, a wave of change had begun in the industry that would ultimately dramatically reshape the role of the investment banking coverage officer, or relationship banker. The Fed had taken the first steps toward dismantling Glass Steagall in late 1996 and Congress would finally finish the job in 1999, making it possible for commercial banks and investment banks to once again coexist under a single roof. The first megadeal in response to this regulatory change was my old employer Bankers Trust's $2.1 billion acquisition of the Baltimore-based midmarket firm Alex Brown in February 1997. The trend reached its mad climax in late 2000 with CSFB's $14 billion acquisition of my almost-employer DLJ. In between, almost every independent advisory firm and brokerage house that wasn't nailed to the ground was gobbled up by one bank or another.

And as soon as this round of deals was consummated, these beefed-up super-banks started merging with each other.

The outcome of the DLJ acquisition highlighted the dangers inherent in all these transactions. At the time of the transaction, DLJ had been a significant force on the street for less than a decade. The proprietors of DLJ had always overcompensated for the youth of the firm by filling its offices with colonial furniture and antiques. The founders themselves were reputed to have invested much of their startup capital in an expensive oil painting, to give visitors the impression of an establishment firm. DLJ did not even have a formal M&A group until 1994 and the previous year had generated far less than $100 million in M&A fees. By 1999, DLJ's M&A fees exceeded $1 billion, and the price paid by CSFB suggested a naïve belief that this and the rest of the revenues that had been quickly built up over the previous five years represented a solid, secure franchise upon which to grow further. Instead, the entrepreneurial, transactional culture DLJ had cultivated ensured that once the employees had been cashed out by the lumbering Swiss giant, they would soon scatter to seek out their next opportunity.

The foreign acquirers involved in this frenzied consolidation could be excused for not having been up to date on the practical implications of the Constitution's 13th Amendment. But most of the acquirers during this period were homegrown. Although the foreign acquirers did as a group pay even more ridiculous prices, the deals engineered by BankAmerica, BankBoston, Nationsbank, and Chase Manhattan were almost as bad, and they had no excuse. It is not a coincidence that only one of the U.S. banks involved in these transactions survives today as an independent entity. As all of these empire builders learned the hard way, the ban on slavery places significant constraints on the ability to keep the critical business assets in place once a deal for a "people" business closes.

In just about every case, the shareholders of the acquirer paid the price as the newly enriched employees of the target cashed their checks and sold themselves off to the highest bidder. For pure shareholder value destruction as a percentage of purchase price, it took Bruce Wasserstein to top what DLJ wrought on CSFB just a month later. Having already lost Joe Perella to Morgan Stanley in 1993 and many of the other most productive bankers in his firm the following year, he pulled off the deal of his career by selling the carcass of Wasserstein Perella to Dresdner Bank for $1.37 billion in 2000. Wasserstein himself predictably quit the following year and took the top job at Lazard where he managed to cash out again in 2005, this time with public investors as the source of capital.[14]

What do all these deals, entertaining as they are, have to do with the job of being a coverage officer, you may ask? The justification for mergers, such as those between investment banking firms and commercial banks, is that the "synergy" between the merging entities makes the whole greater than the sum of the parts. At base, the fundamental problem with being a salesman for a financial supermarket is that one of the products you sell, and the most central product at that—namely, providing solid independent advice—is structurally in conflict with the other products. For if you were providing truly independent advice, there should be no "synergy" between this service and your bank's other products, since those should not be given any advantage over competitors' products.

But banks trying to build credible investment banking franchises on the back of expensive acquisitions felt obliged to put significant pressure on their historic bank lending clients to give them investment banking business. Having once happily provided capital for all of a client's balance-sheet needs—from backup credit and commercial paper facilities to senior bank lending and long-term bond underwriting—it might now be suggested that this level of support should not be taken as a forgone conclusion. Now such continued sponsorship might be implicitly or explicitly made contingent on being hired for any future M&A activity.

Although some lending can be an attractive business, it is more capital intensive and less profitable than M&A and underwriting. "One-stop shopping" would become code for leveraging the least attractive aspects of traditional bank lending to secure higher margin investment banking business. The relationship banker is left stuck in the middle potentially trying to sell assorted financial products that may or may not be in the client's best interest. And sometimes the banker might even be put in the position of threatening to withhold needed credit from a "trusted relationship" unless additional banking services are purchased.

The follow-on megabank mergers that these misguided deals spawned caused a corporate credit crisis that made the tactic of using access to credit as a tool to obtain investment banking business all the more effective. After the crash in 2001, this credit crisis would be exacerbated by the unprecedented number of high-profile bankruptcies. The result would be that during the bust even blue-chip corporate clients could have difficulty putting a basic credit line in place. And many companies themselves concerned about future liquidity now make participation in their backup credit facility—a true loss leader for banks that agree to play this role—a necessary but not sufficient condition for receiving any investment banking business.

With respect to the use of their balance sheets, the nonbank investment banks (namely Morgan, Goldman, Merrill, Lehman, and Bear) are at a huge disadvantage in relation to the major commercial banks like Citigroup (which swallowed Salomon Smith Barney), Credit Suisse (now owner of First Boston and DLJ), J. P. Morgan (including what was once BankOne, Chase, Hambrecht, and Beacon), UBS (having subsumed Warburg, Dillon Read, and PaineWebber) and Deutsche Bank (which has acquired Bankers Trust, Alex Brown, and Wolfensohn). For one thing, pure investment banks do not have the diversity of credit exposures that a traditional bank does. More important, nonbank institutions, unlike banks, are forced to "mark to market" their positions in debt securities. This means that rather than being able to hold a loan on its books at cost (as long as it has reason to think the loan will be paid back), investment banks must adjust their books to reflect the actual "market value" of the holding, which is subject to increasingly volatile swings. As a consequence, a pure investment bank could be forced to report a multimillion dollar loss simply because of a relatively minor change in interest rates or other temporary market anomaly.

The result of the mark-to-market requirements is that pure investment banks typically hedge or immediately sell their holdings, either of which is hugely expensive. In addition to the expense, clients don't like to see their sponsoring financial institution dumping their securities in the market, which then defeats the whole purpose of having undertaken the exposure in the first place.

The effort to compete in traditional bank-style lending is an expensive nuisance for investment banks, but it illuminates deeper issues. This may explain why each of the investment banks has changed its perspective repeatedly on whether and to what extent it is in the traditional lending business. The increasing frequency and intensity of these requests has created a kind of schizophrenia over whether investment banks' core product is their financial capital or their intellectual capital. In an investment bank, even a request to have it participate nominally in a client's backup credit facility triggers endless internal memos and meetings for investment bankers. The focus is on whether the cost of fulfilling the client's request is greater or less than the expected value of potential business forgone by not fulfilling it.

Investment banks and investment bankers had always thought of them-selves as providing a highly differentiated value-added service—strategic advice selected based on quality. This is in contrast to lending, which invest-ment bankers viewed as something of a financial commodity, selected purely on price. Clients, however, have now shown an increasing tendency to choose, or at least winnow down, their list of prospective strategic advisers based on investment banks' willingness to provide credit. This has subtly under-mined banks, and bankers', sense of their own worth, as well as the clients' own belief in the value being added. It has contributed to the general decline in prestige of the investment banks.

But back in 1997, this phenomenon was in its early days. It would only become overwhelming after the full combined impact of the bank mer-gers and the crash was felt. And since my own experience was exclusively on the sell-side of transactions, I spent almost no time thinking about financ-ing issues beyond making sure a purported buyer had enough money to pay. So, when I returned from vacation (not coincidentally the day after the check cleared) I left Thornton a message letting him know what I would be doing.

Thornton happened to be in New York and I agreed to meet him at his room at the Carlyle at 7:00 AM before I went in to announce my decision. Thornton, who had ascended to the Executive Committee but was still formally only in charge of Asia, asked me to stay on long enough to allow him to complete his planned global reorganization of CME. I thanked him for his help and support but said it was time for me to move on. He could always hire me back if he took over the firm, I offered. Thornton reminded me of the cultural taboo at Goldman against hiring back anyone who has left the firm. I suggested that if he ran the firm, this would probably not be the most important cultural taboo that would have already been swept aside. He promised not to tell anyone about my decision before I had given my resignation, but asked me to give him a full report at the end of the day as to how everyone—particularly Peter Weinberg—reacted.

I headed from the Carlyle to Morgan Stanley near Times Square. My employers-to-be were worried that Goldman would "turn" me and figure out a way to stop me from leaving. Morgan insisted that before I notified my supervisors I was resigning, I go through a formal coaching session with them and a headhunter named Laura Lafaro whom they had on retainer. Since Laura was going to be paid for my hiring anyway they figured they should get some use out of her expertise. Their basic message: be firm, don't leave any openings, and get out as fast as you can. This was harder than it sounded. If you attempt to seriously answer an open-ended question like "Why are you going to Morgan Stanley?" or "What could we have done better?" you will quickly find yourself in the middle of a negotiation you never wanted to start. I racked my brain for irrefutable but polite responses and could only come up with things like "They have a gym" or "I can walk from my house" but decided these might be viewed as flip. Instead I opted for the simply vague "It's time" or "It's something I want to try."

Although from my perspective I knew there was no likelihood of my staying put, Morgan Stanley's concern that I would never return from the exit interview at Goldman was understandable. Something approaching half of those who accept jobs at other banks either never make it there or go back to wherever they started within a few weeks. This is because many never wanted to leave in the first place but wanted some sign of recognition or other from their home institution. They scheduled a lunch for me with banking chief Joe Perella back uptown, to force me to leave Goldman quickly. And they had Laura drive me down to 85 Broad Street and wait for me in the car to ensure that I came back.

Peter Weinberg was not happy. He had treated me well, paid me at the top of my class, and now I was leaving. This would undoubtedly be used by equally ambitious peers to suggest that Peter's management skills were not what they should be. He said that he had suspected something like this when I had politely declined to return from Christmas vacation early to lead a pitch meeting at the *New York Times*.

"Is there any chance of changing your mind?" he asked halfheartedly, already knowing the answer.

"It's something I want to try," I responded.

I thanked him and the firm profusely for taking me in and making me a banker, but Peter was not listening. When I was done, he looked at me coldly and made a surprisingly personal speech of the Michael Corleone "You are dead to me now Fredo" variety. He told me I owed it to Kiernan and Zimmel to tell them personally and that I also needed to tell Bob Hurst, the head of investment banking. He asked if I had told Thornton. When I said yes, he made a grimace that suggested he thought Thornton was planning to use this against him in some way. We were done.

Part of the intensity of Peter and the firm's response was that I was going to Morgan Stanley, widely viewed as their closest competitor. But this was also the great irony of Peter's speech about loyalty, for Peter had started his career at Morgan Stanley. Many at Morgan had objected to his hiring on the theory that he could be a potentially dangerous double agent who would eventually leave to join the family firm. Morgan was so angry when Peter did just that several years later that then-investment banking chief Joseph Fogg III, one of the latter-day "grumpy old men," issued a short, bitter, and unprecedented internal memo to the entire firm: "Effective immediately, Peter Weinberg has resigned from the firm to join Goldman Sachs, a firm with which his family has been involved for many years."

Despite the intensity of Peter's reaction, our meeting was mercifully short. But getting out of Goldman would not be quite that easy. I had explained as planned that I needed to be back in Midtown for my lunch with Perella. But they insisted that I return in the afternoon to meet with Hurst and have a formal exit interview with personnel. So Laura dutifully chauffeured me up and back.

The meeting with Hurst, who I had gained a lot of respect for from a number of accounts we had worked on together, was relatively painless. He began with "they already told me I'm wasting my time" and ended with what seemed like a genuine warning. "It is a jungle up there, not like here. They are brutal."

"It's something I want to try," I said.

The meeting with personnel was comic. After asking a number of pro forma questions about why I was leaving, the junior functionary handed me a single piece of paper titled "Continuing Confidentiality Requirements of Departing Employees" and told me to sign it. At the time, when Goldman was still private, the firm paid its employees in cash without any deferred compensation element. And as the sound of my bonus hitting my bank account was still ringing in my ears, the firm had absolutely no leverage to make me sign anything.

"Why would I sign this?" I asked.

The functionary seemed genuinely shocked. "Everyone does," he said as if he were stating the obvious. There may be some truth to this. I later called Alan Mnuchin, another former Goldman banker then at Bear Stearns, to laugh about the fact that they really seemed to think I would just agree to this. "Just sign it," Mnuchin said. "You don't want these people mad at you."

I scanned the page filled with small print and lots of legalese. The document did not just focus on confidential client information or even confidential information about Goldman's business. It was equally concerned with departing employees saying anything that might embarrass the firm or any of its partners. So just to be safe, the document seemed to say, you shouldn't even disclose that you worked at Goldman Sachs.

"I'll show it to my lawyer and get back to you," I said and got up to leave.

My most difficult meeting ended up being with my closest friend at Goldman Sachs at the time. Adrian Kingshott was a sardonic Brit who ran the junk bond origination business. The entrepreneurial personalities looking for junk bonds were not generally a great fit with the typical Goldman IBS type. Adrian's self-effacing wry sense of humor and fondness for midday martinis, on the other hand, was much appreciated by this constituency. Adrian converted me both to martinis and to consuming them midday.

Adrian had a sharp eye for the foibles of the people and the place. Although he was well respected and had some strong supporters, his irreverence kept him from the inner sanctum of power at Goldman. Like most of my peers, Adrian had never worked anywhere but Goldman and really couldn't imagine leaving voluntarily. And although I had already told him what I was thinking about doing at one of our occasional afternoon gripe sessions at a nearby seedy bar, I don't think Adrian actually thought I would leave. He was the first person I had called when I came in that morning and he was stunned. I promised we would go for a final drink at our favorite haunt before I left. We had our traditional two or three martinis and he walked me back to my car, where Laura was still patiently waiting after the sun had set. I had explained Laura's role to Adrian. When we got there, Adrian started banging violently on her window.

"Get out of here," he screamed, "leave us alone!"

Laura was startled and smiled awkwardly through the glass. I took this to be a typical jest of a slightly inebriated Kingshott, but when I looked up at him I saw that he was crying. Goldman was a source of enormous pride and comfort for those who drew a sense of belonging from it but could be a particularly lonely place for those who did not quite fit in. For Adrian it was both. I was certainly awed by Goldman's power, efficiency, and professionalism. I was also thankful for the opportunity to have learned as much as I did in such a short time. But I knew if I stayed much longer it could only end badly. I would get more frustrated over Goldman's refusal to allow me to play a broader role and Goldman would get more exasperated by my unwillingness to quietly play the role deemed to be my highest and best use within the Goldman machine.

I thought of Hurst's warning, and was reminded of how little I really knew of the investment banking world outside of Goldman. I hugged Adrian and got into the car. My last view of Goldman Sachs was of the silhouette of Adrian angrily railing into the night at our departing limousine as I pulled away from 85 Broad Street for a final time.

THE RISE OF
JOHN THORNTON

WHEN I LEFT Goldman Sachs in early 1998, neither I nor any of my peers really thought the firm would go public any time soon.[1] Of course, I knew that every few years in Goldman's history the firm would reconsider the issue. But the last time had been quite recently—in 1996—and had been so overwhelmingly rejected, despite Corzine's support, that another push in the near term seemed unlikely. As a partner quoted in the *Wall Street Journal* at the time pointed out, whatever Corzine's personal preferences, "like anyone in that kind of position, he wants to keep his job."[2]

In the end, Corzine didn't keep his job. Much has been written about Jon Corzine's departure from Goldman Sachs in 1999, shortly after the firm ultimately went public. Less has been said about the extraordinary ascent and subsequent departure of John Thornton. Thornton rose with stunning speed from virtual pariah among the Management Committee to president and heir apparent to CEO Hank Paulson once Corzine had been sidelined—only to be pushed out by those with whom he had engineered Corzine's fall a few years earlier. The arc of Thornton's career at Goldman is reflective of how the boom and subsequent bust reshaped not just the firm but the entire landscape of investment banking.

Thornton's early years at Goldman were in some ways as unconventional and controversial as his later ones. Thornton came to Goldman in 1980 from Yale's fledgling School of Organizational Management (SOM), which offered something called an MPPM (a Masters in Public and Private Management) rather than a traditional MBA. Undergraduates at Yale

College mostly knew SOM as a place where easy courses and grades could be found. Originally conceived of as an innovative approach to graduate business studies that would integrate the study of the public and private sectors, SOM quickly became a repository for disillusioned public servants desperate to get into business. The weak mathematics and economics credentials of these returning students made it difficult for them to gain admittance into more traditional MBA programs. So what was originally billed as something new and different was soon viewed by prospective employers as something quite familiar—a second-rate MBA program. This was hardly a feeder school for Goldman Sachs.

Thornton was the rare SOM student who actually was interested in going into government. He had settled on this aspiration during the two years after graduating from Harvard that he spent pursuing an advanced degree in jurisprudence at Oxford. After a summer job at Goldman while at SOM, however, he changed his mind. Once he joined the firm full time, Thornton quickly gained a reputation for being an iconoclast. By any standards he was a maverick; by the steadfastly buttoned-down standards of Goldman, Thornton was clearly beyond the pale. Even as an associate, Thornton was famous for acting like a senior partner not only to peers and clients, but to *actual* senior partners.

All this raises the question of how Thornton could have survived at all if Goldman Sachs were really as monolithic culturally as I have suggested. This is explained in part by the fact that Thornton has spent almost his entire career at various international outposts of Goldman, a circumstance that was initially fortuitous. As a young associate, Thornton had tried to revive a failed divestiture of a small industrial company, Alpha Metals, by interesting a number of international companies in the asset. When the following year the purchaser of Alpha, a British company called Thomas Tilling, became the object of a hostile bid, Thornton camped out at their offices for days and secured a co-advisory role for Goldman. At the time, in 1983, Thornton was a third-year associate still in his twenties.

Thornton was then able to convince the leadership of the then 12-person M&A Group to establish himself as the "senior" M&A professional on the ground in London. Although he did not officially move to London until 1985, he spent most of his time there, first living at Claridge's Hotel and then a succession of service flats, from 1983. The decision to allow Thornton to establish roots so far away from the central office of Goldman in New York was probably viewed as a no-lose proposition.

On the one hand, Thornton's brash brand of M&A banking would at least provide a change of pace in a market in which Goldman had made little impact. On the other hand, if Thornton were to fail in his long-shot assignment in London, as many expected and some hoped, he could easily and quietly be severed from the corpus of Goldman Sachs.

As it happened, Thornton did not fail. He soon brought a number of high-profile banking assignments to Goldman after a wave of U.S.-style hostile takeovers were launched in the United Kingdom. Thornton extended Goldman's established takeover defense franchise "across the pond" applying aggressive tactics to the defense of British corporate mainstays like ICI and Storehouse that had been previously unheard of in "the City." Thornton even used controversial private investigator Terry Lenzner to dig up dirt on whichever raider or greenmailer was in his sights. Lenzner, a former counsel to the Senate Watergate Committee in the 70s, reinvented himself as the king of "opposition research" in the 1980s and 90s, having investigated whistle-blower Jefferey Wigand for tobacco manufacturer Brown and Williamson and dug through Microsoft's trash on behalf of Oracle.[3]

Thornton's methods were just as alarming to the genteel bankers of Britain as they were to the old guard at Goldman Sachs, but they brought in so much business that both groups were forced to take notice. And another aspect of his accomplishment was vintage Thornton: he used nontraditional means arguably to defend traditional values and used this fact to blunt any criticism of his methods. In this case, he was after all pursuing Goldman's traditional raid-defense business on behalf of traditional British companies. His success in London was rewarded by admission to the partnership in 1988.

Thornton used the press not just to fend off unwanted suitors for clients but to promote himself, in a manner even more unsettling to Goldman. According to the *Independent* of London, "Colleagues say that right from the day he arrived in London in 1985, Mr. Thornton focused on getting his name around, ensuring that he personally took credit for deals."[4]

"The fact that he not only talked to journalists but seemed to enjoy their company," the *Independent* continued, "was regarded as a cardinal sin by a firm that in the not-too-recent past had, as a matter of policy, refused to allow journalists even to set foot on the premises."

When Thornton was quoted in the *New York Times* in 1995 as saying he would consider going to Lazard Freres, but "only for the top job," many of us assumed his days at the firm were numbered. I remember being stunned that summer, when Management Committee member and Investment

Banking head Bob Hurst held a forum for summer associates to ask ques-tions. One asked how the firm squared its general abhorrence of the press with allowing Thornton to negotiate through the media. "Well, that's just John," replied Hurst with an awkward laugh before he moved to the next question.

In fact, Thornton's use of the press to accelerate his climb up the corporate ladder was remarkably effective. Within a few months of his infamous quote, Goldman revamped its governance structure, forming two new 18-person decision-making groups: a partnership committee and an operating committee. Thornton would be appointed to both. More important, in September of the following year, Thornton would be named as a new sixth member of the Executive Committee—this ultimate decision-making body had been shrunk and its previous appelation, Management Committee, changed in connection with his appointment as head of the Goldman's Asian operations. Thornton never actually moved to Asia, but used the position to move his acolytes to positions of responsibility throughout the region. (I was in New York by that time and my wife insisted that I politely decline the offer to run the Asian media practice out of Hong Kong.)

The most important factor in this unlikely chain of events was the arrival in London in 1995 of John Thain as Thornton's co-head of Europe. The explosive growth in Europe, combined with the extent to which the bank-ing franchise there was personally identified with Thornton, was a source of increasing management discomfort. It was certainly no longer possible for the Executive Committee simply to pretend that Thornton represented a cultural aberration that could be safely ignored. To Corzine, sending his protégé Thain, the youngest member of the Executive Committee, to Europe to keep an eye on Thornton must have seemed like a prudent move.

Thain could not have been more different from Thornton. Thornton was a charismatic salesman who had not only a very un-Goldman-like taste for publicity but also a laser eye for the strategic pressure point in any situation. Thain was a shy, meticulous detail-oriented chief financial officer and "the quintessential low-key Goldman executive who strenuously eschews the limelight."[5] Although Thain was originally a banker, he had also worked on the sales and trading side of the business in mortgage-backed securities, which gave him particular credibility with the increasingly powerful fixed income division. Thornton, by contrast, was viewed as treating anyone from sales and trading—since they were unlikely to hold sway with the key corporate decision-makers Thornton considered central to the franchise—with a certain disdain, and the feeling was mutual.

If what Corzine was hoping for in throwing these two opposites together was to establish organizational checks and balances in London, he was sorely disappointed. What he got was a powerful alliance that would alter the direction of the firm and ultimately cost Corzine his job.

By quickly exploiting the extent to which the strengths of each complemented the other, Thornton and Thain became a force to be reckoned with. It was only a few months after Thain arrived in London that Corzine first pressed the partnership to consider an IPO. After the turmoil of 1994, Corzine was particularly sensitive to the importance of securing the firm's capital base before another market downturn. Thain, the youngest member of the Executive Committee at the time, emerged as an unlikely and reluctant leader of the opposition to the IPO in 1996. Many have speculated as to the extent of Thornton's role in establishing Thain's position, which seemed to come as a surprise to Corzine. What is indisputable, however, is that the lack of unanimity among the Executive Committee made approval almost impossible. As the only member of the Executive Committee who, like most partners, opposed the IPO, the soft-spoken Thain established himself as a formidable presence there. What's more, there is little doubt that Thornton would not have been promoted to the Executive Committee later that year without the strong support of Thain. Ironically, part of what attracted Corzine himself to Thornton was precisely the fact that he was so controversial with his investment banking colleagues and potentially less likely to align with them against fixed income interests.

Thornton fully appreciated the real implications of joining the Executive Committee. Within the partnership structure, these six individuals had almost plenary authority to do anything they liked, including changing the leadership of the firm. As the press release announcing the formation of the two new "decision-making" bodies the previous year made clear, "except for matters which require a vote of the partnership or the consent of the individually affected partner," the Executive Committee was the firm's "final decision-making body." With Thain as a solid ally, the pair only needed to attract one additional vote to block any unwanted measure.

With Thain and Thornton on the Executive Committee, the next time the issue of a possible Goldman IPO was placed on the agenda in 1998, the pair were well prepared to wage a campaign to thwart Corzine's efforts. Thornton and Thain emerged as the driving force behind the efforts to halt the offering. It was no small touch of irony that Thornton cast himself as the preserver of Goldman Sachs tradition. It undoubtedly made many of his New York partners cringe to see Thornton cloak himself in the mantle of former chiefs John Weinberg and John Whitehead. And although Thornton's preference for a private Goldman Sachs was surely genuine— after all, his vision of the firm as the leading strategic adviser to the world's corporate and financial leaders did not require outside capital—the politics of his positioning was nothing short of brilliant. If he won, Thornton would be the de facto leader of the firm, morally if not literally. If he lost, Corzine would need to quickly offer him a leadership position to present a unified face to the outside world.

In the battle that ensued, Corzine's need to secure the IPO's approval by the partnership led him to agree to two things that precipitated his downfall.

The first was the deal he made with the "limited partners." When a Goldman partner retired he "went limited" and slowly withdrew his capital based on a pre-agreed formula based on the book value of his holdings over a number of years. Relations with these senior members of the firm who had formally retired from the partnership but nonetheless still had a significant amount of continuing equity in the enterprise was always a sensitive topic. Many of the previous private banking partnerships had not survived precisely because of their failure to establish such a mechanism for the gradual withdrawal of capital. Faced with a run on the bank from too many simultaneous retirements, these institutions buckled under the resulting financial pressure.

Now, the prospective Goldman IPO looked like it would provide existing equity holders with as much as five times book value. Although the "limiteds" knew they were not entitled to the same value for their stakes as continuing partners, they wanted some kind of financial "kiss" for their contribution to positioning Goldman to command such a value in the public markets. And the last thing the current partners wanted was the legendary bankers from Goldman's past picketing the NYSE on the day of the listing with signs saying "Goldman Unfair to Seniors."[6] To avoid any such unpleasantness, Corzine agreed, after much negotiation, to guarantee the limiteds a payout of two times book value.

Second, just before the vote, in an embarrassingly public display of apparent quid pro quo, Corzine announced that Hank Paulson would move from being his number two to being his co-CEO. Although Paulson had supported the IPO in 1996, this time around Paulson had refused to declare himself. Soon after his promotion, however, Paulson announced his support for the IPO and Corzine secured a bare majority of the Executive Committee.

Although Thornton and Thain did maintain the support of a number of the higher profile limited partners like Weinberg and Whitehead, as well as many younger partners who had not had a chance to build up much equity in the firm, these groups were by definition those with the least influence from a numerical perspective. Corzine knew he had the votes when the Executive Committee announced publicly in June that they were proceeding with the IPO.

But then something happened that any IPO underwriter warns his client about. The markets turned south. Well before the announced date for the IPO, it became clear that achieving five times book value was out of the question. Then four times looked unrealistic. Then three times. Then it looked like the limiteds, with their guaranteed payout of two times book value, might make *more* than the continuing partners. The IPO was pulled in September 1998, indefinitely.

Corzine was badly weakened by these events. How could the head of Goldman Sachs have agreed to a fixed price for the limiteds while everyone else was taking market risk, many asked? And now in Paulson he had a permanent co-CEO who had already demonstrated that his loyalty was, if not explicitly for sale, at least potentially negotiable. Shortly after the offering was withdrawn, Corzine ally Roy Zuckerberg resigned, leaving the Executive Committee with just five members. Thornton and Thain realized that there was now a clear path for them to wrest control of the firm from Corzine, and quickly made an alliance with Paulson to allow him to become sole CEO with them acting as co-COOs. When the smoke cleared in January 1999, Corzine's services were no longer required. With the markets stronger, the new leaders allowed the IPO, which had after all garnered the support of a majority of the partnership, to go ahead. Corzine would be allowed to continue at the firm to assist in managing that process, but would leave altogether once the offering was completed.

The brutality of the coup left many partners stunned. This was not the way that partners treated each other, particularly in public. Lisa Endlich's overwhelmingly laudatory and largely uncritical history of Goldman Sachs —"Goldman Sachs has been run by men of extraordinary vision" is a typical sentiment—had the misfortune of being pushed into the bookstores just as Corzine was being pushed out. A new chapter Endlich added for later editions sounds like she is describing an entirely different organization. She begins her description of the infighting and tensions leading to the IPO by candidly noting "you can include my name on the list of those who remain astonished."[7]

It was less astonishing to those on the Executive Committee, where tensions had been brewing for some time. Corzine's style contrasted with the historic consensus-based decision-making at Goldman and was reflected in his assigning himself the previously unused title of CEO and restructuring the once 12-member Management Committee into a tightly-controlled 6-member Executive Committee. Ironically, it was precisely the new more centralized governance structure that Corzine himself established that had allowed Paulson, Thornton, and Thain to execute their bloodless putsch.[8]

Even before Corzine was forced to resign, it had been clear that significant cultural changes were afoot. And after his departure, the Executive Committee moved to enforce a much rougher version of the old partnership culture. At Goldman, every two years new partners are elected and a new partnership agreement signed. Coincidentally, 1998 was a partnership election year. Whereas in the past, the Management Committee might have gently suggested that a particular partner move to a new area and make room for young blood, negotiations could drag on for a very long time before the committee would force the issue. Now, with the IPO deferred until after the new partnership agreement was signed, the Executive Committee had all the leverage, and exercised it with previously unheard of ferocity. Partners were given terms under which they would be invited to sign the new partnership agreement or be forced into early retirement if they didn't consent—depriving each one of tens of millions of dollars that would be realized in the IPO. So this time, for instance, Pete Kiernan was not given the option of staying where he was. He could either move to Private Wealth Management or retire now. Given the financial stakes involved, his decision to become a very high end hawker of stocks at this late stage of his career was not really surprising.[9]

Goldman ultimately went public in May 1999, with Thornton firmly ensconced as president and co-COO and, along with Thain, heir apparent. To say this would have been unthinkable only five years earlier when I had joined the firm is an understatement. It was a source of both amusement and satisfaction to Thornton that partners who had cursed him now treated him with respectful deference. Astonishingly, even in private, individuals who had displayed unvarnished contempt for Thornton and what he represented now spoke in hushed tones of his visionary leadership. Even his once-heretical views on coverage were now treated as mainstream. As a laudatory *Business Week* profile just after the coup described, "Associates say that an important ingredient in Thornton's banking prowess has been his determined pursuit of the rich and powerful. Thornton preaches to his minions that there are only a few hundred CEOs and other key decision-makers around the world worth Goldman's trouble."[10]

Bankers at Goldman came up with increasingly creative rationales to justify their radical change of perspectives on Thornton. One version of the conventional wisdom that emerged after Thornton's ascent was that the problem had been that on the outside looking in, Thornton's ferocious aggressiveness was directed toward his own personal advancement. Now, this line of thinking went, with Thornton's personal ambitions aligned with Goldman's corporate ambitions, everybody benefits!

The truth, as usual, was far more complex. What changed was not Thornton, but whether the values he represented were consistent with the Goldman ethos of the time. In chapter 8, the impact of the boom in technology and telecommunications on the culture of investment banking generally is explored more fully. For now it is sufficient to say that, by 1999, this unprecedented explosion in deal activity that had been quietly sneaking up on them was clearly stretching the resources, systems, and mores of these institutions. Goldman's partners realized that to maintain their leadership position in this new environment would require abandonment of the consensus-based decision-making processes that had been previously relied on. Whether the decision making dealt with how to manage a senior partner's exit, whether to offer a Goldman partnership to someone at a competing firm, or which companies Goldman would do business with or even underwrite, it was clear to the partners that a more aggressive and frankly more brutal regime was called for.

There is a derisive phrase in investment banking—a "boom hire"—to refer to bankers who were added during the overwhelming rush to satisfy the needs of this period but whose credentials would never have otherwise passed muster. Thornton was the antithesis of a boom hire. Long established, with an enviable track record at the firm, Thornton was not only brilliant but arguably the most creative banker of his generation. But, political machinations aside, Thornton's rise within the Goldman power structure could be described in some ways as a boom phenomenon. Although recently derided internally as a cultural anachronism, Thornton's relentless, unsentimental style of leadership suddenly seemed to precisely and uniquely satisfy Goldman's new needs.

The imminent IPO was not only used to twist the arms of less productive Goldman partners, but to attract new blood. Just as many technology startups of the era did, Goldman used potential IPO currency to lure the best talent from its competitors. But Goldman was anything but a start-up and the value of the currency was anything but speculative. It was not surprising, then, that Jack Levy of Merrill Lynch or Michael Carr of Salomon would join Goldman. That the firm would offer these outsiders closely guarded partnership interests and even accord them senior management roles, was surprising, however, and another sign of the sea change within the organization.

In a global deal environment that at its most heated was supporting well over 100 IPOs and 3,000 M&A transactions each month, the standards applied both at the Commitments Committee and more generally would need to be relaxed—at least if Goldman were not willing to cede its historic market share in these products. And with an IPO of its own imminent, it seemed a particularly imprudent moment to abandon market leadership. Still, many former Goldman partners were shocked by the various revelations to emerge recently from New York Attorney General Elliot Spitzer's investigations of the practices of that period. Among other indiscretions, Goldman had gone so far as to offer "hot" IPO allocations—shares in Internet offerings that were sure to skyrocket in value immediately after coming to market—to CEOs as an incentive to attract their business.

Sidney Weinberg's successor, Gus Levy, had coined the maxim that what set Goldman apart was that it was long-term greedy rather than short-term greedy. The simple and honorable notion was that investing in long-term relationships at the expense of short-term business opportunities was both what distinguished Goldman and made for a superior business model. During the boom, there was little about the way that Goldman operated that supported that distinction.

The view that Thornton's ascent was made possible only by the uncontrolled growth experienced by Goldman in the late 90s is at least consistent with his fate once the firm's unrelenting expansion stopped. The business "bust" that inevitably followed the "boom" began in late 2000, and Thornton's standing in the firm and relations with Paulson deteriorated as Paulson became clearly less inclined to move on. In March 2003, Thornton announced his retirement from Goldman.

The nature of Thornton's departure from Goldman might suggest simply that Paulson had learned his lesson in power politics from Thornton too well. It was a poorly kept secret that Thornton had limited respect for Paulson's capacity for strategic thinking. Paulson was, however, sole CEO. And as we will see again in the case of Morgan Stanley, effective board management is a skill that does not necessarily rely either on strategic thinking or on investment banking expertise.

At the time of his initial ascension, Paulson had indicated an intention to turn over day-to-day management to Thornton almost immediately and then to move on altogether within a couple of years. That this informal timeline soon became a "rolling" two years was the source of gallows humor between Thornton and Thain. Around the time Thornton moved back to the United States in 2002, he began to press Paulson on the succession timetable, saying effectively that unless Paulson would commit to stepping aside at a certain point, Thornton would leave the firm. By early 2003, however, Paulson had decided he enjoyed being CEO after all, and told Thornton he had decided to stay indefinitely. Paulson had already lined up the support of outside board members, leaving Thornton little choice but to make good on his offer (or on his threat, depending on your point of view).

There has been internal debate over the extent to which Paulson deliberately undermined Thornton with other board members. If that was the case, there is no question that Thornton's iconoclasm made Paulson's job easier. It probably was not that hard to make all of those bold Thornton initiatives of the bull market now seem excessive and out of step with the current difficult environment. Even those projects that represented Thornton at his visionary best—like hiring the head of General Electric's world famous management development center at Crotonville to establish a leadership academy at Goldman—could easily be derided when wave after wave of layoffs were being announced. In a market in which investment banking was responsible for less and less of the firm's overall profits, Thornton's historically poor relations with the suddenly much more important fixed income division also became a dangerous vulnerability. Paulson ultimately promoted the head of that division, Lloyd C. Blankfein, to the board, replacing the departing Bob Hurst and further consolidating his own power. Thornton's retirement came only a month after Blankfein joined the Board.

Thornton's departure did not and could not really signal a return to the Goldman Sachs of yore. The original social contract of the Goldman partnership had been broken and too few of those who had been a party to it remained. Paulson continued to consolidate his power and less than a year later, Thain would leave to lead the New York Stock Exchange. Lloyd C. Blankfein would be promoted to president and COO of Goldman. There is no remaining serious competition for the leadership of the firm.

Goldman continues to be the best of the "bulge-bracket" investment banks, whether judged by their market share in the most value-added products, their prestige among corporate decision makers, or their profitability. But the difference has become one of degree rather than one of kind, and what was once an ingrained cultural competitive advantage has been reduced to something much more tenuous. With investment banking now only representing less than 10 percent of Goldman's profits, and Goldman's other now more profitable principal businesses increasingly competing with investment banking clients for opportunities, this is likely to get worse before it gets better.

The unique "long-term greedy" model of the old Goldman Sachs partnership is one of the sadder casualties of the boom and bust that followed. Some of this loss can be attributed to the decisions of Goldman's own leaders, beginning with Steve Friedman's abrupt decision to abandon the institution just at the dawn of the boom. Other permanent changes in the regulatory and business environment—such as the new restrictions on board members' ability to do business with the companies on which they serve —have put a cramp in the traditional Goldman style of doing business. And it is at least open to question whether long-term greedy is a sustainable model for a public company, given investor pressures and mounting disclosure requirements.

Can another kind of institution—a boutique investment advisory firm, another kind of service firm, or Goldman itself—recapture some element of the unique franchise and service that Sidney Weinberg's Goldman Sachs provided to corporate leaders and investors? It would take another market shock to test the integrity of any such institution before either the public or corporate executives could be convinced. There is always hope. As the pages that follow demonstrate, however, the behavior during the last market shock of all potential institutions that might fill this role should not fill anyone with optimism.

· 8 ·

THE HOUSE OF MORGAN

ORGAN STANLEY HAD initially seemed the least likely of my options. If I was on the outer fringe of culturally acceptable at Goldman, I thought, Morgan had to be a nonstarter. I associated Morgan with wood paneling, private club memberships, an initial as a first name, and something like IV as a last (as in T. Bartholomew Blowhard IV). And to be sure, after the enforced split from J. P. Morgan in 1935, even if these bankers were not quite "the homogeneous, money grubbing, white-shoe lot that the public took them to be," the bankers of Morgan Stanley were at the very least "[c]losest to the stereotype," as Cary Reich put it. "Morgan Stanley was, just as J. P. Morgan & Company had been before it, the godhead of securities underwriting, in total control of the bluest of blue chip issuers. And the men who ran it were, in the best tradition of Pierpont Morgan, stubborn, hardheaded, and imperious; accustomed to leadership, unaccustomed to challenge."[1]

When the 1930s Glass Steagall Act forced J. P. Morgan to choose between being an investment bank or a commercial bank, it had considered securities underwriting as an unreliable "byproduct business"[2] to the core commercial banking franchise, much as later firm leaders in the 1950s and 60s would see M&A as a loss leader byproduct business to securities underwriting. In addition, the partners were concerned about potential liabilities from the new regulatory regime. But most fundamentally, they dreamed of one day being able to put Humpty Dumpty back together again. And with almost all of the hard assets in the commercial bank, this would only be possible if the investment banking operation were spun off rather than the other way around. The firm actually waited a year after Glass Steagall was in effect, thus forgoing any underwriting business for that entire period, in the vain hope that somehow the government would reverse itself and allow the happy family to remain as one. Morgan Stanley formally came into being on September 16, 1935, opening its doors just down the block from J. P. Morgan on Wall Street.

Concerns about the robustness of the securities business generally or the ability of an independent Morgan Stanley to participate in it without a commercial banking operation were quickly dispelled as the new firm underwrote $1 billion of securities, representing a quarter of the market, in its first year. In the insular and highly profitable banking world of the 1950s, Morgan Stanley established itself as the "trend-setting firm and social arbiter."[3]

During this heyday of relationship banking it was a very good thing to have the legacy relationships of the old J. P. Morgan. And if being the "care-taker of a cache of crown jewels" during an era of low volatility and high spreads might not have required an advanced degree, the firm's leader during this period, Perry Hall, made the most of a great situation.[4] Although stylistically about as dissimilar to Sidney Weinberg as conceivable, Hall, a physically imposing Ivy League patrician, played a role at Morgan Stanley that most closely paralleled Weinberg's at Goldman. After Morgan obtained General Motors as a client through its relationship with the du Ponts (who had accumulated a large stake and control of the finance committee), Hall considered his relationship banking role to extend to personally persuading the distraught chairman's daughter not to marry a Pakistani.

By the time Morgan Stanley would go public in 1986, the firm was already dramatically transformed from what it had been at Hall's retirement in 1961. For much of the intervening quarter century, the firm had been under the direction of the volatile but visionary Robert H. B. Baldwin. So revolutionary was Baldwin's reign that Ron Chernow concluded, somewhat overheatedly, that he "probably saved the firm and destroyed its soul."[5] Baldwin saw the need to shake up the complacency of Morgan Stanley in the more volatile and competitive markets of the 60s and 70s.

During this period, the historic differences between Goldman Sachs and Morgan Stanley, as the leading Jewish and Yankee houses, respectively, began to blur. Where what Ron Chernow calls the Gentleman Banker's Code had once ensured that each firm kept its own historic client base to itself, those mores had begun to break down.[6] Starting in 1979, Morgan's longstanding Fortune 500 client base had begun to question the firm's insistence on exclusivity. By this time many of Goldman's once more modestly sized clients, like Sears, had grown into Fortune 500 clients. Now for the first time, Goldman aggressively, and sometimes successfully, sought to take over Morgan franchise accounts like AT&T. Morgan, for its part had not only started a trading operation but forcefully attacked Goldman's historic leadership in initial public offerings of younger companies. Both Goldman and Morgan competed directly in the emerging M&A and junk bond arenas. "The new transaction-oriented environment of today," *Institutional Investor* would observe by the early 1980s, had changed the basic understanding between these institutions and their clients, "setting customers free and producing internal tensions as corporate finance, capital markets and mergers and acquisitions people battle for turf."[7]

Baldwin's 1971 decision to establish Morgan's own trading operations —rather than continuing to place its clients' equity and debt securities through other firms—probably had the greatest impact on the firm's culture and subsequent growth. From a cultural perspective, the introduction of the kind of rough-hewn ethnics that typically populate a trading floor came as something of a shock. The firm had only hired its first Jew in 1963, and Baldwin had called Sidney Weinberg to crow about this watershed event in Morgan's history.

"That's nothing," deadpanned Weinberg after listening patiently to Baldwin's description of how he was changing Morgan's culture by breaking the taboo of Jewish hiring, "we've had them for years."[8]

From a business perspective, the trading operations strengthened Morgan's underwriting franchise at a time it came under unprecedented competitive attack. When IBM rejected the firm's traditional insistence on being the sole underwriter on its historic $1 billion debt offering in 1979, the firm was much better positioned to withstand the more aggressive competition even for "house accounts" that followed. In addition, the trading operations gave the firm the confidence to take the principal risk that would later be the source of its success in "merchant banking." Merchant banking was the fancy name given to taking principal positions in companies, usually alongside a lot of debt, all naturally underwritten by Morgan Stanley.

If Morgan Stanley had changed dramatically from its patrician roots, it still bore the weight of that legacy. My own dealings with the firm in the mid-90s across the negotiating table while at Goldman Sachs, suggested that vestiges of the Waspy snobbishness of the early era continued to thrive in at least some corners of the firm. And Goldman had been plenty "white shoe" for my taste, leading me initially to look elsewhere for an alternative platform. But in addition to its strong reputation as the clear second to Goldman in overall banking strength, Morgan had leading equity research analysts across the key media sectors—broadcasting, entertainment, and, particularly relevant to me, publishing. So back when I had been talking to DLJ, I made a cold call to the head of Morgan's media group, Jeff Sine, whom I had never met. Sine returned the call from Asia where he was traveling and suggested I come in to meet his partner Beatrice Cassou.

Although I did not realize it at the time, by 1997, when I began talking to them, the culture at Morgan had indeed changed radically. In addition to the events described leading up to its IPO a decade before, just a year earlier the firm had allowed itself to be taken over by Dean Witter Discover (although they were still in denial about this having been an acquisition rather than a "merger of equals" as they liked to imagine), a firm with about as plebeian a pedigree as one could imagine in the world of banking and brokerage and cash-back credit cards.

My meeting with Bea completely shattered my preconceptions of Morgan Stanley. First, and most obviously, she was a woman. There were no female senior coverage officers in the global Goldman media and communications firmament, and none of any consequence within the entire IBS sales force. Bea did not come from money (humble Kentucky origins), did not live in Greenwich (hip Manhattan apartment), had not gone to an Ivy League college (University of Colorado, where much skiing and partying appeared to have transpired), or gotten an MBA from Harvard, Wharton, or Stanford (she enjoyed her two years at Berkeley's Haas School of Business very much thank you). And she was knowledgeable, funny, completely at ease with herself, and utterly unpretentious. As she walked me to the elevator after our meeting, Bea introduced me to her colleague who headed the investment banking Retail group, an African American woman. Morgan Stanley had clearly changed.

At the time, after a number of meetings at all levels of Morgan, our conversations had trailed off, as I had focused on DLJ and then decided to stay at Goldman, and Morgan had turned their attentions to negotiations with a more senior banker. But when they contacted me again toward the end of 1997, I was ready. I sat down with Jeff and Bea and went through a list of a hundred or so company names I had come up with, predominantly in the publishing sector, where I knew some senior executive or other by having sold something to or for them or just come across them. Of this list, which included some pretty small companies, almost half of the names had never been called on by Morgan. About half of the balance had been called on but had never given any business to Morgan. Between these two groups, I had my coverage list. Now my job would be to go out and get business from these people. It was as simple, or as hard, as that. The prospect of trying to build a business with two like-minded, media-focused bankers and the institutional support of Morgan Stanley was irresistible.

Although I met others in the course of my interviews, it was clear that huge deference was paid to what Jeff and Bea wanted to do with their business. Whom they hired was ultimately up to them. (By contrast, Goldman's standard process, for any hire but particularly for a lateral—notwithstanding my anomalous experience—involved dozens of interviews throughout the firm and required consensus prior to an offer.)

The diversity of styles and cultures was reflected nowhere more dramatically than in the emergence of Joe Perella as the head of Investment Banking at Morgan Stanley. Perella was a legendary figure in the industry. He founded First Boston's M&A department in the early 1970s and had hired a young lawyer named Bruce Wasserstein in 1978 to help him build what became a preeminent practice on the street. The two left to start their own firm—Wasserstein Perella—in 1988.

An explosive, funny, utterly unpredictable character who wore classic hats and an occasional cape, Perella surprised skeptics[9] by quickly rising through successive senior management positions at Morgan Stanley. He joined as simply another senior banker in 1993, became head of Corporate Finance two years later in 1995, and then was made head of Investment Banking in 1997. None of this would have been conceivable at Goldman, where the potential order of succession for key management positions was well established and the notion of recruiting a more highly qualified outside candidate would have been cultural anathema at the time. Indeed, when Perella fell out with Wasserstein and began to explore rejoining one of the established investment banks, Goldman was the only firm that refused even to talk with him about joining in any capacity.

A meeting in Perella's office could go on for hours and was accented by shouts for Barbara, his longtime assistant (to whom he would deliver whatever he was editing one page at a time), emotional calls to friends, relatives, clients, or bankers, dozing off, and occasional flatulence. You could not go to Joe's office on any subject without being prepared to be drawn into whatever other personal or professional crisis was consuming him at the moment. If Joe had to leave for an appointment, he was famous for taking whoever he was talking to with him, whether to dinner or a board meeting. In one of my first meetings with Joe, I learned about this habit in a distinctly unglamorous context. Joe bolted up suddenly in the middle of a sentence and motioned for me to follow him from his office as he continued talking. He had unfortunately already positioned himself comfortably in the bathroom stall with the newspaper before I realized that he expected me to continue our conversation from the sink. A few minutes later his number two (no pun intended) at the time, Terry Meguid, took the stall next to him and struck up a three-way dialogue. It was the last time I agreed to follow Joe from his office during a meeting.

Although Perella had made his bones in the industry as an M&A practitioner, he had demonstrated extraordinary effectiveness as a senior coverage officer. An impressive number of Morgan's high-profile banking successes across many industries—from the combination of Sandoz with Ciba-Geigy to the AOL Time Warner merger—would have Perella's fingerprints on them. Despite his formidable track record, and Perella's willingness to go to any meeting if asked, many bankers thought twice before calling Perella in as "senior air cover" on an account. Perella refused to be used as a mere prop for new business pitches. If you called him in, he was on the client team for good. So, if you screwed up later or made the even more dangerous mistake of not keeping him posted on the progress of the account, you could become the object of Perella's famously volatile temper. If a banker annoyed him, it could take Perella days to cool down, and his invective could fill hours of airtime in totally unrelated internal meetings.

The other source of caution cited by bankers reluctant to secure Perella's assistance was the unpredictability of his performance. When Perella was "on," there was no one more effective than he in a pitch. But when he was "off," the results could be disastrous or sometimes just bizarre.

Some of this could be managed. Companies or situations that were unlikely to hold Joe's attention were always a bad idea. I once asked Joe to come to an IPO pitch for a mundane business-information company. Somewhere along the way, Joe decided that the nature of the silverware we had used in the lunch meeting was more intriguing than the presentation being given by his colleague on the state of the equity markets. At first, as he carefully examined each piece of his own place setting, it was possible to pretend nothing was amiss. When Joe got up, however, to examine others' utensils, I knew I would be having an interesting conversation afterwards with the company CEO.

But even if a banker selected the situation thoughtfully, and carefully rehearsed the presentation with Joe and the team beforehand, there was always the risk that Joe would become preoccupied. And that could mean that whatever preoccupied him at the time—whether something that had recently happened to him, something he had just read, or some long-ago connection to the company that he had just been reminded of—could end up filling the entire time allotted to the team to make their pitch.

Nonetheless, I would come to love working with Joe. At the end of the day, no one was smarter or had better judgment or was more generous with his time or cared more about coming to the right answer. Even when Perella—known affectionately as Joey Pa—was "off," he somehow managed to communicate to the prospective client both his unpretentious common sense and his fundamental decency—both qualities in short supply on the Street. And, from my selfish perspective, win or lose, there was no one I learned more from or who was as much fun.

Despite Perella's idiosyncratic style, he was also a remarkably effective leader. Like one of his heroes, Ronald Reagan, Perella cared about a few overriding principles deeply, and he made sure everyone knew what they were and knew the penalty for violating them. It was generally understood what he thought constituted effective client coverage and what kind of parochial behaviors he thought dysfunctional. He also had an unerring eye for bullshit and generally could tell the good guys from the bad guys. He had a strong deputy in Meguid who made sure that Perella's guiding principles were reflected in compensation and personnel decisions.

Finally, and critically, for effective management of any professional services organization, Perella made sure to stay involved with the day-to-day selling effort. Research has shown that it is very difficult to lead professionals whose own worth is judged by business-getting ability if you have not demonstrated such ability yourself.[10] In investment banking, in particular, where money is unambiguously the coin of the realm, a manager who has not shown a proclivity for "ringing the cash register" himself quickly loses the respect of the troops. He is overhead, a mere bureaucrat; key decisions are consistently second-guessed; as he becomes more isolated, the resentment grows. Being a senior member of key client teams across industry groups also provides invaluable context for making personnel and compensation decisions and for credibility once those decisions are made. And although it is axiomatic that good business getters are rarely good managers, in investment banking at least, continued tangible productivity ends up being a necessary if not sufficient condition to effective leadership. Despite the fact that everyone had a story about a client meeting with Joey Pa that had gone strangely awry, no one could seriously contend that he was not overall the most effective rainmaker that Morgan Stanley had.

Having Perella (or someone with similar judgment and credibility) sitting on top of the somewhat unruly collection of industry groups and functions at Morgan Stanley seemed to me to be critical to ensuring that the organization did not spin out of control. And we seemed to hit it off from our first meeting when Perella gave me his personal assurance that if I joined, he would do whatever he could to make me successful.

Although this more "entrepreneurial" culture at Morgan Stanley was perfect for what I was trying to achieve professionally, it came at a cost. Specifically, the challenges associated with communicating among groups and marshaling resources were significantly greater than at Goldman, where the culture of teamwork was unrivaled in the industry. In my first week or so at Morgan Stanley, I actually thought my voice mail was broken. Following up on a variety of leads from Jeff and Bea I sent out a slew of messages introducing myself and trying to track down the institutional history relating to a number of the accounts to which I had been assigned. As I was starting from ground zero, I wanted to make sure I took advantage of any existing relationships between Morgan and these companies. But my voice mailbox remained suspiciously empty. At Goldman, any banker (no matter how junior) would not think twice about leaving a voice mail for any banker (no matter how senior) to seek information relevant to a project he was working on. And he would get a prompt, concise, responsive reply. In the more balkanized environment of Morgan, I soon discovered, bankers only share information and resources across groups if an explicitly symbiotic relationship has been established between the bankers involved. So, before I could expect my voice mails to be returned, I needed to make the rounds, initiate personal connections with counterparts in different groups and demonstrate that I could be of use to them in some context or other.

This single factor—the ability to efficiently access and mobilize its store of institutional intellectual capital—is the principal reason why Goldman was and, by a smaller margin, still is the best investment bank on the street.

For me, however, this was a small price to pay for the ability to have free rein to call on a list of clients that were my own and see whether I could generate any business. I had a committed group of media professionals with complementary skills and relationships, I had solid equity research support and I had air cover from Joe Perella and other senior bankers who had been involved in my move. It was hard to imagine a more hospitable platform to try what was essentially a completely new job for me.

A final advantage I had as I launched my career as a senior coverage officer at Morgan Stanley was a certain Goldman "mystique" that allowed me, at least for a while, to do pretty much whatever I wanted. The Morgan Stanley I joined was obsessed by Goldman Sachs. Morgan liked to think of itself as one of the two premier investment banks and at worst a very close second to Goldman. And although it was probably correct that Morgan is one of the two leading investment banks, there was no evidence that this competition was in any sense close. So, for instance, although it is true that since 1990 only Goldman or Morgan have been number one in the Global M&A rankings, Goldman has secured this position thirteen times to Morgan's three. The last time Morgan was number one in M&A was 1996. In Global Equities during this period, Morgan typically trailed not only Goldman but Merrill and sometimes others as well. This dichotomy between self-perception and reality created a certain cognitive dissonance with respect to all things Goldman and a deep self-consciousness at Morgan with respect to the firm's own relative standing in the world.

So intense were these feelings of competitiveness that they sometimes manifested themselves in childish or petty ways. A few months after I arrived, Media Group head Jeff Sine giddily called me into his office to tell me that a friend of his had seen Pete Kiernan act boorishly at a charity horse show in Greenwich and get into a fight. The story, involving Pete rudely refusing to put out his cigar at the request of a woman who turned out to be the hostess of the event, was amusing enough. But then Sine decided it would be a good idea to call the *New York Post* to plant the story. When the story appeared atop Page Six under the headline "Cigar incites horsey hooliganism," it certainly could not have helped Pete's negotiations over his continuing role at Goldman as the IPO approached.[11] What Sine thought it did for Morgan Stanley, I don't know.

These subconscious feelings of corporate inadequacy were exacerbated by the fact that no one from Morgan seemed to know very much about Goldman. Because so few people ever left Goldman, most intelligence came from snippets gleaned from the few former Morgan Stanley employees who had gone over to the other side. When I was interviewing, Morgan dragged out Walter Bopp—a fine senior banker who had nonetheless left Goldman in 1985, when he worked in debt capital markets—presumably to comfort me that I would not be the first. The result was that Morgan's internal conventional wisdom on its chief competitor was both badly dated and slanted to diminish Morgan's feelings of inadequacy. As the only person with any credibility on the subject, I was routinely called on to "spin" bankers thinking about leaving for Goldman or recruits trying to decide between the two firms.

My recent association with Goldman gave me implicit standing to express my views on all sorts of matters on which I would otherwise be an unlikely authority. I would occasionally be pulled aside by someone in investment banking management and asked in hushed tones how Goldman succeeded at one thing or another—as if there was some obvious technique that they had somehow overlooked. I was also not above using my Goldman mystique in more trivial ways. The first time a senior colleague came by to complain about my messy office I made a big show of pointing out how much less "uptight" Morgan was than Goldman and how the fact that I was free to keep my office as I liked was reflective of the Morgan entrepreneurial culture so lacking at Goldman. This bought me almost two years' relative peace on the subject.

And in other respects my first couple of years at Morgan were great. I didn't bring in much business in my first year as I went around reintroducing myself to media executives in my new Morgan Stanley coverage officer persona. But I was still able to work on a couple of large transactions to make me appear productive while I tried to build a broader business base. Morgan had been hired by Viacom to sell Simon and Schuster just before I arrived. I had known the S&S CEO, Jonathan Newcomb, who was interested in getting me involved in its sale to Pearson for $4.6 billon. And I used my relationship with my former client and colleagues to help us get hired by Reed Elsevier, which was very interested in owning Times Mirror's legal publishing assets, being sold by Goldman at the time.

When we got to year end, I was a little self-conscious about how little tangible fruit my aggressive calling effort had made so far. I had negotiated only that I be considered for managing director at year end (at least a couple of years ahead of when I would have been up for Goldman partnership) and be paid in the top quartile of my class. Unsurprisingly, I was not made managing director. But what did surprise me was that I was paid substantially more than required under our agreement.

Starting the following year my investment and theirs began to pay off, with me being responsible for, or at least associated with, between $60 to 80 million of fees each year thereafter. That level of business was more than respectable even in a great year for the firm and industry and was exceptional in only an O.K. or bad year. In addition, the consistency of the revenue made it more valuable in a business with inherently lumpy results.

The politics of which fees appear on which banker's "revenue sheet" in a given year and how this translates into actual compensation is more art than science, and highly contested. Because any other alternative would have resulted in fistfights between bankers in the hallways, there was not even a theoretical limit to how many bankers could claim credit for the same deal. A distinction is made between "primary" and "secondary" responsibility for a transaction, and it was an open secret that even fairly tenuous connections to a particular transaction could earn a banker secondary credit. The reason this system is allowed to persist is that the alternative is excruciating—endless arguments about the extent of each person's contribution to a particular deal. At the end of the day, there is only a general connection between the revenue sheet and year-end compensation, and decision makers can always adjust based on their perceptions of the true value of the contribution. And since there is always an argument about annual bonus compensation anyway, there is little incremental cost to deferring these other arguments to the same time.

Some bankers were famous for getting revenue credit for a wide range of transactions to which their connection was obscure at best. Referred to internally as "velcro bankers," because they would stick their name on any deal in the general vicinity, it was said that they engaged in "hoverage" rather than "coverage" of accounts. These bankers consistently managed to get revenue credit on deals even where there they would fail my own "police-lineup" test for awarding secondary revenues: if the client could pick the banker out of a police lineup, he gets secondary credit.

The reason why bankers were so generous with each other on revenue credit is that it cost them nothing (it didn't diminish their own contribution) and provided some significant upside: the thankful banker who had got unearned secondary credit on your deal could be trusted to do the same for you on his. So revenue sheets, which should be the core management tool in any professional services organization, are reduced to a huge ponzi scheme that need to be subjected to intense metaphysical deconstruction at year end. But without a genuine culture of teamwork at Morgan, as a practical matter it was a necessary ponzi scheme to get bankers to cooperate with each other.

The actual evaluation process itself was also subject to extensive jockeying by the participants. In theory, reviews were divorced from consideration of the revenue sheets and related only to the feedback obtained. The process was described as a 360-degree review because reviews were completed by individuals at all levels—above, below, and lateral to the person under review. But Morgan bankers select who they want to review them. It was, accordingly, far less objective than it was made out to be. Even your superiors would get in on the act, as strong reviews for their direct reports make them look good and make it easier to get their people paid. Your boss might suggest which colleagues to rate hard or easy on the review forms, or even point out that one person or another may not be such a good friend after all based on his or her previous reviews. I found it was also not unusual to get a call from a banker asking coyly whether he should put me down as a reviewer. This was a not-so-subtle code for asking, "Will you say nice things about me?"

To counter such gaming of the system, individuals not selected as reviewers are free to submit voluntary reviews. As a practical matter, voluntary reviews are rarely submitted. Once a banker I had worked with extensively on a project from a different group had neglected to put me down as a reviewer. This was not surprising, as he was up for managing director and I had made no secret of my disappointment in his work. I gave his supervisor my assessment of the banker and asked him whether he wanted me to fill out a voluntary review form. As it turned out, the supervisor wanted the banker promoted and preferred that I keep my views to myself. Because class ranking and compensation are determined through an iterative process in which that supervisor would have a role, if I had nonetheless submitted a voluntary review on his banker, it would have undoubtedly cost me or someone who worked for me money. This was just how the game was played.

Because the majority of my coverage list and revenues were associated with companies that Morgan had never done business with before— revenue sheets at Morgan for a time actually separately categorized "first-time business"—I was generally treated quite well in this process. Reviews by their nature are presented in terms of "strengths" on the one hand and "development needs" on the other. As long as you were in favor, the former would be emphasized and if you were not, it would be the latter.

My basic observation is that individuals' reviews don't change much, and mine certainly didn't. My reviews tended to laud me for my "industry knowledge," "CEO impact," "commercial instinct," and "relentless pursuit of business." My "colorful/unorthodox personality," it was said, made for a "great work environment" and as such I served as an "important leader and mentor to junior professionals." On the other hand, I needed to "temper" my "sometimes irreverent style," which could "sometimes be too blunt and rub people the wrong way." Because my "straightforward, no-nonsense style can shock," I needed to exercise "discretion in expressing views" and "tone down [the] overly aggressive approach." And although I got through the first formal review cycle without mention of it, by the end of 1999 I was being reminded annually of the importance of "clean[ing my] office and desk daily."

Through the boom, the "style" development areas identified were seen as charming idiosyncrasies. In addition to being paid extraordinarily well, I was rewarded with a supplemental package of options at the end of 1999, messy office or no. These perceptions would change dramatically along with much else when the bust turned everyone's world upside down.

CRACKS IN THE FAÇADE

ALTHOUGH the beginning of the Internet era is usually dated from the 1995 IPO of Netscape, it did not begin to deeply infect the rest of the investment banking world until 1999. To be sure, we were all aware of it: after Netscape, Yahoo had gone public in April 1996, Amazon.com in May 1997 and eBay in September 1998. And one could hardly miss the Morgan Stanley technology group's seemingly endless self-promotion in trade magazines. Many groused that the group paid a senior banker with no client responsibility to manage public relations. Such observations were of course typical of the kind of snide comments you might expect in a decentralized organization where petty intergroup jealousies abound.

It was in late 1998 that the floodgates opened. Early-stage technology companies—companies whose lack of historic operating results would have been an absolute bar to public flotation only a few years earlier—were now coming to the market in droves. These newly liquid entities, flush with cash from their overvalued stock offerings, fueled an unprecedented merger boom.

The impact of this technology binge on the overall investment banking business—both in terms of the sheer magnitude and the changing composition of the industry's business mix—would first be realized in 1999. The number of U.S. technology IPOs would approach 400, over double the previous year and a rate of more than one a day. In M&A circles, the 1980s had been remembered as the modern boom era. But in 1999, Goldman Sachs, Morgan Stanley, and Merrill Lynch each worked on over $1 trillion of M&A

deals, more than the total volume of mergers consummated in any year during the 1980s. Indeed, the combined transaction volume represented by these three firms in just 1999 exceeded that of all firms combined for the entire decade of the 1980s.[1]

At this point, the technology boom could no longer be smugly dismissed by bankers in other sectors. This was not simply a function of the fact that the technology banking business was growing so much faster than other sectors. The problem stemmed from the fact that the valuations in the Internet world were not only astronomically higher than in any other industry, but appeared to be based on entirely new methods of calculation. Although analogous to or modeled on more conventional methods, the precise contours of these mysterious valuation techniques were known only to a close-knit group of technology bankers fully immersed in these dark arts.

At bottom, traditional valuations are based on some assessment of current earnings or cash flow and future prospects. Current earnings are, by definition, more certain than future, so methods grounded in the former are less speculative than those grounded in the latter. For this reason, the least precise of traditional valuation methods is the "discounted cash flow" or DCF, which estimates the present value of cash flows projected five or even ten years out. DCF valuations can swing wildly based on relatively minor changes in assumptions on growth and interest rates. Typically, the majority of the DCF value is found in the "terminal value"—the value assigned the last, and thus most speculative, year of projections. The value is calculated by multiplying the projected cash flow in that year by a factor—called the "terminal" multiple—that implies a view on the ability of the cash flows to continue to grow in perpetuity at a certain rate.

Applying this valuation method to Internet companies that were not currently profitable and whose ultimate business models were uncertain at best, exacerbated all of its intrinsic weaknesses. It would not be unusual for over 90 percent of the total estimated value to be in the terminal value, which could only be based on a wild guess as to what these young money-losing companies might look like in a decade. Internet bankers then tweaked the traditional DCF by making up new methods with catchy acronyms like the DEVA ("discounted equity valuation analysis") that justified pumping up the terminal valuation even further.

When not relying on fantastical projections, Internet bankers looked to other operating statistics at these companies. It is true that, in certain industries, financial or even operating metrics other than earnings or cash flow are used to estimate value. But this is only the case where there is a well-established relationship between this data and earnings and cash-flow generation. In the Internet world, the metrics relied on—like the number of "clicks" or "eyeballs" or the "stickiness" of a given Web site—had no known relationship to earnings.

This ascendancy of technology had three main implications.

First, clients in every industry from media to pulp and paper became convinced that yesterday's small, money-losing technology investment was tomorrow's (or today's) hidden multibillion-dollar jewel to be sold, IPO'd, spun off or otherwise monetized. As much as bankers tried to temper their clients' fantastic visions of wealth, the prospect of a payoff not typically available to, say, a pulp and paper executive was hypnotically compelling. When the employees of businesses that had never turned a profit—or in many cases, never even sold a product—could be worth millions, who was to say the pulp and paper executive's dream was irrational?

Second, the sudden expansion of the technology sector created capacity constraints within banking firms, which now depended on those individuals who had what obnoxiously came to be called "internet DNA." In a manner strangely reminiscent of the 1970s EST craze, this era of irrational valuation metrics established a world divided between those who "got it" and those who didn't. The views of the former were all that mattered. And as the phrase "Internet DNA" suggests, the general presumption was that you were not capable of being trained in the mystic arts of Internet valuations: you were either born with it or not. It was not enough to ape the Internet-speak of technology-group peers or master the intricacies of a DEVA calculation. And more problematic, not only didn't the technology bankers take nontechnology bankers' views on such matters seriously, clients insisted on hearing from the "real" Internet bankers.

Old-school bankers were now at the mercy of Internet bankers to deliver the kind of advice their clients wanted. To use another analogy, this was as if the prototypical "organization man" woke up one morning and found that every Fortune 500 company was now run by hippies. Capacity constraints aside, the recent jealous derision with which Internet bankers had been treated by their peers further aggravated the tension created by this state of affairs.

Third, compounding both the capacity constraints and the internal tensions was the fact that in the broader world, investment banking as a whole was no longer viewed as a "hot" profession. Bankers may have been viewed internally as integral to the Internet economy, but to those entering the job market that function seemed, almost by definition, one step removed from the real action: actually working at or investing in Internet companies. As a result, the best and the brightest coming out of the top colleges and top business schools no longer had top investment banks on their employment wish lists. Those who did end up at investment banks —in addition to being of lower overall quality—no longer were pumped up about beating out their peers for that coveted I-banking gig, but rather were resigned to accepting their backup plan. More incredibly, established bankers were leaving in record numbers for Internet-related positions. To respond to this changing environment, top investment banks started to engage in two practices long considered taboo: they cut special financial deals with Internet bankers at all levels to keep them from leaving, and recruited lower quality Internet bankers from midtier banks. Indeed, with respect to the latter, individuals who had been initially turned down for jobs at top investment banks were now being recruited laterally to a higher level than they could have achieved if they had come directly, simply because they had secured internet DNA somewhere along the way. Soon, this modus operandi was extended to other banking groups as well.

The subversiveness of negotiating special individual financial arrangements, particularly below the managing director level, to the cultures of the major investment banks cannot be overstated. As suggested earlier, one of the ways that these institutions successfully manage troops of "superstars" is by allowing *all* of them to think that they are in the top quartile of performance. When you are trying to build a "team" culture rather than a "star" culture, this fib may seem harmless, even helpful, at the margins. Indeed, given the intelligence of those being lied to, they must fundamentally know it is a fib but suspend disbelief because it is in both their and the institution's interest that they do so. At investment banks, even more than at other companies, money is viewed as a proxy for performance—one's relative standing in the organization is tightly correlated with the relative size of one's bonus in a given year. As a result, until bankers become relatively senior, the vast majority are compensated within very narrow ranges based on the year they graduated business school and joined the firm. This provides at least a colorable basis for the white lie that 100 percent of the firm is in the top 25 percent. Once management begins negotiating preferential financial arrangements on an ad hoc basis—particularly among a group that is viewed as generally of lower quality—the covenant of "team" culture is shattered.

Back in the 1970s, controversy had surrounded the creation of the early M&A departments at the major firms because of concerns about potential conflicts with established "relationship" clients. In order to break into this new business line, these firms took on clients that would not otherwise be admitted to the "franchise" and whose interests might be antithetical to a longstanding customer. Morgan Stanley, which was held to a higher standard because of its pedigree and traditions, came under particular scrutiny. As Morgan rapidly expanded during that period, its management "found it harder to screen people or instill the old culture,"[2] although this was nothing compared with what the firm was to experience during the Internet boom. At the time, in an effort to reinforce the traditional Morgan values and respond to critics, Bob Baldwin resuscitated Jack Morgan's slogan about the firm only doing "first-class business in a first-class way." Thirty years later, during an even more controversial period, the phrase would find its way into the vernacular once again. Only this time, it was used for internal consumption and with heavy irony. The expression was usually accompanied by a roll of the eyes as a way to indicate the latest decline in standards.

The general lowering of hiring standards, both for starting and mid-career bankers, had a number of follow-on effects. Some were obvious and predictable, like the deterioration of the quality of work product. Hiring practices aside, the sheer volume of business made it less likely that work would be reviewed and more likely that material that went to clients would be prepared by less seasoned bankers. But the truly incendiary element that was added to this already dangerous mix was the more subtle weakening of the cultures of teamwork that had prevailed to a greater or lesser degree at the better investment banks. In its place grew a more individualistic, celebrity-oriented culture. Feeding this shift was the increasing willingness of the banks to pay bankers on an individual rather than a class basis. Furthermore, as turnover increased with the demand for new bankers, an increasing percentage of the workforce had little or no historic cultural connection to their firms. Finally, the investment banks reflected the culture at large, which had begun to celebrate the good fortune of the individual Internet millionaires rather than the value of the institutions they founded.

To the extent that an investment bank's reputation is both central to the long-term value of its franchise and closely tied to the perceived quality of its people, the danger these phenomena posed were acute. Almost by definition, the danger to an institution is greater the more senior and high profile the banker that is revealed to be less than stellar. Yet ironically, at Morgan Stanley, the potential for trouble was realized most explosively in a situation involving the most junior of banking professionals—an analyst. In the strange and misunderstood case of Christian Curry, the issues of lowered standards and the obsession with celebrity converged. Morgan Stanley's mishandling of the troubled young analyst ultimately even managed to play a role in the power struggle at the top of the company and the incident was used by then president John Mack's loyalists to force out Morgan Stanley's general counsel, long closely associated with CEO Phil Purcell.

When it was reported in 1998 that Morgan Stanley had fired a young African American analyst the day after he appeared on newsstand covers of a gay magazine, it confirmed most people's presuppositions about homophobia and racism in investment banking. The true story of Christian Curry, and of Morgan Stanley's comically bad handling of the case, has very different morals and implications. Curry was the troubled child of privilege, hired despite the reservations of many who interviewed him, whose father had a connection to one of the senior bankers at Morgan Stanley. Indeed, Dr. William Curry, a surgeon at New York Presbyterian Hospital, and Bill Lewis, then head of Morgan Stanley's Real Estate Department, were among the first blacks admitted to the exclusive Shinnecock Golf Club, where they became friends. In other words, Curry was hired in much the same way scores of troubled white children of privilege have been hired into prestigious firms for years. The fact that a screwed-up rich black kid can make as much of a fool of himself as his white counterparts is, in a perverse way, a positive sign for race relations generally and investment banking specifically.

If it were not for a combination of bad timing exacerbated by remarkably bad judgment, Christian Curry would have disappeared into oblivion, known primarily to his disappointed family and creditors. On the timing front, Joe Perella was presented by Morgan Stanley human resources with the overwhelming evidence of Curry's alleged misappropriation of funds in April 1998. The beginning of the end had been when someone in operations decided to call the phone number on one of the many "meal" receipts for reimbursement that Curry submitted with the top ripped off. When it was determined to be a "night club" called Cheetah's, further investigation ensued. When they were done Morgan estimated that fully half of the receipts submitted during Curry's ten-month tenure, representing over 150 expense submissions, were fraudulent. "Meals" had been claimed for purchases at Cole-Haan, Blockbuster, FAO Schwartz, Lots of Linen, and liquor stores.

This seemed like an easy case. If the alleged fraud weren't enough, Curry often did not arrive to work until noon and left early. But because Curry's file noted that he was a "Bill Lewis hire," Perella suggested waiting until the following Monday, when Lewis would return from vacation, before firing Curry. Unfortunately for Morgan Stanley, when Curry was fired as scheduled on Monday, the issue of *Playguy*—featuring Curry and his semi-erect penis—had hit the newsstands over the weekend.

But the Curry case also reflects the inability of any of the major banks to maintain their standards and cultures in the face of their then insatiable appetite for people. This demand was created both by the unprecedented number of transactions they were called on to process and by the unprecedented turnover among many of their best and brightest who were leaving for Internet start-ups and venture capital firms. The result was in part to make membership in these once-elite clubs seem rather pedestrian. And Curry himself, a self-absorbed mediocrity with an overblown sense of his own importance and an unhealthy taste for celebrity, became the perfect poster child for the investment bankers of that era.

Curry's time at Morgan Stanley, however, was an unexpected catalyst for the institution to recognize that it was running a very different kind of club from what it once had. That experience demonstrated unambiguously that the internal controls that had been established to manage significantly smaller businesses with a significantly higher caliber of employee were no longer adequate to the circumstances.

Related but distinct from the issue of hiring standards is the issue of the internal standards of behavior enforced by these institutions. Top-tier investment banks, whatever the popular impression, are rather staid places. At least within their banking divisions (as distinct from their trading operations, which have always had a more freewheeling culture) these institutions have a relatively low tolerance for aberrant or abusive behavior. Scandals, whether sexual or otherwise, were relatively unusual and dealt with swiftly and quietly. The image of the out-of-control white male executive harassing female co-workers, yelling profanities in the hallways, and throwing things at cowering subordinates may have some basis in reality, but it was rarely found at the top investment banks.

As one delves deep into the lower tiers of banking, however, it is easier to find examples that more closely mirror common stereotypes. The reason for this, I think, is that in these institutions one was more likely to find a single industry group responsible for a wildly disproportionate share of the revenues and profits. The lower rated an investment bank, the larger and longer-term the financial guarantee required to attract high-quality bankers, the more likely that an individual or group has real leverage over the entire institution. If a badly behaving group is responsible for a quarter of overall investment banking revenues and all the bankers have three-year guarantees that are triggered upon dismissal for any reason, management will be unlikely to kick them out short of proof of embezzlement.

This is another area in which the boom muddied the distinctions between the best and the rest. The story of Bob Kitts at Morgan Stanley highlights this phenomenon. Kitts co-headed something called the Business Development Group (BDG) that was responsible for coming up with creative banking ideas and marketing them to other groups but also, most important, to the LBO firms the group also covered. The stocky Kitts was aggressive, combative, and likable in a mischievous sort of way. He kept a pair of boxing gloves in his office and fought hard internally to get the industry group experts to come up with actionable acquisition ideas for Kitts' LBO clients. He had an operations chief named Lauren Bessette who was as aggressive as Kitts but who shielded the junior staff from his rough edges.

And Bob Kitts had a lot of rough edges. Someone once told me that Kitts had the worst case of "short man's disease" he had ever seen. He drank a lot. He had an explosive temper. And the married Kitts had a weakness for young women who worked at Morgan Stanley.

Some of this came to light in 1998 in a way that was hard to ignore. During a group outing, a drunken Kitts took offense at something a young male analyst said and lunged at him. During the struggle that ensued Kitts bit the analyst's ear. Once separated, Kitts left abruptly only to return later in a cab to pick up a young woman in the group with whom he was having an affair. The woman, Elena Drill, a statuesque Russian blonde, had graduated with honors from NYU but had not been admitted to the regular analyst program. Drill spoke with a thick accent, had been a model in her native country, and seemed more than a little out of place in the analyst bullpen. Kitts had nonetheless hired her as an "administrative assistant" in the group. Within days everyone on Wall Street had heard about Morgan Stanley's "Hannibal Lecter" (or sometimes "Mike Tyson").[3]

In a different era I have no doubt that a Morgan Stanley or a Goldman Sachs would have fired Bob Kitts, no questions asked. But this was a time when all investment banks were fighting a losing battle to keep the bankers they had, on almost any terms. Sabbaticals were routinely offered. Administrative jobs for which the bankers had no apparent aptitude. Flex-time. Anything. Letting a banker as productive as Kitts go was seen as madness. So instead, Kitts was given a month leave and told to get help.

According to the *Wall Street Journal*, Kitts was given a huge raise only a few months later in early 1999 after a competing midtier bank tried to "bid" him away (he was reportedly offered a 5×5 package, which means $5 million guaranteed each year for five years). Kitts apparently swore to Morgan's management that his affair with Drill was over and the entire thing was dropped.

Later that year, I was invited to an off-site BDG function and ended up sitting next to a drunken Kitts against the wall at an after-hours club. A few feet away from us, standing on the dance floor, was Elena Drill.

"You see that?" Kitts said confidently, gesturing toward Drill.

"I own that," he said. "She's mine."

Finally he asked, "You want some?"

I was friendly with Bessette and we would meet in the cafeteria at odd hours every month or so to check in on what was going on in each other's lives. Lauren was one of those rare people within the Morgan Stanley culture who reached out to help across groups without needing to establish an up-front quid pro quo. And within BDG , she was an adored den mother who protected her staff from Kitts' outbursts, counseled them on career and personal problems, and helped everyone keep a sense of perspective. Bessette had been thinking about leaving banking, possibly joining Hillary Clinton's campaign. Although Lauren often thought about life after banking, something seemed more urgent about her musings this time. When I related what Kitts had said to me earlier about Drill, Lauren just breathed a sigh and shook her head.

"He is trying to make me promote her," Lauren said quietly.

Lauren was torn between her personal friendship with Kitts—who despite his troubled, self-destructive nature was an engaging and lovable rogue—and her deep feeling of responsibility for the junior bankers who were horrified at the prospect of Drill becoming a full-fledged analyst. Over the next weeks I tried to convince Lauren that it was Kitts who had put her in this untenable situation and that she should not feel obligated by the bonds of friendship. Eventually, Lauren went to Perella and Kitts was told to start looking for another job. Once Lauren told Drill that she was not going to get a promotion, Drill threatened to sue and Kitts was finally asked to leave in July 1999. Whether he would have been kept on even then, at least in the absence of the negative publicity around the Curry case and another very public EEOC inquiry into Morgan Stanley's promotion practices, is open to question.

In the months after Kitts left, both Drill and Bessette would die in a pair of surreal tragedies. Drill was killed in an apparent murder-suicide committed by her Russian boyfriend. Lauren died with her sister, Carolyn, and John F. Kennedy, Jr., in the ocean off Martha's Vineyard. At Lauren's memorial service, I couldn't look at Kitts, knowing how painful he had made the last year of her far-too-short life. The following year I suggested to Perella, with the support of a number of Lauren's friends, that we establish an award in Lauren's name for community service at Morgan.

But it was not to be. Perella took the idea to the Management Committee where it was quietly and indefinitely tabled. Although no one in the media made the connection between Lauren and Elena, both deaths were the subject of intense public speculation. Drill's death was said to be connected to the Russian mob.[4] Morgan Stanley was accused of causing Lauren's death by making her work late.[5] Internally at Morgan Stanley, where Lauren's involvement with the Kitts and Drill situations was widely known, bizarre theories abounded—had the Russian mob shot down JFK, Jr.'s, airplane? No matter how deserving Lauren's memory and legacy, this was a chapter that Morgan Stanley did not want to be reminded of.[6]

For every banker like Lauren, who kept her feet on the ground during the boom, there were many who didn't. Bankers by nature are a delusional lot, each imagining they are responsible for much more of any success with which they have some affiliation than an objective observer would consider fully rational. As discussed earlier, allowing multiple bankers to claim credit for the same transaction allowed life to go on without forcing bankers to confront the mutually inconsistent nature of their respective fantasies. In the unprecedented bull market of the era, this tendency manifested itself in ways as various as the bankers themselves. At the extreme, some developed full-blown messianic complexes: *L'Internet c'est moi*, to paraphrase Louis XIV. And institutions unwilling to lose productive bankers tended to humor such beliefs, which of course only fed them. As the culture of celebrity asserted itself institutionally, there were fewer and fewer structural protections that would otherwise mitigate the unhealthy manifestations of each banker's personal psychosis in this regard.

In the Media Group, this phenomenon manifested itself particularly in the behavior of Jeff Sine. Sine had been a lawyer and made his bones at Morgan Stanley in the rather technical corporate restructuring area before joining the Media Group at its inception. In between "restructuring" and "media," during the last industry downturn in the early 90s, Jeff served briefly as the "operations officer" for the Investment Banking Division. Many of the media bankers were fired during the layoffs instituted during this period and Jeff subsequently emerged as the new group head. It was widely assumed that Jeff had used his administrative post to engineer his subsequent assignment by cleaning the firm out of media bankers.

Jeff was a bit of a loner and prided himself on having a deep knowledge of both the structural deal minutiae and various pieces of gratuitous trivia relating to media companies and their managements. Jeff had a lot of outside interests and invested in everything from theater productions to trendy nightclubs. Shortly after I joined Morgan Stanley, Jeff finalized his second divorce and energetically reinvented himself as something of a bon vivant, renting a stunning suite at the Trump Plaza just beneath The Donald himself and dating young models. Even his hair was reminiscent of The Donald's. Those qualities that made Jeff think of himself as a kind of Renaissance man made other bankers think of him as a bit of a nerd.

As something of a theater aficionado and media trivia buff myself, I initially got along well with Sine. Where others found his relentless consumption of trade rags and blizzard of follow-up notes annoying, I considered his immersion in the industry useful and a welcome change from the telecom-oriented environment I had experienced at Goldman. And I think Jeff considered me a kindred spirit. He would wander into my office and reflect on whether one day he might like to go work on voting rights cases for the Southern Poverty Law Center. I never knew if he was serious, trying to impress me, or genuinely conflicted, but I liked that he felt the need to do it.

As the boom grew, so did Sine's view of himself as more International Man of Mystery than investment banker. Sine loved to travel internationally and, much to the annoyance of bankers overseas, he would turn up and demand to join whatever meetings were going on that day regardless of how disruptive it was to whatever coverage plan the primary banker was trying to execute. Then he would disappear, never to be heard from again.

At home, Sine began to treat and see all his colleagues as there to serve him, Jeff Sine: King of All Media. By 2000, as my efforts to build a business of my own really started to bear fruit, I was not interested either in being Jeff's sidekick or having him intrude himself at whim into my relationships with accounts.

This conflict reached a head in connection with the Thomson account. Thomson, you may recall, was the company that purchased West, and had been a longstanding Morgan Stanley client. Sine used me to execute Thomson business and help him prep for meetings, but did not want me to call on the company independently. I had been pressing Sine to allow me to pitch the sale of their newspapers and he had continued to put me off, partly, it seemed, because he had never worked on a newspaper transaction and wasn't comfortable with the subject matter. After it was announced in February 2000 that Thomson had hired Goldman to sell their newspapers, I stewed for a while and then scheduled a lunch with Sine to clear the air.

The lunch was a disaster. Sine simply couldn't understand why I wasn't perfectly happy being on call for him. He thought I was being disloyal, that I was the one with an overblown sense of his own importance. To be fair, he had some reason to be upset. Sine, along with Beatrice Cassou, had supported my promotion to managing director in 1999 and seen me paid well beyond what I ever thought I could justify: $1.3 million in 1998 and $2.25 million in 1999. And although I had managed to define a profitable little niche that managed to generate a steady stream of deals and revenues, I certainly didn't have the media or banking industry expertise he did. In fact, I had been a banker for barely six years, which hardly made me an éminence grise. And there is no question that I myself had been infected to a certain degree by the boom virus. No doubt I subconsciously overemphasized my own role in whatever bull market success I had experienced.

But none of this mattered to me. I had become a banker by accident and stayed a banker to see if I could build a business. I had been a "buttboy," as eager and obliging junior bankers are derisively called, earlier in my career and even enjoyed it while I was learning my way in the business. As I got older, my willingness to serve in that capacity diminished and my standard for anyone seeking me to play that role was correspondingly higher. And as talented as Jeff Sine was, he did not come close to meeting that standard.

The problem with the divalike behavior the star culture created was not just its impact on relations among bankers. Clients liked it even less. In the entertainment industry there is a saying in effect that when the suits start to confuse themselves with the stars, all is lost. One thinks of Walter Yetnikoff morphing from geek business development lawyer at CBS Records to drug-addled leader of all of Columbia.[7] More recently, the New York Stock Exchange's deposed chairman and CEO Dick Grasso is an egregious example of an executive who apparently came to believe he was more important than his clients and thus deserving of as much money and perks, regardless of the modest size of the business he actually ran. In a service business like investment banking, it is dangerous to give clients the impression that you are more concerned with yourself than them. This may sound inconsistent with the eighth of John Whitehead's legendary ten commandments of IBS coverage: "Important people like to deal with other important people. Are you one?" Wanting a banker who is a hitter, though, is not the same as wanting a banker who is self-absorbed, delusional as to his place in the value chain, and only marginally interested in the prospective client's business and concerns. At the end of the day the key to effective sales is the ability to put oneself in the customer's shoes. Empathy is not consistent with the self-obsession that is characteristic of a star culture. As Whitehead's fifth commandment states: "The client's objective is more important than yours."[8]

Throughout the industry, mediocre bankers were coming to consider themselves superstars and genuine superstars thought they were wasting their lives as mere investment bankers. Some of this latter group took well-compensated, high-profile operating jobs for which they had no apparent qualifications. Tom Casey had been a deal lawyer at Skadden Arps when he was tapped for a senior banking job at Merrill. After being promoted to co-head of the Global Communications Investment Banking Group, he quit to become vice chairman and then CEO of Global Crossing.[9] When the talented Michael Price left Lazard in 1998, he had worked on four of the seven biggest telecom deals in history. He convinced a consortium of the largest private equity funds to give him over $1 billion to build a European broadband backbone network called FirstMark Communications. The start-up even attracted an all-star board that included Henry Kissinger and Microsoft's chief technology officer, Nathan Myhrvold.[10] Neither of these enterprises ended well. Global Crossing filed for bankruptcy in 2002 and the remains of a restructured FirstMark were sold in 2004 for a tiny fraction of the original investment.

Even more typical than actually trying to run companies, investment bankers at the top of their game in the bull market became convinced and convinced others of their investing prowess. Although it may not be obvious, being a good investment banker is not synonymous with being a good investor. In fact, a strong case could be made that an investment banker is about the last person you would want to make investments. Investment banking is, fundamentally, a sales job. And the very best sales people are so good that they are capable of convincing even themselves that whatever they have on offer, no matter how meager in reality, is a must-have item. This sort of person may be one you want to show your house to a prospective buyer, but it is not one whom you would want investing your money.

The discipline of investing involves not only meticulous analysis of the financials but a deep understanding of the dynamics of the operating business involved. Where a banker's job ends once the deal closes, an investor's job is just beginning once the investment is made.

Yet every major bank had high-profile defections to the worlds of private equity and venture capital. Rex Golding, the able head of Morgan Stanley's technology group, went to be a partner at a venture fund backed by Softbank. Chris Flowers, leader of Goldman Sachs's financial institutions practice, joined up with Ripplewood Holdings. Steve Rattner, the hugely successful media banker from Lazard, raised $1 billion with three partners. Bruce Wasserstein's well-earned nickname, "Bid 'em up Bruce," might sound attractive if one had a company to sell but much less so if one had money to invest. And the early indications are that where Wasserstein has diversified into the investing business, the results have been uneven at best. My point is not that investment bankers can't be good investors, only that the apparent assumption that they necessarily *would be*, seems deeply flawed.

Given the ability of private equity investors to delay revealing the results of their investments—particularly the bad ones—it will be some time before a general conclusion can be reached about the success of this group overall. But some anecdotal evidence of investment bankers' investing abilities should be cause for concern. So great was the brain drain into private equity that the investment banks began providing investment bankers with opportunities to make substantial direct investments under terms that allowed them to keep much of the upside while the firm was saddled with the bulk of the risk. These investments were often made without the same careful oversight and due diligence that is typically associated with such investments. The argument was that these were opportunistic situations that bankers came across that were simply too good to miss out on by imposing such bureaucracy. The results were predictable.

When Jeff Sine pushed through investments in start-ups with names like 360hiphop.com, both Bea and I declined to participate. The firm went ahead anyway. At least Sine's investments were small. In the technology and telecom sectors, these investments ran into the hundreds of millions of dollars. In some cases, banking groups were making bigger investments than huge internal funds set up for that purpose with actual investing expertise and disciplines. Sine's telecom counterpart, Chris Harland, invested $300 million in the space of a couple of years. "Like a drunken sailor," was how one of those who nominally reviewed some of these investments described the atmosphere. Bankers were stars, after all, and did not like their judgment on such matters questioned. The 1999 vintage telecom investments at Morgan Stanley have yielded around 16 cents on the dollar.

The delusions of this era were varied and deeply held, extending to the wider business community. Indeed, one of the reasons prosecutors have had such a hard time obtaining convictions in cases brought against Wall Street figures for many of the worst excesses of the period is that the perpetrators believed in what they were saying and doing. The line between the delusional and the criminal is a surprisingly fine one.

Within investment banking, these delusions went to the very top of these organizations. Although until recently Hank Paulson had been viewed simply as a solid Midwestern Goldman Sachs corporate coverage officer, by mid-1999 he was the unlikely leader of the newly public premier global investment bank. Paulson's remarks to the captains of industry in Silicon Valley gathered one evening around this time at a fine Palo Alto Italian restaurant are reflective of how integral these delusions were to the way these businesses now operated.

Although no one had ever accused Paulson of being a philosopher or grand strategist, his new role, growing confidence—and what he had seen earlier that day—led Paulson that evening to speak of revolution. That afternoon, Paulson had watched as a huge high-tech warehouse in Oakland, chock full of intertwined conveyor belts, spit out perfectly packed crates of groceries to be delivered by an army of little trucks. Paulson's enthusiasm for the enterprise, a start-up Internet grocer called Webvan, was apparently not diminished by the fact that what he was watching was simply an advanced beta test in which groceries were sent at specified times to company friends and family, not goods being sold to actual customers.

Paulson saw the contraption going at full tilt and declared he had seen the future.

The future that Paulson felt he had seen was not limited to supermarkets specifically or even retailing generally. The revolution that Paulson spoke of that evening related to investment banking. Unless it changed the way it did business, he warned that evening, Goldman Sachs could become the Safeway of investment banking. And, Paulson made clear, Goldman would not become a "dinosaur" on his watch.

Paulson was obviously premature in providing an epitaph for the country's large grocery chains. As I write this, Safeway, Albertson's, and Kroger's together have revenues of over $150 billion. Webvan, on the other hand, filed for bankruptcy in July 2001—but only after Goldman, at Paulson's personal urging, had sunk $100 million of its own money into Webvan and sponsored the company's initial public offering in November 1999.

Paulson was not the only CEO to make misguided messianic prophecies during the height of the Internet boom. One thinks of Time Warner's Jerry Levin hungrily accepting AOL's wildly inflated stock so that he could lead the combined colossus proudly into a convergent future.[11] In 1999, however, for Goldman's chief to speak of revolution was in itself revolutionary. This was once the ultimate conservative investment banking house. At one time, the firm wouldn't sponsor a company without a track record of at least five years of profits. Now it would not only underwrite but invest in businesses without a single year of meaningful revenues. And Paulson's prediction about the changing nature of investment banking itself is interesting both in that it reflected changes long underway in the industry and foreshadowed even more dramatic changes to come.

The Thomson account proved to be Jeff Sine's Waterloo. In late 2000, we organized a closing dinner for the successful $1 billion acquisition by Thomson of a financial information company called Primark. The entire senior management team from Thomson attended. Sine showed up for cocktails, blew some air kisses and said he had a more important dinner elsewhere. At the end of the evening Thomson's CEO, Richard Harrington, pulled aside Stuart Epstein, a well-liked media M&A specialist who had worked on the Thomson account for some time. Harrington told Stuart that if Morgan Stanley wanted to do business with Thomson again, Sine had to go.

Stuart set up a lunch for Harrington and his CFO with Joe Perella at which they laid out their litany of complaints regarding Sine: completely inattentive, only called when he wanted something or to complain about not getting a piece of business; the list went on. A new coverage team was agreed upon with me in charge of day-to-day contact and another senior banker to be named later to be introduced to Harrington for "air cover." It was left to Joe to break the news to Sine.

After Joe laid out the situation, Sine had only one request. He wanted to be the one to tell me of the change in coverage strategy, so it would seem to be his idea. Joe agreed but realized that it would be impossible for anyone to cover the company effectively without understanding fully the history of the relationship and the rare chance Thomson had given us to get back into their good graces. So Joe told me everything and made me promise to act surprised as Sine magnanimously handed over the reins of the Thomson account.

All of the cultural phenomena described here relating to the boom's impact on investment banking and investment bankers generally sometimes took outsized shape at Morgan Stanley because of a single individual: Mary Meeker, Queen of the Net.[12]

Mary Meeker had been a fairly undistinguished PC and computer software research analyst in the early 1990s, slaving away on reports covering companies like Microsoft and Compaq. She had joined the equity research division of Morgan Stanley in 1991, and prior to the Internet boom had never appeared in the rankings of the *Institutional Investor* magazine's prestigious survey of analysts. Indeed, because of some bad market calls she had made, at one point Meeker had come close to being fired.

But Meeker had discovered the Internet early and championed its potential as coauthor (with her then colleague Chris DePuy) of *The Internet Report* just four months after taking Netscape public in 1995. The following year HarperCollins commercially published the report as a book—a first for a research report. This book and its successor volumes became the standard reference for venture capitalists but, more important, played a key role in legitimizing for public investors this entire sector, which had yet to demonstrate an ability to generate profits. When *Institutional Investor*'s influential annual survey first created an Internet category in 1996, Meeker was ranked number one and stayed in that position for four straight years, being displaced by Henry Blodget of Merrill Lynch in 2000. Meeker then disappeared from the rankings altogether once the bust hit in 2001.

As a kind of unofficial spokesperson for the entire sector, Meeker became Morgan Stanley's not-so-secret weapon in the market-share wars for technology banking business. Other investment banks belatedly tried with varying degrees of success to establish their own ready-for-prime-time celebrity Internet analysts, but Mary had an insurmountable first mover advantage during a boom that would only last a few short years. Ironically, these jealous competitors probably never suspected the extent to which at Morgan Stanley many not so secretly wished they could give her away.

The problem was that having Mary Meeker at Morgan Stanley created client expectations that simply could not be fulfilled. This was partly a function of the overwhelming demand for all things Meeker. But it was exacerbated by Meeker's stubborn insistence that she be consulted on any decision touching on her "space." And her celebrity was such that Morgan Stanley acceded to a very broad definition of the realm within which Meeker had unchallenged authority.

The impracticality of any single person playing the role that Meeker reserved for herself was apparent. During the height of the craze, the Morgan Stanley switchboard received many hundreds of calls for Meeker in any given day. These calls were from well-intentioned individuals who thought if they could just get 15 minutes of Mary's time she would be happy to sponsor their venture in the public markets and make them rich. The problem was that a single research analyst can reasonably cover at most around 20 companies. And Mary's existing responsibilities simply precluded the possibility of her sponsoring any but a few companies. Still, so overwhelming was Mary's value to the franchise that she was rumored to have made as much as $15 million annually during the height of the boom, an unheard of sum for a research analyst.

Many of the calls directed to her—not to mention the many thousands of e-mails—were from bankers within Morgan Stanley who had important clients that wanted just a moment of Mary's time. Some wanted to take a subsidiary public, others wanted investment advice and a few just wanted to meet the celebrity of the moment. Needless to say, a very small proportion of the calls, even from relatively senior people inside the bank, were answered, much less were the requests satisfied.

Morgan Stanley generally had a system of banking "gatekeepers" for its research analysts. Any requests for an analyst's time were screened by the banker most knowledgeable about the industry. For example, I was the gatekeeper for publishing analyst Doug Arthur. This took very little time for me but helped Doug manage his time and ensured that I was aware of whatever was going on in my sector. Ultimately, regulators would target the ability of bankers to improperly influence supposedly independent research analysts' views for particular scrutiny. As a result of the reforms instituted in the wake of these controversies, today no banker is likely to be able to speak with an analyst without a lawyer present. Then, however, research analysts were treated and compensated as if they were part of the investment banking team.

Mary required three gatekeepers. One of these, Ruth Porat, was a talented and aggressive banker in her own right and had three secretaries to screen and schedule incoming requests. Another was Andre de Baubigny, a relatively junior banker from midtier Robertson Stephens whom Mary took a liking to and had hired as Morgan Stanley's chief Internet strategist to satisfy overflow requests for Internet expertise. The gentle, shy de Baubigny burnt out under the pressure after about a year, shortly after his second marriage foundered in a matter of weeks.[13]

Because relatively few people at Morgan Stanley spoke to Mary with any frequency, having access to Mary became viewed as an extremely valuable commodity, both internally and with clients. In the absence of any realistic possibility of getting Mary's time, bankers turned not only to official gatekeepers to get some sense of her possible perspective on a particular idea or topic, but to other individuals perceived for one reason or another to have Mary's ear or her respect. An entire informal social hierarchy grew up based on how close or far from Mary a banker was thought to be. This was complicated by the fact that bankers had every incentive to pretend to be close to Mary, not just because of the status it bestowed but because of how difficult it was for anyone to verify one way or another.

These issues were not unique to Morgan Stanley but they were exacerbated by Meeker's star power and her relative unwillingness to delegate. Many of our competitors dealt with this problem by hiring a legion of Internet research analysts each focusing on some alleged Internet subspecialty or other—e-commerce, portals, B2B, entertainment, software, and the like. The problem at Morgan was that Mary held that any company even tangentially related to the Internet required her personal approval before the firm could sponsor it regardless of whether she actually covered it. As more and more companies were trying to reposition themselves as Internet businesses, this exponentially expanded Mary's potential reach. And given her unique place in the new economy, no one, it seemed, was willing to say "no" to Mary Meeker.

In my world, media, the problem this created became quite acute, as it seemed every client we had was trying to recharacterize themselves as some kind of Internet play. We came up with the bright idea of organizing an "Internet Media Conference" in part to satisfy our clients whom we could never actually get invited to Mary's "real" Internet conference—one of the street's hottest tickets—but also as a subtle way to credentialize our traditional media analysts as having all-important Web savvy. I was responsible for organizing the conference and kept Mary and her "gatekeepers" informed. By early 2000, I had already gotten commitments from Viacom chairman Sumner Redstone and AOL Time Warner CEO Jerry Levin to speak and had sent out save-the-date cards to investors announcing the conference for that summer. Then I got the call I had been dreading. "Mary says you can't call it Internet Media," said the gatekeeper. "Why?" I asked. "It will confuse investors," said the gatekeeper, "and besides she really hasn't been involved in the organization." "But," I pointed out innocently, "you and gate-keepers number two and three have been involved from the start, and we have copied Mary on everything." "She doesn't want it," said gatekeeper number one. Q.E.D.

After many months of negotiations it was finally agreed that we could call it the "Digital Media Conference." (The conference was held in June 2000 at the New York Hilton, quite successfully.)

Although Meeker's celebrity was a source of frustration to bankers hungry to exploit every revenue-generating business opportunity, it is clear in retrospect that in many instances she saved Morgan Stanley from itself. By enforcing her role as the ultimate bottleneck for doing Internet deals, Meeker ensured that there was *some* consistent quality control in an era in which there was often none. The evidence is that as a group, the companies she took public did better than those of other banks. And the reason ultimately that Meeker, unlike Henry Blodget, her counterpart at Merrill, never became a regulatory target is that she actually chose companies to take public based on quality. Her singular focus was determining which company would be the leader in its category.

Of course some of these "categories" turned out not to support any business at all. Nor were the calls that she made universally right or even necessarily based on a depth of analysis that an investor should expect. It is hard to justify Meeker's continuing insistence, long after the Internet jig was up, that any company she sponsored should almost by definition be rated as an "outperform."

The fact that Meeker was committed to taking only the highest quality companies public in their respective categories did not mean that her work in pursuit of that goal was always of the highest quality itself. A comparison of the depth of financial analysis undertaken on comparable companies by, say, Richard Bilotti, Morgan Stanley's cable analyst, and Meeker reveals a huge gulf. To be fair, the direct demands on Mary's time plus her insistence on keeping ultimate authority over any significant decision touching on the Internet meant that she almost of necessity could only fly by any particular situation at a fairly high level. This had ancillary effects on the quality of work produced by bankers who, as noted earlier, were by now of lower quality overall, also faced incredible demands on their time in the boom, and were desperate for the Internet "street cred" that Mary's imprimatur bestowed.

Accordingly, bankers hungrily waited for the latest set of standard pages that Mary used in her standard investor presentations so that they could mindlessly incorporate them into their own banking pitches. Flipping through the pages to their often rapt audiences, these bankers would then gravely intone that this was the way the royal "We" think about the "Space." The good news was that the pages Mary produced were easy enough to follow, even for a relatively junior banker with little Internet experience. The bad news was that they often bordered on the platitudinous. One of my favorite pages, which I saw reproduced literally hundreds of times for banker pitch books, appeared under the provocative heading "Who Will Emerge to Dominate the Internet?" The subheading continued authoritatively, "History of Media Has Taught Us . . ." The body of the page then followed:

#1 is Awesome
#2 is OK
#3 is Tough
#4 is Pits
#5 is Huh? Who? Forgot . . .[14]

These handful of words were supposed to capture Mary's Internet *Weltanschauung* and leave the listener breathless. In many meetings I attended, it did. Of course, it is a perfectly valid observation that having leading market share is a good thing and that the further one is from that goal the worse off one is. It is something else altogether, however, to suggest that the particular gradations offered here were derived from careful study of the history of media or that they added to the general pool of human knowledge.

In a 2001 article, *Fortune*'s Peter Elkind argued that "Mary Meeker got so caught up in the allure of the Internet—the celebrity, the money, the thrill of dealmaking—that she forgot that she was supposed to be analyzing companies."[15] Elkind also quoted an unnamed "friend" of Meeker as claiming that the reason she had not left Morgan Stanley in 1996 to follow Frank Quattrone—then head of Morgan Stanley's tech banking group and Meeker's mentor—was that she wanted to become a "star" in her own right. The desire to be a star, of course, had by this point become a fairly commonplace aspiration on Wall Street. But while there is evidence that the extraordinary pressures of Meeker's celebrity undermined the quality of her work, there is no evidence that she used it to pursue an untoward agenda. If anything, her stardom may have made her all the more driven to be sure that she only picked winners. At worst, Meeker's fame caused her to personalize the stock calls she made in a way that made it difficult for her to admit mistakes later.

To see how someone else might have exploited his celebrity to simply maximize revenue in the same environment, one only need look at the actions of Meeker's former colleague Frank Quattrone during the same period. Quattrone successfully appealed a criminal conviction reached after a first jury was unable to agree as to his culpability. These recent trials, and the next one, should prosecutors seek to retry Quattrone, hinged on the very narrow legal issue of whether a single e-mail he forwarded constituted an attempt to obstruct justice. By the time that e-mail was sent on December 5, 2000, Quattrone had generated hundreds of millions of dollars for himself and the succession of investment banks at which he worked.

The fact that this e-mail, rather than anything that preceded it, proved to be his downfall reflects both the ambiguous nature of the regulatory environment in which the boom transpired, and Quattrone's ingenuity in leveraging the short-term financial opportunity that ambiguity represented. The longer-term impact on the institutions at which he practiced and, indeed, the industry he represented did not seem to be major considerations. There was a once-in-a-lifetime chance to make a short-term killing for himself. Any longer-term financial or reputational costs to investment banking as a whole would be spread across many institutions and individuals. And besides, given the magnitude of the potential spoils, some version of what happened to investment banking standards during the boom would have happened anyway. On this theory, Frank Quattrone's only offense was being the absolute best at getting more than his fair share of the booty available to investment bankers during the era of Internet euphoria. As such it is worth considering just how he committed this offense so magnificently.

Stories about Frank Quattrone invariably speak of his working-class South Philadelphia roots, his scholarship to Wharton as an undergraduate, and his regular-guy fondness for singing karaoke in general and "Rocky Raccoon" in particular.[16] Quattrone had been an analyst for two years at Morgan Stanley before going to get an MBA at Stanford and returned there immediately afterward as an associate in 1981. Quattrone took leadership of the tech banking effort and moved the group to Silicon Valley in 1994.

By the time Quattrone left in 1996, Morgan Stanley had established a reputation for sponsoring very high-quality companies such as Silicon Graphics in 1986, Cisco in 1990, and, most notably, Netscape in 1995. But there was a cost to limiting yourself to high-quality companies, particularly when the Netscape IPO established for the first time a public market for early stage companies with little operating history and no immediate prospects for profitability. The public had clearly lowered its standards for investing in IPOs; if investment banks followed suit and lowered their standards for underwriting securities there was a lot of money to be made.

To understand the dangers inherent in this line of thinking, it is worth considering the fundamental differences between the two most profitable areas of business in investment banking: M&A and IPOs. In advising on an M&A transaction, investment bankers take no real risk, financial or even reputational. They provide advice (tactics, valuation, structuring, likely market reaction, company positioning post-transaction) and help manage the process. The closest thing to financial exposure is when advisors provide a "fairness opinion." This is a formal written statement of the investment bank's view that the price paid or received, as the case may be, is financially "fair"—not the best possible, the highest or the lowest, but simply "fair" —to the shareholders. But, fairness opinion or no, the bankers are indemnified by their client for all but the most egregious acts. And if you actually ever read a fairness opinion—with its boilerplate language about relying on whatever information the other guy gave me as being true— you would not walk away thinking these bankers were really putting their neck on the line. On the reputational side, the parties to an M&A transaction are sophisticated companies who should know better. Even if shareholders are harmed, individual retail investors have not been sold the deal directly as in an IPO—their mistake was trusting the company's management to make smart decisions and their ire rarely runs to the bankers who advised the company in question. Even if a deal goes disastrously wrong, the bankers usually walk away largely unscathed. The banker to whichever side was overpaid gets bragging rights and the other banker usually blames the client ("I warned then") and moves on. To take an extreme example, the performance of Morgan Stanley's advisors to Time Warner on the AOL Time Warner transaction—even after multiple books were published demonstrating with some precision just how badly their counterparts at Salomon Brothers bettered them—has had no apparent negative impact on their franchise. The same group was even hired subsequently by Time Warner itself to divest its music business.

The economics of IPOs are in some ways similar: just as an M&A banker gets his fee when the deal closes regardless of its long-term wisdom, the investment bank gets to keep 7 percent of the proceeds from the offering regardless of how the stock performs. But there are three other constituencies whose interests force investment banks to take a broader view before agreeing to sponsor a new public company.

First, individual investors cannot be expected to have the sophistication of corporate or institutional ones, a fact at the heart of much of investment banks' recent regulatory scrutiny. The charges against the investment banks focused on the fact that the research analysts' independence was not adequately protected from the influence of bankers looking to ingratiate themselves with clients. One of the most surprising aspects of these research scandals was how little complaint was heard from the institutional investors who are the biggest customers for stock offered by investment banks. The reason: they never took the research report recommendations seriously in the first place. These investors had their own analysts who used a variety of sources and if they wanted to know what the analysts really thought, they picked up the phone and called them. To be fair to the investment banks, what changed during the Internet era was not so much the quality of research, which had always been shamelessly biased toward stocks the firms were underwriting, but the nature and sophistication of the readership interpreting these reports. From 1983 to 2002 the portion of American households that owned equities of some kind grew from under 20 percent to around half.[17] It is this shift that makes a truly independent research function so critical.

Second, young companies can do irreparable harm to themselves by going public too early. You (usually) only get to go public once. This is your chance to tell your story to the market, establish financial and operating metrics that you want to be judged by, and describe your strategic direction. A company that goes public before these elements are ready risks returning to the very investors who bought its stock in the IPO and saying, "Never mind." It is almost impossible to recover credibility from this fundamental breach of trust. The number of "fallen angels"—highflying issues that fail to meet expectations and become penny stocks—that ever come back to life can be counted on one hand. This is the corporate finance equivalent of changing your clothes in public—very few have the body to justify the practice. You might attract a crowd but they are highly likely to walk away in disgust. And something like this is what happened with legions of companies that went public during the boom. Did I say judge me on revenue growth? I meant profitability. Did I say we were going to be an advertising model? I meant subscriptions. Of course some companies knew they shouldn't ever be public but were looking for someone to help them exploit a market anomaly. Maybe they could use their stock currency to buy some real assets before the market came back to earth. This brings us to the third constituency.

Investment banks face several structural challenges. Their investment banking teams are generally judged and compensated by the fees generated by their corporate clients—the 7 percent mentioned in the case of IPOs. In any given year, bankers' pay is tied closely to the number of transactions, not the quality of transactions. But the overall long-term health of an investment bank, and its sales and trading operations in particular, is tied to its reputation and its ability to consistently offer quality new issues. If many of the offerings led by a firm quickly trade down, the sales force will start to lose customers and commissions and even the investment bankers will find it harder over time to secure financing mandates. But investment bankers are financially incentivized to ignore the long-term cost to the institution of a weak offering, particularly if a competitor will likely underwrite it. A truly independent research function and an internal "commitments committee" process that incorporates the views of internal professionals with a broader perspective and less skewed incentives minimizes the risk that the firm will agree to sponsor IPOs that are not ready for prime time.

This brings us back to Frank Quattrone. He viewed the structural counterweights to an investment banker's short-term pecuniary interests as unacceptably constraining. Before deciding to leave Morgan Stanley, Quattrone had unsuccessfully pressed the firm to give him more control over the technology bankers and research analysts and to share more directly in the trading revenues of stocks his group had IPO'd.[18] The deal Quattrone cut with Deutsche Morgan Grenfell (DMG), as the firm was then called, gave him direct supervisory oversight of the research analysts and bankers, a blank check for hiring, and 50 percent of the group's profits to be distributed to his team as he saw fit. This deal allowed Quattrone what he euphemistically referred to as the "flexibility and autonomy"[19] he needed to generate revenues unconstrained by the traditional checks and balances of an investment bank.

It is hard to imagine Quattrone coexisting with Meeker at Morgan Stanley during the boom years, given his singular focus on profiting in the post-Netscape world. With this incentive scheme in place, Quattrone rather unapologetically marketed himself as the un-Meeker in a sense. Using what *Investment Dealers' Digest* called his "virtuoso spin control," Quattrone effectively argued that quality may be all fine and good in normal times, but we have a gold rush on and quantity is king.[20] Meeker and her ilk were "out of capacity," Quattrone argued. In under five months at DMG he had hired 90 people, a third of whom were in research. The relevant metric for choosing an investment bank was the "ratio of people to clients" and by that standard "[w]e have the most capacity in the industry." It almost sounded as if each company might get its own personal research analyst.

Although there is no denying that Quattrone was an excellent marketer and effective banker, it is clear that he offered not only extra capacity but a lower quality bar. Quattrone targeted companies Morgan Stanley and Goldman Sachs told to "wait a quarter or two" before they were ready to go public.[21] Admittedly, this would seem an eternity to an entrepreneur whose peers have already gone public and become rich, particularly a sophisticated entrepreneur who knows "waiting a quarter or two" is investment banker-speak for "I don't know when or if you'll be ready, but you sure as hell aren't now." This strategy in turn put pressure on Goldman and Morgan to weaken their own internal procedures and lower their standards. Soon companies hungry to join the IPO orgy would claim, not always truthfully, when seeking sponsorship from Morgan or Goldman to have been offered to be underwritten by Quattrone. Sometimes the blue-chip banks could convince the company that waiting was in its own interest. Sometimes they passed and Quattrone did the offering. And sometimes they lowered their standards. Given how amorphous the standards were in this era, bankers could always manage to rationalize their decision and satisfy themselves that the criteria had not been altered. But no one can seriously claim that the competitive environment failed to have an impact on which companies these institutions underwrote and when.

In July 1998, two years after leaving Morgan Stanley and only a few months after sending a letter to clients that ended, "We are here to stay. Please trust us," Quattrone jumped ship from DMG to Credit Suisse First Boston (CSFB). According to Quattrone, his previous German employers were apparently looking to renegotiate his deal after the first full-year profits they had to split with him were $143 million. CSFB offered the same "autonomy" and not only a piece of the revenues his group generated but an ability to invest in the companies beforehand—in case any more incentive was needed.[22] Following the same pattern, two years later rumors started circulating that Quattrone was planning to leave CSFB,[23] but despite early signs of the extended technology winter that would follow "he managed to negotiate an enormous new pay package" for three years.[24] It was not until July 2001, that CSFB, under intense regulatory scrutiny, announced that research analysts would no longer report to bankers. That decision was made by CSFB's new leader John Mack. Mack was the same person who had refused to accede to Quattrone's requests in the early and mid-90s as then president of Morgan Stanley.

As the boom era moved to an end in the latter part of 2000, among its casualties was the culture of excellence and client service that had once prevailed at the leading investment banking houses. In its place was a culture of celebrity that had countenanced a systematic lowering of standards. These included hiring standards, underwriting standards, research standards, standards for conflicts, work quality standards, teamwork standards, and standards of behavior. These lowered standards were apparent to both employees and clients. As the industry faced an extended contraction, some wondered whether these institutions could recapture the values that had been lost or whether the breach was too deep. As we shall see, much of the era of retrenchment was spent settling old scores rather than reestablishing old business principles.

· 10 ·

DRAMA OF THE GIFTED
BANKER

I N CONSIDERING the poor job that investment banks did in responding to the pressures of the boom, it is worth looking more
closely at the kind of people these institutions attracted and the kind of
training they had received. For some time, the major investment banks have
overwhelmingly recruited from a small group of top business schools.
The notion that a graduate degree in business might be a sensible pursuit
for smart and ambitious young people is a relatively new one. An MBA
had been viewed as a glorified vocational certificate, a weak second choice
for those not up to a proper professional career like law or medicine. This
perspective began to change in the late 1970s and early 1980s and corresponded with new attitudes toward business in general and CEOs in
particular.

During this period business topics became an integral part of mainstream
public discourse. In 1983, for the first time, the top four titles on the
New York Times nonfiction bestseller list all fell under the broad heading
of "business books."[1] The greater public interest in business can be traced
in part to the emergence of the celebrity CEO as a cultural icon. Lee Iacocca,
who was elected as chairman and CEO of Chrysler in 1979, will likely be
remembered as the first celebrity CEO of the modern era.[2]

In addition to changed public perceptions, there was a dramatic
increase in recruiting at graduate schools of business by high-paying
consulting firms and investment banks. In the 1970s, barely one out of ten
new CEOs had MBAs but, by the 1990s, well over a quarter would.[3] These

phenomena combined to make it socially acceptable for a high-powered college graduate to pursue an MBA. In fact, an MBA became viewed as the graduate degree of choice for those who were not just bright but true "go-getters."

More traditional professional degrees were now derided as excessively narrow and technocratic. An MBA, by contrast, was associated with a more entrepreneurial spirit. It allowed ambitious overachievers to simultaneously do precisely what was expected of them and yet suggest that what differentiated them from the merely intelligent was their courageous pursuit of so open-ended a calling. Rather than learning about the painful details of civil procedure or organic chemistry, MBAs would be trained to be all-purpose leaders, armed with the secrets of modern management. These skills, it was implied, could be applied to any industry or situation. And the fact that this magical degree could be had in a mere two years without the troublesome requirement of a final qualifying test like medical boards or a bar exam made it all the more attractive.

The reality of both the pedagogy and the people involved in the MBA factories was something different altogether. And the output became highly predictable.

The core MBA curriculum seeks to introduce graduates from the widest possible range of undergraduate majors to the mysteries a more than a half dozen distinct disciplines. Any one of economics, accounting, marketing, organizational behavior, finance, manufacturing, or statistics could usefully fill up two years of serious graduate study. But with the first year taken up primarily with core requirements that represent a smattering of each of these and the second year primarily concerned with job search, it is not surprising that faculty often view the entire MBA program as an ugly, if highly profitable, stepchild.

Part of the problem is that there is no general agreement as to what precisely these students are being trained for. Indeed, the multiplicity of subjects covered in part reflects this lack of consensus. But rather than making a genuine effort to synthesize these various disciplines, MBA programs often leave it to the students to figure out what connections, if any, exist between these subject areas.

Ironically, the success of business schools at recruiting highly regarded faculty from each of these subject areas has made it harder rather than easier to create a truly integrated two-year course of study. Superstar faculty are famously more concerned with their own advanced research than spending time teaching or otherwise dealing with students. This is particularly true with respect to MBA graduate students, who are viewed as less than serious in the first place. The fact that these students are not known for their humility and that many will soon be making more money than the faculty themselves exacerbates the problem. As a result, investing in developing a truly thoughtful, comprehensive curriculum for this constituency is not a real faculty priority.

So, like most interdisciplinary courses of study, the MBA falls apart in its execution—the equivalent of an Evelyn Wood speed-reading course on every topic arguably related to the problems of business without any attempt at integration. It would not be unusual, for instance, to be told one day in finance class that there is no value to diversification (on the theory that investors can obtain diversification themselves by investing in multiple pure-play companies) and have the virtues of just such diversification extolled the next day in a manufacturing seminar (based on the benefits of evening out capacity utilization and smoothing a company's results). What would be unusual is for the respective faculty to talk to each other to give students tools to form a coherent way of reconciling these views.

One might expect the bright young go-getters who are getting MBAs to blow the whistle on this charade. In fact, they are very much in on the joke. Honest MBAs will tell you that they pursued it primarily to signal future employers of their worth and secondarily to develop friendships that can be exploited later in life. For them, the focus is on getting their tickets punched and networking. One widely cited recent study suggests that with the exception of the very top MBA programs, where the networking is truly first-rate, an MBA is one of the poorest educational investments one can make.[4]

When I was getting my MBA in the late 1980s at Stanford University, the most intellectually stimulating course I took was the core macroeconomics class. That year my section was taught by Thomas Sargent, a distinguished visiting faculty member who is one of the fathers of the "rational expectations" school of economic thought. Sargent did something unexpected. He decided not to simply offer the usual slightly souped up version of the traditional macro course offered at every liberal arts college in the county. Instead, he recast the class as an introduction to game theory in which the Federal Reserve, the Congress, and consumers were each cast as players. Rather than being stimulated by this provocative approach, my classmates revolted. This was not what they had signed up for. They had lots of other classes to prepare for and job interviews and they really didn't have time to debate the applicability of the prisoner's dilemma to the macro economy. Just provide some sample questions for the final exam and they would take care of the rest.

For all of the talk of leadership, entrepreneurship, and innovation, by the mid-1980s almost half of the graduates of the nation's top MBA programs went to either consulting firms or investment banks. This would climb to well over half by the mid-1990s. Having invested so much into satisfying the cultural expectations around being a true go-getter, these graduates seemed paralyzed by the fear that they would make a career choice that might undermine their hard-earned social status.

I recall how I felt when I saw the bulk of my business school classmates march off to become investment bankers and consultants. I had come to know the Stanford Business School class of 1987 as an eclectic and in many ways remarkable group of people. At our initial class orientation, I remember thinking as the director of admissions rattled off the accomplishments of my classmates—astronaut, successful entrepreneur, professional golfer, captain of a small boat that sailed around the world—that I had somehow slipped through by accident. But as our two years drew to a close, this same group of brilliant, ambitious, creative people were transformed into passive followers as they competed for the interview slots of the investment banks and consulting firms that dominated the campus recruiting schedules.

It's not that interesting people can't want to be bankers and consultants. It's just that nothing about these particular interesting people suggested it would be their overwhelming desire as a group.

Given the passive, risk-averse tendencies of these MBA graduates, it may seem surprising that despite the fact that investment banks were making more, and paying more, than ever before during the boom, investment bankers were leaving the profession in record numbers. Rates of departure were up 50 to 100 percent or more across the board, from young analysts—who sign on for a two-year commitment straight out of college—to very senior managing directors—who typically have the most to lose by walking away from millions in unvested stock and options.

Even more curious, these bankers were often leaving to work not at competitors, but at Internet-related start-up companies. It is hard to imagine a job more unlike being a banker at an established firm than being an executive at an early stage operating company. It is as different as, say, being a plastic surgeon is from running a chain of hardware stores. While one person's making such a career change might not seem altogether shocking, why it became an industrywide craze is puzzling.

Nonsense, some will certainly say, what's the mystery? Bankers are the greediest people in the world, this argument goes. The Internet suddenly became the quickest way to become a gazillionaire. Why should we be surprised that bankers fell all over each other on the way out of one set of doors and through the other? To be fair, some version of this explanation is by far the most popular not only among the general public, but also among bankers themselves.

Yet there is something unsatisfactory about this theory—let's call it the Greed is Good theory after the famous Michael Douglas line from Oliver Stone's *Wall Street*. If the theory were true, it would suggest one could simply get bankers to stay by paying them more. And this is precisely what the major investment banks tried to do. They began gingerly with a variety of "quality-of-life" initiatives that tried to emulate the imagined work environment at Internet companies. They instituted casual dress year round, after escalating in stages from casual summer Fridays, a move viewed as revolutionary at the time. When this did not have the hoped-for effect, the concept of life quality was broadened so that companies were offering everything from free fruit and coffee in the pantry to paid leaves of absence. But before long the investment banks turned to the currency they knew best: cash. Each institution soon announced a variety of incremental compensation plans involving cash, stock, and a multitude of ways to participate in these firms' private equity investments.

It is always problematic to assess the success of such schemes because it is impossible to know what would have happened in their absence. The extent to which the flight of bankers to Internet companies eventually slowed could easily be attributable to the ultimate collapse of the Internet IPO market. Luckily, the unique compensation arrangements surrounding Goldman Sachs' own IPO in 1999 do allow us to draw some conclusions regarding the impact of the pure greed factor. All Goldman Sachs employees received significant stock grants at the time of the IPO that would be forfeited if they left the firm within three years. The incremental compensation plans of other banks, no matter how generous, were no more than a fraction of the payoff that the Goldman IPO represented to those who stayed with the firm. If the Greed is Good theory were true, one would have expected dramatically lower personnel turnover at Goldman Sachs—even ignoring that Goldman has had lower historic turnover anyway.

But Goldman experienced the same attrition rates as its peers. This happened despite the fact that Goldman had instituted one of the more generous incremental compensation plans (on top of the IPO stock distribution) to stem the exodus of bankers. Although Goldman's competitors were undoubtedly tempted to gloat, any gloating likely turned quickly to horror. For if Goldman couldn't hang on to its people by using the stick of taking back its IPO largesse, how could others ever afford a carrot big enough to do the job?

What can explain the odd group dynamic that first drew these overachievers to banking and then to the Internet? At the time, I groped for a theory less simplistic than Greed Is Good but more persuasive than, say, mass hysteria. Surprisingly, I stumbled onto a clue in the journey of personal self-discovery embarked on by Al Gore, who then was in the midst of his unsuccessful quest to succeed Bill Clinton as president of the United States.

After his disastrous 1988 presidential run and his son's near-fatal car crash, Al Gore had a midlife crisis. He undertook an intensive study of family dysfunction, enlisting the help of a University of Tennessee clinical psychologist who supplied the reading materials. The book that Gore felt captured his own internal struggle was *The Drama of the Gifted Child: The Search for the True Self* by Swiss psychoanalyst Alice Miller. Gore not only began handing out copies to friends and colleagues, he asked job applicants if they had read it.[5]

Miller's book deals with the special problem of exceptionally gifted and sensitive people "who have been praised and admired for their talents and their achievements" from an early age but who are prone to "suddenly get the feeling they have failed to live up to some ideal image and measure they feel they must adhere to."[6] The source of the problem, Miller argues, lies with parents who unconsciously use their gifted children to satisfy their own narcissistic needs. The children in turn are condemned to continually seek the parents' love by piling on achievement after achievement while secretly harboring the fear that what the parent loves is the achievement rather than the child. Such children never develop their own sense of self, separate from their need to please, and can experience wild emotional swings. Once the euphoria of the latest achievement wears off, they are filled with the shame and emptiness that comes with being alienated from their own feelings and needs. And soon they are off conquering the next challenge in the vain hope of filling that void permanently.

As syndromes go, this one sounds like it could at least partly explain why waves of overachieving business school graduates and investment bankers would blindly pursue whatever career is publicly associated with success at the moment regardless of whether it holds any intrinsic interest for them, regardless even of economic incentives as powerful as the Goldman IPO.

Even if Al Gore himself had explained the crisis, it is still not clear what the banks could have done about it. At first blush, Dr. Miller's likely remedy—psychoanalysis for bankers to get in touch with their true feelings—seems impractical. On the other hand, compared with some of the "quality-of-life" perks that were offered up to keep bankers happy, psychoanalysis might have had the added benefit of having the right people leave banking for the right reasons. And who knows, maybe a banker in touch with his inner self would not just be happier, but a better banker as well.

Given who became the investment bankers of the 1990s and why, the impact of the basic shift at these institutions toward a more transactional culture is easier to understand. The IBG YBG ethos was an almost predictable outcome of the collision between this new pecking order and the overwhelming desire to please among the troops. All across the Street, personal relevance was now achieved not by excelling at being a team player or some other quaint notion. The goal was to do deals, generate revenue, and be noticed. To avoid, in Paulson's vernacular, becoming a dinosaur. To be a player, a star, whatever the cost, particularly when someone else bore that cost. And there would be significant costs indeed.

This context is helpful to understanding what came before and what unfolded next. Bankers who would lose their jobs in the imminent downturn felt worthless, empty, and confused. And more broadly, the decline in social status of investment banking over the last decade that corresponded in part with the decline in standards left those whose personal and professional identity had been intensely identified with the industry feeling betrayed and, well, a little bit grumpy. The more important societal implications of the transformation of the investment banking industry lie elsewhere. But it is the "drama of the gifted investment banker" that gives our tale a certain poignancy.

TAKE A WALK ON
THE BUY-SIDE

ONCE THE MARKET downturn came, the challenges to playing the role of a relationship banker in the era of the financial supermarket were brought into sharp relief. This was particularly true when representing a client looking to make a purchase—acting on the "buy-side," to use the banking vernacular—something I had rarely done before joining Morgan.

Because of my "sell-side" focus, I also had spent relatively little time learning about the financing side of investment banking. Beyond making sure that the buyer secured adequate financing commitments to pay for what I was selling, I was not that interested in the details of the loan documents. When representing the buyer, however, actually providing the financing to make the purchase is central to the engagement. In these circumstances, the investment banker plays two different and potentially conflicting roles: objective advisor on all aspects of the transaction and conduit to the internal lending product specialists who want to actually provide the money. The obvious conflict arises when the lending terms offered are not competitive and the best objective advice is to seek financing elsewhere.

In the era of the financial supermarkets, in which every possible opportunity to sell every possible product and service to every possible client is the strategic imperative, even when you are representing a seller in a broad auction designed to get them the highest price possible, similar conflict-of-interest issues arise. Sellers' advisors increasingly offer "stapled financing" packages to potential buyers. This is analogous to getting store credit to buy a refrigerator. The key difference, however, is that it is not the "store" itself that provides the credit package, but the investment bank. This raises two serious problems.

First, although buyers are not required to use the package, and in theory are free to find better financing elsewhere, they will be understandably reluctant to get on the wrong side of the investment bank managing the process. Often the fees associated with the stapled financing are greater than the M&A advisory fees. The investment bank accordingly has a large financial incentive to direct the property to a party who will use its stapled financing package. This creates a deep structural conflict between the client and the investment banker. Even if the client will make the final call, in close situations a little extra information or inside push can make the difference between winning and losing in a hotly contested auction.

Second, once a deal is signed there is usually a period of time— typically 30 to 90 days—during which government approvals are obtained and the financing is put in place, before the transaction actually closes and money changes hands. The seller's interest is in ensuring that they get their money as quickly as possible no matter what. But in precisely those difficult circumstances that a seller will be most worried about, this will not be in the investment bank's interest if it is responsible for delivering the funds. Financing documents have vague escape clauses that allow the lender to get out of the commitment if there is a "material adverse change" in the business or the market environment. The investment bank as lender will have different interest in both negotiating and interpreting such phrases. And if the normal method by which the investment bank lays off its risk—known as the syndication process, where other institutions take on pieces of the commitment—goes poorly, it will want more time to finish whereas the seller will want the buyers to provide the funds and close immediately. The "objective advisor" and the client are literally on opposite sides of the table in such circumstances.

But it is on the buy-side where the tensions are greatest. Bankers always seem to be groping to seem busy and useful on the buy-side—producing endless timetable and working group lists and pages of analysis on hypothetical deals. On the sell-side, the bankers have a process to run and plenty to do. On the buy-side, there isn't much to do beyond helping with due diligence, doing a little financial analysis, providing a point of view on the likely market reaction to a deal and sourcing intelligence about other buyers. Buy-side fees reflect this fact and are often heavily reliant on the potential financing.

My own experience on a significant acquisition in 2002 was a painful initiation into the world of financing and the buy-side. The year 2002 was not a great time to be a banker and this was certainly true for those of us focused on the media industry. The media industry is about fun and fame, politics and personalities. As an investment banker, I wasn't attracted to the invitation to work in the media industry rather than, say, forest products because I thought it was necessarily a better business than cutting down trees. It was sexy.

But the public markets during the bust had begun to reward safe and boring, not sexy. On the whole, for society at large that was a good thing. The renewed focus on free cash flow, strong balance sheets, and moderate risk was certainly a welcome and even necessary change. But the media business, or at least what most people think of as the media business, is all about hits. Blockbuster movies, platinum albums, *New York Times* bestsellers, number one rated TV shows. And there is still no such thing as a sure thing when it comes to hit-driven businesses. It is hard to argue that anyone who produces such products has a sustainable competitive advantage of some kind. How many go to a movie or buy a CD based on the studio or record label? Accordingly, in the environment of 2002, media businesses were in almost as much disfavor as Internet start-ups.[1]

Yet even within the media industry, there are some businesses that have the operating characteristics that were now of most interest to investors. The funny thing is that these businesses were once the ugly ducklings of the stock market. Rarely spoken about, their cash flow often abused to finance other more speculative endeavors by their corporate parents, these businesses were suddenly the belle of the ball.

The business that epitomized the postbust media industry aesthetic was the yellow pages. In place of the celebrity gossip of a glossy magazine or the provocative prose of a bestseller, the "content" of yellow pages is page after page of classified listings and advertisements. Unlike sexy media companies such as the entertainment conglomerates, yellow page businesses pretty much never experience double-digit organic revenue growth. But they don't usually dip much in a recession either. If the local pizza delivery or moving company wants to stay in business, they need to advertise in the yellow page directory no matter how bad things get. Yellow pages require almost no capital expenditures. They typically have cash-flow margins of greater than 50 percent. Although there are threats from on-line competitors and independent upstarts, these established directory publishers seem unruffled and just continue to churn out cash.

The story of R. H. Donnelley (RHD) perfectly captures how much the media sector had changed between the 1990s and 2002. This tale actually begins in 1917 when the company was formed out of its predecessor, the Chicago Directory Company, which had published yellow pages in Chicago and the surrounding region. Dun and Bradstreet, a conglomerate that epitomized the nonstrategic build-ups that took place in the 60s, had purchased the company in 1961. With conglomerates out of favor, in 1996 the company announced what would be only the first in a series of split-ups and spin-offs that would continue over the next five years that would result in eight different companies: IMS, Moody's, AC Nielsen, Nielsen Media Research, Gartner Group, Cognizant, D&B, and RHD.

RHD was always viewed and treated as the very poor relation of this otherwise fairly distinguished group. When RHD was finally spun off as an independent entity from D&B in 1998, it was saddled with most of the parent company's debt and many of the legal liabilities from various predecessor companies. The company was barely a shell of its former self. Its two primary assets were now a contract to sell the advertising and provide other ancillary services for Sprint's directories and a 50 percent stake in a joint venture with SBC Communications called Don Tech, which published yellow pages in Illinois and Indiana. The terms of the Sprint contract got progressively worse as it moved toward expiration, and Don Tech operated totally independently, requiring RHD executives only to show up a few times a year to pick up a check. This was not a great equity story and the market capitalization of the company (the total value of its shares) had been as low as $350 million.

RHD executives considered just about everything to reinvigorate the company. But their debt constrained what they could buy, and it seemed like nothing could turn around the trend of yellow page publishers bringing the functions once outsourced to RHD in-house. So in early 2000, the company basically gave up and hired Goldman Sachs to sell itself. Then, in the ultimate humiliation, on December 5, 2000, the company issued a press release announcing to the world that during the hottest bull market in history, it had been unable to find any buyer at all.[2] This was truly a company that could not get itself arrested.

Then in early 2002, something happened that offered a possibility, maybe the only possibility, for RHD to transform itself into a company with its own yellow page operations rather than just dissipating contracts with and equity stakes in others. Word began to leak out that Sprint was running out of cash and might need to sell its directories business. Here was a chance for RHD, if it could buy the directories from Sprint, to become master of its own fate. But by the same token, if the scenario unfolded another way, it had the potential of putting the final bullet into the forehead of the already weak company. For if someone else, particularly a tough LBO buyer looking to cut costs, got hold of the Sprint directories, there was no chance that the RHD contract would be renewed. And in the interim, it was likely that relations with Sprint would deteriorate as it tried to convince potential buyers of how much more profitable the business could be once the RHD contract were eliminated.

At the time, RHD was a small company with few prospects, so very few bankers spent any time covering them. Even Goldman, once the failed sale was announced, had kept its distance. I knew enough about RHD's plight and relationship with the Sprint directories to conclude they were an asset RHD *had* to own. And the best buyer to represent is one for whom the deal is a matter of life or death.[3] I had met RHD's CEO, Dave Swanson, while I was selling a small independent directories company called Worldpages.com the previous year. Another banker knew the new CFO at RHD, Steve Blondy, from his previous job. This was enough for an audience, and I thought it might be enough to get the engagement. But there were two challenges, one related to RHD and one related to Morgan.

RHD was at this point a tiny company and getting smaller. Although it had paid down a lot of debt, it still owed around $300 million and its market value was just over $800 million. The Sprint directories might cost as much as $2 billion or more. We ran numbers and concluded it could probably be done with a lot of leverage, but it was not a slam dunk. Two critical factors would be the receptivity of the markets to RHD becoming so highly leveraged, and the willingness of the RHD board to bet the company on this deal.

LBO firms had for some time represented a hugely important constituency for investment banks because of their relentless generation of fees both directly and through their portfolio companies. Investment banks even came up with a more benign sounding name for them—just as "junk bonds" were now referred to as "high yield," leveraged buyout firms were transformed into "financial sponsors" in investment banking parlance. During the bust, as corporate America turned inward and became skittish about doing any transactions, "financial sponsors" saw a buying opportunity. In this period of retrenchment, LBO firms came to represent a historically unprecedented percentage of all M&A deals that got done. And yellow pages were the perfect LBO target: high, stable cash flows to support high leverage, and the most obvious strategic buyers (the phone companies who owned the incumbent directories) unwilling to invest more in a business that they had always thought of as noncore. To the bankers who covered the sponsors, the fact that RHD was obviously a better buyer didn't matter. They wanted to use the opportunity to get closer to their client base, win or lose, and at this point in the cycle they had as much clout as anyone.

In the end, we were offered and accepted the appointment as coadvisor to RHD alongside Bear Stearns, which had been one of the few firms that had bothered to actively cover the company. Bear Stearns is a midtier firm with an uneven history and reputation, but like all such firms, Bear Stearns has its areas of strength—in their case particularly on the trading side.[4] In 2001, the legendary trader, 73-year-old chairman "Ace" Greenberg, handed over his title to 67-year-old CEO "Jimmy" Cayne, although Greenberg remains on the board and acts as chair of the Executive Committee. Bear also had a handful of very strong senior bankers. The trouble with midtier firms is that they cannot attract the best graduates, and to recruit established bankers to leave top-tier firms, they have to pay a significant premium under long-term contracts. The result is that the drop-off in quality from the very top is quite precipitous.

For Morgan, the RHD bid was a potentially nice piece of business, but hardly one to stop the presses. It would take a lot of time over several months, and RHD was a modestly sized company that might or might not win the auction. I led the team that included a solid but new managing director from mergers, Adam Shepard, and our associate, Todd Davison. At Bear, this project was taken a little more seriously. My counterpart on the Bear team was Allan Schwartz, president and COO of Bear. Adam's counterpart was Lou Friedman, head of Global Mergers and Acquisitions. And Todd's counterpart was Davies Beller, a senior managing director who had been in investment banking since he and I had left Stanford Business School together almost 15 years earlier.

Throughout the ensuing months that included full-day board meetings and even occasional all-nighters, I could not believe how much time Bear's senior banking management team spent on this project. It would have been a highly foolish career move even to ask Morgan's president to help cover a sub-$1 billion equity value company, much less have him help execute a transaction. In the end, having a corporate decision maker on the team paid off for Bear in a big way. The trouble for Bear and other firms like it, however, is that this is not a highly efficient business model—you can only rely on the president of the company to cover so many clients and go to so many meetings.

Over the next months we got the board comfortable with a transaction, but both the company and we became nervous about how much debt the company could support. We couldn't be sure how either the market or the credit agencies would react to this small, moderately leveraged outsourcer to yellow page companies becoming a highly leveraged multibillion dollar publisher overnight. So, to hedge our bets in case the required debt would be more than the company could practically support, we decided to see whether we might be able to attract equity from financial sponsors on reasonable terms. Accordingly, we let it be known that we would consider taking in a couple of hundred million dollars in private equity for a non-controlling stake in RHD.

Word of our potential openness to private equity spread rapidly. Literally dozens of funds contacted Morgan, Bear, or the client directly. We organized presentations at which senior partners from all the major financial sponsors presented as to why RHD should let them invest in the deal. What became clear, however, was that this money would be very expensive as these firms were looking for returns at least twice as high as required from lenders. The company understandably wanted to keep the option of just using debt to finance a transaction if possible.

As the final bid day for the Sprint directories transaction approached, I started seeing disturbing signs about Morgan's stomach for financing the deal. Although underwriting securities is typically undertaken on a "best efforts" basis, providing a financing commitment in a situation like this —although potentially quite lucrative—did carry some risk. First, the participating banks would need to underwrite not just the junk bonds that would be marketed to investors but also would need to provide a bank loan. Although the idea would be to immediately syndicate this loan to other institutions, there was a risk that this might not go as planned. Second, if it was not possible to get investors to buy the junk bonds at even a very high interest rate, the banks would need to commit to provide a "bridge loan." This was necessary because Sprint would never be willing to take the risk that its directories sale would only close if RHD's debt placement were successful. Although the terms of these bridge loans—so-called because they are meant to serve as a "bridge" to getting more permanent financing—can be quite punitive to the issuer, underwriters dread being forced to hold these. Their view is that it is almost impossible to adequately compensate them for taking this kind of risk. Third, even in a "successful" junk bond offering, the lead underwriters are expected to provide liquidity in the securities afterwards—known as "making a market." If the markets turn south, they can end up holding significant amounts of debt whose value has decreased.

As RHD's investment banker, my internal points of contact on the financing were the product specialists in the high yield department. High yield departments at investment banking firms typically sit on or near the trading floors, but are actually simply marketing departments to promote the firm's prowess in high yield. They have no authority to make credit or underwriting decisions. Their job primarily is to work with investment banking coverage officers and reel in the business and secondarily to serve as a kind of go-between communicating to the banker the views and concerns of those who actually would make those decisions. Others have final say over what business to do and what to charge. At Morgan Stanley at this time there was literally a wall with a locked door that separated this marketing department from the real traders and senior executives who were ultimately responsible for making decisions relating to the firm's balance sheet.

The fact that these high yield bankers sat on the same floor as the traders did have an impact on the culture of their group. A little more swagger, a little more macho, slightly louder, a few more sports metaphors. But really it was all show. These guys had no ability to commit the firm's capital. And the more worried they got about their ability to deliver the firm in a situation, the more aggressive their style to overcompensate for the fact that they had nothing.

So I started getting nervous when the high yield department started trash talking what lousy M&A bankers we were to have to pay as much as we were talking about to own the Sprint directories. By definition, the higher the price, the more leverage would be required and the riskier the financing.

"What are you guys, fucking idiots?" had become a fairly common greeting when I would arrive at the high yield department to check on the status of our proposal. This was big commitment and everyone on the floor, even those who were not working directly on it, seemed to have a point of view.

"They're playing you, man. No one else is there!"

"Do I need to explain M&A 101 to you, or what?!"

We were in the process of preparing for our presentation to the firm's Commitments Committee as the final bid day approached. In theory, the Committee is the source of final approval before a banker can provide a commitment to underwrite a security on specified terms. One morning, as we were preparing to visit RHD, the banking team got a call from the high yield team asking us to come downstairs for a brief meeting before we left. When we arrived, Mitch Petrick, head of high yield sales and trading, had come over from the other side of the wall to take a look at the updated financing materials we would be presenting. Mitch had run the distressed debt trading desk and had ascended to successively senior management positions. These were more or less the same materials we had been presenting for the last several months and, I assumed, not controversial. That was a bad assumption.

"Who the hell gave you these numbers?" Petrick shouted. The investment banking team had incorporated all the leverage levels, market judgments, and pricing information from the high yield team who had been coordinating with their counterparts at Bear Stearns to present a consensus view. As the rest of us turned toward the head of U.S. high yield, who had been on the RHD team from the start, he turned quite pale. Before he could fully collect himself, Petrick cut him off.

"This is the first fucking time I am seeing this," he said. "You're talking about more than $2 billion, for Christ's sake!"

We were running late for our meeting with senior RHD management at their offices in Westchester and had to leave. While we were in the car, Mitch called to continue the conversation.

"You should have come to me sooner," Mitch told me.

"That can't be the right answer, Mitch," I said as the rest of the car's occupants, including the high yield head, pretended not to be listening. "Why the hell do you have a high yield department if I have to go directly to you each time to make sure they're not full of shit?"

To the annoyance of my high yield counterparts, I had always encouraged RHD to get competing financing proposals. But the slim corporate staff was already overwhelmed by the demands of this massive deal and managing the deluge of financial sponsors who were offering to invest in the deal. And besides, they couldn't believe that at the end of the day we wouldn't step up.

In the days leading up to the board meeting to approve the final bid, our high yield team tried to craft something with Petrick that would be acceptable to the Commitments Committee. But they would need to get Bear Stearns on board as well, since the idea was that each of us would underwrite half of the deal. At the end of the day, we needed to propose the same terms. Bear was a relatively small institution and a minor presence in the high yield market and could never commit to the entire financing. It was in their interest to present a common front with Morgan because—even if they really thought we were being too conservative—they represented only half a deal. And if RHD went outside to others for potential financing proposals, a large bank might insist on taking the whole deal or nothing, cutting Bear out altogether.

Because of the usurious terms associated with many of the private equity proposals, RHD very much wanted a proposal that was not contingent on taking in new equity, and both Bear and Morgan had indicated a willingness to do this. But Sprint's were now not the only directories on the market. Another phone company facing financial peril, Qwest, had announced it was divesting an even larger portfolio of yellow pages. And scuttlebutt had it that a massive junk bond issuance would be used to finance this sale as well. At this point, it was still unclear which of the yellow page financings would come first. Morgan started to convince itself that there was a real risk that if the Qwest deal did come first, high yield investors would not be willing to buy any more yellow page junk bonds, almost regardless of the pricing. In this nightmare scenario, in which the market literally ran out of capacity, the underwriters in theory would be left holding billions. So the Morgan high yield guys tried to scare the Bear high yield guys into agreeing to a joint proposal that was not actually contingent on new equity, but became dramatically more expensive to the company if new equity was not raised within a very short time frame. Then for good measure, they added a provision that made the company pay an additional fee to the extent that the underwriters were unable to syndicate more than a certain amount of the debt. In essence, the underwriters were trying to get the company to insure them against the risk of a difficult offering. I asked my high yield counterparts for any precedents to justify such a pricing structure. They could not produce one.

Despite loading up all of these off-market protections on an asset that had the lowest risk profile and highest cash-generation characteristics of any company you could imagine, such was the environment at Morgan that the Commitments Committee meeting was highly contentious. What was most clear from the meeting was that no one on the committee or otherwise in attendance, wanted their fingerprints on the transaction. Ironically, the one exception was Mitch Petrick, who despite his early skepticism, now strongly advocated the deal—at least certainly on the remarkably off-market terms we were now talking about proposing. Everyone wanted to be on the record for asking at least one tough question. No actual vote was taken at the session, as no one seemed to relish being on record for making a decision either way.

Mitch assured me after the meeting that he would get me the official O.K. in time for the RHD board meeting the next morning at which the final bid would be approved. He just needed to make a few phone calls.

The next morning I stopped in to Mitch's office on my way out to get the official approval.

"I'm waiting to hear back from George," Mitch said.

"Who the hell is George?" I asked. George James, I learned, was Mitch's immediate supervisor in the new fixed income hierarchy.

"Just call me from the car," he said, "don't worry about it."

So I called from the car.

"George wants to talk to Zoe," Mitch informed me, referring to Zoe Cruz, who was in charge of all of Fixed Income. "It should just be a few minutes."

Just before entering the board meeting I ducked into a private phone booth across the hall.

"Zoe needs to speak with Vikram." Vikram was co-head of the Institutional Securities Division into which Fixed Income reported.

"You have got to be kidding me!" I cried. "None of these fucking people are even on the Commitments Committee! Why did we even bother?"

Luckily, the board meeting would run several hours, with the financing issues not covered until well into the agenda. Steve Blondy, the CFO of RHD, cornered me on the way in.

"You guys got through Committee?" he asked.

"We should be fine," I said trying to seem as nonchalant as possible. "I'm waiting on one final approval, which we should get well before the meeting is over."

As we approached the financing agenda item, I pretended to go to the bathroom and tried Mitch again.

"Now don't get upset," Mitch began with an uncharacteristic sheepishness, "but Vikram wanted to check with Steve and he's out of the office playing golf or something. They're tracking him down." Steve was Steve Crawford, the young CFO of Morgan Stanley.

"I am sitting in there with my dick in my hand," I told him. "You've got to help me out here."

"We're finding Crawford."

I returned to find RHD CEO Dave Swanson directly asking Alan Schwartz, the Bear Stearns COO, whether the financing proposal was contingent upon an equity infusion.

"Absolutely not," Schwartz said.

At this point I wanted to clarify that although our offer was not contingent upon equity, the failure to get equity would cost the company a great deal more money. But since I still didn't have authority to offer up any proposal, no matter how ridiculous, I really had no standing to insert myself into this conversation.

"They're just getting hold of him now," I assured the board, feebly. "He was out of cell range."

Alan got up to go to the bathroom and I followed. By this time everyone certainly thought I had diarrhea anyway.

"You really should clarify that it triggers other fees if they don't get equity," I said to him before he stepped back in to the board room. Alan said he wasn't really that familiar with the details of the proposal.

"We'll work it out," he said, seeming unconcerned as he went back in. I headed back to the phone. Of course when they finally found Crawford, he in turn wanted to just touch base with Purcell.

We were coming to the end of the meeting. My cell phone rang. I stepped out. We were a go. It would be too little, too late.

When RHD management finally saw the terms of the financing commitment, they were understandably apoplectic. When Swanson confronted Schwartz claiming that he had misled him at the board meeting about the equity contingency, Schwartz waived those terms as well as the usurious provisions providing penalties if the syndication went poorly. Just like that. It's good to be the king. Or at least to have access to a real decision maker. Morgan Stanley was convinced that this had been part of a massive conspiracy by Bear to get us out of the deal. But Bear was not that smart. More important, Bear had every incentive to work with us and get as many fees as possible. The Bear high yield guys were of course happy to receive the additional fees if they could get them. I think they just always thought it was unlikely that RHD would agree to those terms and never made approval internally contingent on getting them. It was also always unclear whether they ever were genuinely as nervous as Morgan with respect to the risks of the offering.

At Morgan Stanley, however, the mingy terms were the only reason we had gotten the deal approved. An understandably angry RHD ultimately submitted their bid to Sprint with half a financing commitment and a plan to get someone to take the other half. It could have cost them the deal. Luckily, Sprint wanted RHD to win and gave them time to get their financing together to support their $2.23 billion bid. Morgan Stanley did not participate in the financing, which was highly successful and led by Bear along with Deutsche Bank and Citigroup. (It included $300 million in private equity from Goldman Sachs.) The financing yielded Bear Stearns more than double the M&A fees they made along with Morgan in the purchase.

In the end, Morgan's decision makers were wrong about absolutely everything relating to this deal. They were wrong about others' willingness to take up our position in the deal (after RHD rejected our terms, I was confidently told RHD would come crawling back to us after being spurned by others). They were wrong about the credit ratings (they insisted RHD would be downgraded two notches by the credit agencies, which in fact maintained their existing ratings). They were wrong about the market capacity (the market showed plenty of capacity for this and all the other yellow page deals). And they were wrong about the market reaction (they argued that RHD stock would spiral downward on the announcement when in fact it went up, and has continued to go up since). Such is the high yield culture, however, that even in the face of this massive and very public debacle, no one in the group ever admitted any weakness or error in judgment. As it became clearer and clearer that the issue was not the business or the market or the credit but Morgan's own peculiar internal risk profile with respect to this type of financial exposure, the high yield team only stepped up their swagger.

"Can't you manage your client?"

"We set it up for you! We put it at the rim! You just had to tip it in!"

"Those guys are just bush league!"

"Do you even understand what we do here?"

Even after the financing went in another direction, every once in a while the most senior high yield banker would suggest something to me that we could propose to RHD to try to get back into the deal. But it was always clear to me that he had no authority and was just freelancing. Indeed, such

proposals would always come on days when the high yield market was particularly hot and he would invariably call back a few days later when it turned
cold to suggest it wasn't such a good idea after all.

Luckily for the company itself, the Sprint directories transaction turned
out to be a remarkably successful transaction. Not only did the stock go
up on the announcement in September 2002, it kept going up and has consistently outperformed the market and its peers—almost tripling in value
since then. Furthermore the company was able to buy out SBC's interest
in the DonTech partnership for $1.4 billion in 2004 and, more dramatic-
ally, announced in October 2005 the purchase of the former Qwest directories that had been originally sold around the same time as the Sprint
directories. Bear Stearns again advised RHD on the $4.2 billion Qwest acqui-
sition. Morgan Stanley did not. J. P. Morgan Chase coadvised and provided
over $10 billion in financing commitments to support the transaction.

My experience with RHD made me realize why my romanticized
notion of being an old-fashioned relationship banker was so unrealistic.
The issue wasn't simply the existence of any particular actual or potential
conflict of interest. Nor was it just the transactional short-term culture. A
person of integrity can manage most conflicts and a person of character
can ignore the culture, assuming he is willing to pay the price. I had always
been willing to suffer whatever trivial consequences were associated with
working on what I wanted to the way I wanted.

The insurmountable problem, however, was that the fundamental
premise of relationship banking was that the banker could deliver the firm
for the client. The banker was trusted, not just because he was a person of
integrity, but because there was no question the firm was behind him. The
RHD experience made me realize that neither I nor anyone else could claim
that ability anymore. There were simply too many other clients, too many
other products, and too many other external and internal constituencies.
Which one would prevail in any given situation was a gigantic crapshoot.
To hold oneself out as being able to meaningfully influence which way the
dice would fall in a particular instance in the era of the public financial
supermarket was a lie.

When I came to this simple realization, I knew that it was time to move
on. But by then I already had other reasons to start thinking about
another line of work.

· 12 ·

"SAVE THE RED CARPET FOR THE TALENT"

THE IDEOLOGY OF THE Internet economy also changed how investment banks actually managed their business during this era. "Save the red carpet for the talent" was a popular saying in the media industry. But because bankers had come to view themselves rather than their clients as the talent, and money was pouring in fast enough that management didn't see the need to correct this view, expense management was not a focus.

A lunch in 1999 that Sine and Cassou organized for the officers of the Media Group with their boss, Terry Meguid, was particularly memorable. Sine was arguing that, although smaller than our tech or telecom counterparts, the Media Group was far more profitable. We had not grown our cost base of either people or expense items (advertising, conferences, client retreats, free car washes, etc.) at near the rate of our peers, and our business required much less of the firm's precious capital. As Sine made his perfectly reasonable case, Meguid became visibly agitated and finally cut him off.

"I never want to hear another word from anyone about profitability," Meguid barked.

"All that means to me is that you are underinvesting in the business. We can worry about profitability, you just tell us what you need."

When Sine tried to protest that we need to balance potential incremental revenue against incremental expenses, Meguid just waved him away.

"We are in a market-share war, a land grab. We are not going to be left behind. Your job is to tell us what you need."

Sine, Cassou, and I couldn't believe what we had heard. But Meguid was clearly serious. We were no longer managing a group profit and loss statement. We were to focus exclusively on how fast we could make revenues grow. We would be faulted for not asking for more resources, but not for compressed profit margins.

So, just like the Internet companies that relentlessly sought to grow the top line at any cost, and even bragged about their "burn rates" (the speed at which they used up capital), investment banks built up their cost structures at a breathtaking clip. We had all internalized the now-ubiquitous Internet management practices and metrics and applied them to our own very different businesses. During the boom, revenue and market share were king. When the inevitable bust came at the end of 2000, the raw magnitude of the infrastructure that had been built up made the extent and duration of the retrenchment that followed all the more painful.

It is rare that anyone knows the exact moment that a bust begins as it is being experienced. In the case of the Internet boom, even in retrospect there is little agreement on when precisely the good times ended. Was it March 10, 2000, the day that the Nasdaq hit its all-time high? Or two weeks later when the S&P 500 peaked? Maybe it was in September or October with the string of disappointing earnings announcements from the likes of Intel, Priceline, Yahoo, Dell, and Motorola and the decision to withdraw the $10 billion Verizon Wireless IPO.[1] Or it could have been as late as the following January when further disappointments in earnings were coupled with massive layoffs at Amazon, Lucent, WorldCom, and AOL Time Warner.[2]

Whatever the exact date, two highly relevant facts are clear. First, through the first half of 2000, investment banks continued their relentless build-up of staff and cost infrastructure. This was not surprising, as revenues were still exploding at that point. At Goldman Sachs and Morgan Stanley, first-half revenues were up 50 percent and 36 percent, respectively, off an already record year. Second, by the last months of 2000, all investment banking business had slowed to a crawl. The last quarter of 2000 was down both sequentially and compared to the previous year at both Goldman and Morgan.

This timing had several implications. First, because most bankers are paid based on something close to calendar-year results (as noted earlier, both Morgan and Goldman's fiscal years end on November 30; bankers typically receive their year-end pay in early January), no one had an incentive to declare the boom permanently over. The first half of the year had been so strong that 2000 would still be most banks' best year on record. And bankers wanted desperately to be paid out on that basis. Announcing to the world that the party was over would have been in no one's interest. Better to consider this a market pause, a brief breather before the inexorable ascent recommenced in the new year.

Second, the relative strength of the overall year's results would temporarily conceal the magnitude of the mismatch between the unprecedented cost base that had been systematically amassed through at least the middle of 2000 on the one hand and the new, dramatically reduced transaction base that would need to be serviced in a postboom world. The full-year effect of these accumulated cost decisions would only be experienced in 2001. In addition, because decisions about new hiring levels are made a year in advance, the entering analyst and associate classes that the firms had committed to hiring for the fall of 2001 would be in many cases the largest on record, further inflating the banks' already bloated overhead.

No longer able to deny what was becoming increasingly obvious about the business environment, the major investment banks began to announce their first layoffs in early 2001.[3] For Morgan Stanley, this first round was particularly difficult, as it had been a full decade since the last time there was a layoff. The firm had made much of the fact that it had treated the last market pause in 1994, during which you will recall that Goldman Sachs had instituted two brutal rounds of cuts, as a "buying opportunity" for talent. The immense disparity between costs and revenues this time made such a benign approach infeasible.

Ironically, this first group to be laid off, representing in many cases the absolute weakest bankers who symbolized the low hiring standards of the boom, would be the lucky ones. The banks seemed to have convinced themselves that this would be a one-time fix and provided relatively generous severance terms. More importantly, before the magnitude and duration of the bust became clear, these employees were generally able to find alternative jobs at either "real" companies or banking institutions a tier below their previous employer. Those better qualified bankers who hung on through the first few rounds of layoffs would face a much less hospitable environment when their time came to be let go.

Outwardly, all of these developments seemed to strengthen my position at Morgan Stanley. I was paid $3.25 million in 2000 and made co-head of the Media Group in 2001. Yet a number of other changes, some specific to my situation and others of more general applicability, were ominous enough that by the middle of 2001 I had begun to suspect that my days at Morgan Stanley were probably numbered.

At the beginning of 2000, Bea Cassou, like many others burnt out by the unyielding demands of the times, had decided to take a sabbatical. Shortly after she returned later in the year, a decision had been made to combine the Media and Telecommunications Groups, making Jeff Sine co-head of the global combined group with Christopher Harland, the longstanding head of the Telecom Group. But Sine was personally quite unpopular with investment banking management. And although the group was quite strong, the Thomson incident gave those who found Sine unbearably arrogant an excuse to act. As a result, Sine would be co-head in name only, giving Harland sole administrative authority over the entire group.

Shortly thereafter, in a breathtaking transaction that finally gained him the respect of his peers that he had always yearned for, Sine secured what was rumored to be a three-year guaranteed contract at $10 million a year from Union Bank of Switzerland (UBS). Ken Moelis, the former Drexel banker who had built DLJ's legendary Los Angeles office, had simply taken it with him to UBS—lock, stock, and lease—once the sale of DLJ to Credit Suisse First Boston closed. Now, as a global head of investment banking, he further exploited the folly of those who overpaid for investment banks thinking that they owned the people. Moelis would simply cherry-pick those individuals and groups who were the most productive from elsewhere on the Street. And even if he paid top dollar and made the occasional mistake, he knew at least he would not make an error on the scale of paying for a business but getting only a hollowed-out shell.

So the Media Group now reported up to Chris Harland, who was sole global head of Media and Telecommunications. Cassou had by then decided to move to the Menlo Park office and establish a West Coast presence for the combined group. The only other pure "media" managing director at the time had been brought into the group at Meguid's direction just over a year before to cover cable companies. Blond and blue eyed, Andrew Tisdale certainly looked the part and had always had solid reviews, but he had most recently worked in the backwater of Morgan Stanley's São Paolo office and had almost no media experience.

I had come to Morgan Stanley to build a business around providing strategic advice to media companies with like-minded peers who shared my focus. Although I had been given the title of co-head of the media portion of the now-combined Media and Telecommunications Group, reporting to Harland, it was déjà vu all over again. Like the situation I had left at Goldman, I was alone and at the mercy of telecom bankers. But even more problematic, as I was to learn, was just how different the brand of banking these professionals practiced was. And how much money they had managed to lose practicing it.

I did not know Harland well, but I was initially hopeful that he would represent a distinct breed from the other telecom bankers I had worked for. Stylistically, at least, Harland was clearly of a different stripe than those I had known at Goldman who covered the large, sleepy, profitable traditional telephone companies. Instead of being a quiet, methodical company man, Harland cultivated an antiestablishment persona. Telecom and Media already sat on the same floor and I would not infrequently see Harland wandering shoeless between offices on the floor, his shirttails untucked, mumbling profanities under his breath. His weakness for profanity was actually memorialized in a nickname—"Chris 'Fucking' Harland." Our occasional conversations tended to revolve around the contempt in which he held various firm bureaucrats but specifically Bill Lewis, a sentiment widely shared but not as loudly voiced by other group heads.

Harland's difference in style from those who spent their days trying to get an audience with the treasury staffs of Bell South or SBC reflected the different client base that Harland was cultivating. Harland had made a name for himself by aggressively building the leading market position in "emerging" telecoms—companies that variously sought to compete with the established providers, sell products and services to those who did or otherwise support the growing need to store, manage, and transport data in the wired environment of the Internet era. This world encompassed Web "hosting" companies like Exodus that managed Internet data centers, Competitive Local Exchange Carriers (CLECs) like XO Communications that competed with the phone companies in selling to businesses in local markets, long-haul access providers like FLAG Telecom that laid miles of underwater cable, and a dozen other categories of company that targeted one perceived niche or another.

During the boom, emerging telecoms was second in size as a business only to technology. Unlike technology, where a company like Webvan that required significant investment in physical infrastructure ("bricks and clicks" was how such businesses sold themselves) was the exception rather than the rule, the emerging telecom segment was highly capital intensive in nature, soaking up money for laying cable, building cell towers, buying switching equipment and so on. These businesses were largely financed on the *Field of Dreams* theory—if you build it, they will come. They didn't come, or at least not fast enough to avoid what were once a multitude of multibillion-dollar public companies from ultimately going bankrupt or being swallowed up for scrap value.

Like their Internet counterparts, these businesses never generated earnings, but they sometimes did show positive EBITDA (which, it will be remembered, means "earnings before interest, taxes, depreciation, and amortization"). In a business like publishing, which has minimal capital requirements, EBITDA actually does approximate the stand-alone cash-generating abilities of the underlying assets. In emerging telecom businesses, with their insatiable demand for capital to build out and upgrade their networks, positive EBITDA masked the fact that these businesses were bleeding cash.

Given Morgan Stanley's legacy as the most traditional of investment banks and its history as banker to AT&T, the most traditional of phone companies (although this role would eventually be lost to Goldman Sachs), Harland took a surprising tack in building Morgan Stanley's telecommunications franchise. He convinced Morgan Stanley to distinguish itself in the sector by becoming the most aggressive in underwriting debt securities for emerging telecoms. As such, again in contrast to the technology business, during the boom the telecom group had generated much of its revenues from underwriting junk debt.[4]

Harland's approach, which for a time appeared to be a stroke of genius based on the fees generated during the boom, had two potential problems. First, traditional phone companies, which had in simpler times been the primary source of banking business, might not take kindly to Morgan Stanley becoming the primary capital provider to unprofitable "emerging" companies whose articulated objective was to turn the established companies into road kill on the information superhighway. Second, although Morgan Stanley had some time ago crossed the Rubicon of participating in the junk bond market, the credit profile of the companies involved here was something else altogether. It was one thing to sponsor a company in the debt markets whose cash flow barely covered interest payments, it was another to sponsor a company that simply hoped to one day have cash flow that might cover interest payments. Since almost none of the emerging telecoms had any current cash flow, Morgan Stanley was jumping into very dangerous waters with both feet where it had once only dipped a toe.

Unlike issuing equity, underwriting highly leveraged companies in competitive markets can involve significant financial as well as reputational risks. Frequent issuers often demanded and received commitments from underwriters to "buy" an entire issue, something that never happened in an IPO where an offering simply prices where the market clears.[5] For a debt security, the counterpart to a share price is the interest rate. Just as an issuer looking for the lowest cost of capital hopes for the highest share price in an IPO, he or she prays for a low interest rate on their junk bonds. "Buying" an issue involves an underwriter putting a backstop on the possible interest rate payable by the issuer: the bank will guarantee to absorb whatever portion of the offering the market will not accept at the specified rate. In the worst-case scenario, if it was badly mispriced, an underwriter could end up literally owning an entire supposedly "public" offering.

Furthermore, because of a regulatory anomaly, bad judgment in underwriting a junk credit is actually more costly to an investment bank than to a commercial bank. Investment banks must "mark to market" the value of any debt securities on their books each quarter. As a result, an investment bank left holding a large position in a leveraged loan or junk bond that trades poorly in the aftermarket could be forced to take a significant write-down almost immediately. A commercial bank would not need to do so until it felt there was some risk the loan would not be paid back.

Harland's push into the top ranks of the most controversial end of the controversial junk bond business made aggressive use of Morgan Stanley's balance sheet and trading operations. This aggressiveness manifested itself in a particularly swashbuckling attitude among all the bankers involved with these questionable credits. Working hand in hand with Dwight Sipprelle, who then headed Morgan's junk trading operations, Harland showed issuers that Morgan Stanley's aggressiveness did not stop with underwriting but also extended to trading. Once Morgan Stanley underwrites an issue, the sales pitch went, they will be there creating liquidity even in difficult markets. Pitch-book charts would be produced showing the high percentage of trading in selected emerging telecom debt that Morgan's own trading desk represented. For a time then, together with his allies in the fixed income division, Harland had helped transform the once-conservative Morgan Stanley into a serious competitor to DLJ as the leading junk bond house on the Street.

In my early days as co-head of Media, Harland was highly solicitous of me and I was at least hopeful that maybe this arrangement could work.

The first serious signs of trouble came when the layoffs began. Only then did I begin to understand what had happened to the telecom business generally and the aspect that Harland had focused his group on particularly.

In spring 2001, the long-dreaded word came down that we would be forced to institute our first layoff in a decade. This posed a number of problems for managers. First of all, when one is in the midst of a market contraction, it is impossible to gauge when the bottom will come. Deciding how quickly to contract is a difficult calculus. On the one hand, you want to be able to tell the troops that the worst is over and avoid the need to come back for a second bite as Goldman was forced to do in early 1995. On the other hand, cutting too many people is costly, given the difficulty in finding quality replacements, and also exacerbates the challenges in recruiting by signaling an unwillingness to take short-term pain on behalf of employees. On the media side, after much debate we decided to err on what we thought at the time was the side of cutting more now to avoid the need later. Although our June year-to-date numbers suggested annualized revenues of slightly more than the roughly $450 million in revenues achieved in 2000, our backlog of business was quickly emptying out and we had staffed up for a much higher level of activity—in part as a result of the message received at the memorable lunch with Terry Meguid the previous year. Accordingly, we offered up six professionals from the Media Group, which represented almost 20 percent of our U.S. bankers above the analyst level.

I knew generally that the telecom sector had been hurt relatively hard in the downturn, but had not seen the detailed numbers, and Harland expressed no intention of showing them to me. After hearing rumors that he might not institute any cuts of telecom bankers, I went to see him. Without knowing any of the numbers, I told him, it would be critical to morale and his personal credibility as the leader of the combined group to include at least some token cuts of telecom bankers. Harland agreed in principle. When the day came to break the news to our six bankers, they were literally walked out of the building. I was informed later by the visibly shaken survivors in the Media Group that no telecom bankers were cut.

"Don't worry," Harland told me when I confronted him on the subject, "all is not as it seems." Harland implied that some number of his bankers would shortly be moved to other groups—a courtesy not offered to those in the Media Group, but at least a potential sign of good faith. Days, then weeks passed. Spring 2001 turned into summer 2001. It never happened.

Then, in early July, we had an all-day business review so that we could learn about each other's business. It was then that I first began to understand the seismic shift in the fortunes of the telecom industry. Morgan Stanley, like all investment banks, has a system for categorizing companies based on their potential fee generation. The Morgan ranking ran from "tin" on the low end, with $5 million of fee potential over three years, to "platinum" on the high end, with $50 million of potential. Understandably, the focus was on the latter, which tended to be multibillion-dollar capitalization companies who either were acquisitive or had significant financing needs. Sitting in the conference room, I flipped through the presentations and noticed something surprising.

There were multiple subsectors within "emerging telecoms," each with their own dedicated coverage teams and strategies, and each had been allocated a full-time slot to present. Looking into these individual presentations, each had some number of companies designated platinum and gold to discuss. But the companies so designated were in many cases at this point tiny—what we called "micro caps," referring to their small equity value. Some of these companies, formerly of bona fide gold or platinum size, had lost 90 percent of their value or more. Yet no one had bothered to change the company designation or, more important, change the coverage strategy or resource allocation. So, for instance, under the subsector discussion designated for Internet/Data Services, 18 public companies and several dozen earlier-stage private companies were highlighted and further segregated into four main sub-subsectors. All 18 public companies together barely represented $10 billion of equity value, usually the minimum size for a single platinum account. One of the silver designated companies, an appellation generally reserved for those companies capable of generating $10 million in investment banking fees over three years had a *total* market value itself of only $10 million. I pulled Harland aside and suggested that some number of these presentations be collapsed together for the obvious reason. He reluctantly acceded to my request, but I could tell that he was not happy.

Looking at these numbers, I finally appreciated just how lopsided the cuts had been. While annualized gross revenues for the Media Group were slightly ahead of the previous year's, telecom annualized gross revenues were only around half of the previous year's. But after the cuts, the Telecom Group had twice as many senior officers in the United States as the Media Group. After the day's presentations, I had to doubt that these bankers were fully occupied. To make up for this, soon Harland began reassigning entire sectors previously covered by the Media Group—movie theater, satellite radio, towers—to these underemployed telecom bankers. He also started reassigning other selected high-profile accounts, such as News Corp., to them and to himself.

I also began to grasp fully the financial and strategic downside of Harland's approach to the telecom sector. As dramatic as the gross revenue numbers already described were, the "net" revenues told an even more shocking story. For media, "gross" and "net" revenues were essentially identical —there was no need to adjust the "gross" fees received to provide a fair picture of the group's financial health. For the telecom group, the gulf between "gross" and "net" represented hundreds of millions of dollars of losses from a mixture of foolish principal investments, junk debt positions in companies we had underwritten and trading losses in the junk portfolio. Just in the first half of 2001, the Telecom Group had racked up almost $250 million in booked losses on barely $300 million in revenues. Because gross revenues were disproportionately European and the losses predominantly U.S. based, a careful analysis suggested that the U.S. business—the only business that Harland managed on a day-to-day basis[6]—actually had negative net revenues. By the time the bust came to ground, some would estimate the total losses associated with this business at over $1 billion.

I hadn't fully appreciated the precarious nature of Harland's position and naively believed him when he said he had no interest in interfering on the media side of things. The only female above the analyst level in Harland's Telecom Group was an administrative person whom he privately derided as being a spy for Bill Lewis but whom he nonetheless used to perform unpleasant tasks. Shortly after the groups merged, he sent her around to inform us that no "media only" meetings were allowed. When Cassou, Tisdale, and I—theoretically tripartite co-heads of media—scheduled a meeting to go over our collective thoughts on managing the media effort, word came back that he would not meet with us jointly, only individually.

While the deep insecurity such behavior suggested initially confused me because of its stark contrast to Harland's self-confident, almost swaggering style, now at least I felt I understood it. Harland had focused on the emerging telecom segment at the expense of building relationships with the traditional large telecom companies—indeed at the risk of antagonizing them by aligning with their competitors—which during the boom were a relatively unimportant source of business. During the bust, these large established companies were the primary source of business left in the sector. Ironically, the other major source of telecom banking revenues during the bust was the restructuring business, which Morgan was usually precluded from participating in because its continuing position as an unhappy holder of the debt of so many of these companies created a conflict of interest.

By the end of 2001, most of the senior bankers associated with the telecom losses had either been fired or were in the process of being reassigned. Harland's enduring influence at Morgan, and indeed accession, in the face of the very bad news about the business he championed is certainly a testament to his political skills. It also establishes Harland as the prototype of another character in the investment banking pantheon that emerged during the bust: the survivor.

As aficionados of the television show of the same name popularized around the same time know, what makes a survivor is not entirely predictable. There is no foolproof blueprint. Certain qualities seem particularly useful, however. Wisdom in choosing alliances and ruthlessness in abandoning them when no longer useful. An ability to discreetly blame others for your own failures and undermine those who might otherwise pose a threat. Positioning yourself as somehow indispensable, whatever your faults.

No single factor explains Harland's longevity. In part, he regularly blamed former junk-bond sales and trading chief Dwight Sipprelle (a predecessor to Mitch Petrick in this role) for the telecom losses, saying it was Sipprelle's trading bets over which Harland had no control that were responsible for half of the losses. This daring strategy was surprisingly effective given that, on its face, the argument was simultaneously disingenuous and weak. It was disingenuous in that Harland had aggressively promoted Sipprelle's willingness to "make a market" in junk debt, even in a downturn, to secure Morgan's selection as underwriter where it should have passed. Issuers and holders value an underwriter's commitment to make a market—that is, provide (hopefully) temporary liquidity in a security where there is a paucity of outside buyers—and this requires a willingness to hold significant quantities of the securities during periods of volatility. In any case, the argument that you are responsible for no more than $500 million in losses is hardly a robust response to the charge that you helped lose the firm a cool billion.

Harland, who had been at the firm for almost 15 years, had formed an early and close alliance with Terry Meguid, who succeeded Joe Perella in September 2000 as head of investment banking. Finally, in a move reminiscent of the old saw about the convicted parent-killer who sought mercy from the court on the grounds of being an orphan, Harland lay quietly in the weeds as all the others associated with the losses, like Sipprelle, were dispatched. Finally, he emerged as the only senior professional who knew anything about the credits underlying the gigantic telecom loan and investment portfolio. Surely, the argument went, you needed him to manage down these positions over time. And, unsurprisingly, in his many years as head of the Telecom Group, Harland had never developed a credible second in command.

Different versions of this drama played out across the firm and throughout the industry as the investment banking retrenchment stretched from 2001, through all of 2002 and into 2003 before it began to stabilize. It would eventually become clear that the sustainable level of business was comparable to that achieved in the mid-1990s, not the enormous volume of the turn of the decade. But just as the investment banks were ill-prepared to deal with the boom of 1990s, they had no road map to manage the bust of the new millennium. As each round of headcount cuts was announced, each assurance that this would be the last rang more hollow. As bonus expectations plummeted, bankers felt more exposed and became more frantically focused on firm politics and internal positioning rather than actually calling on potential clients.

Like their counterparts in other service businesses, successful investment bankers tend to be promoted into management positions for which they are unlikely to be well suited. So, ironically, many of the bankers like Harland who rode the wave of artificially high revenue during the boom were in management positions by the time of the bust—and thus in a position to determine who got paid and who got cut. This phenomenon was not limited to Morgan Stanley. As recently as September 2004, Kevin Kennedy, the long-time co-chair of Goldman's Commitments Committee, described its decision to underwrite companies like Webvan and PlanetRx.com during the boom as "personally embarrass[ing]." "It was the low point in my career," said Kennedy.[7] Yet by the time Kennedy made his comments, Brad Koenig, the head technology banker who had sponsored these and dozens of other failed IPOs that the firm would later seek to distance itself from, had been made head of not only technology, but telecom and media globally.[8]

Intuitively one might expect that, during bad years, actually bringing in new investment banking business would take on increased relative importance within the corporate pecking order. In fact, in a curious way, the opposite was true. Once it became obvious that 2001 was a bust financially speaking, everyone knew that no one would make money of the kind disbursed during the boom. There would be dramatic compression in the range of compensation among bankers overall, particularly senior bankers.

In boom times, money was obviously the yardstick: how much you could generate for the firm (or be associated with) and how much you could convince the firm to pay you. In a downturn, bankers with time on their hands, knowing the short-term payday would be modest by historic standards, feeling vulnerable not just financially but in terms of their status both internally and in the world at large, naturally became focused on the only game in town left to play: politics. This is a parallel to the situation in academia, where, as the saying goes, the politics are so brutal because the stakes are so low. In investment banking, when the stakes become temporarily low, energies are quickly redirected toward honing survival skills, managing upward, looking for internal administrative responsibilities, and generally positioning oneself for the eventual upturn.

The renewed focus on internal bureaucratic processes became a source of constant gallows humor as each week seemed to bring a new, random administrative edict, widely and correctly interpreted as some version of moving the deck chairs around on the Titanic: a new committee, a new initiative, a new reorganization, a renewed commitment to "client-centricity" or some other management buzz word, a new prioritization or categorization of accounts (e.g., henceforth all tin accounts will be called bronze!).

Bankers all over the Street compared war stories with their peers over the latest internal innovation designed to ensure that everyone appeared busy and to direct attention away from the fact that there was no business. Our own new tripartite "management structure" for the Media Group was reflective of a disease that had infected all of these institutions as bankers desperately searched for an official *raison d'être* during the downturn: co-headitis. A senior banker at Goldman would tell me that they eventually conducted an internal review of how much money Goldman could save if a decision were made to systematically remove one of every "co-head" of some group or function within investment banking. The potential savings: $100 million.

Even previously existing bureaucratic processes took on a life of their own during this era. At Morgan Stanley, the quarterly strategic business reviews, or SBRs, involved the chief division bureaucrats assessing the various industry groups' financial progress. Although such an exercise could serve as a useful management tool, under the direction of the Investment Banking Division's bureaucrat in chief, Bill Lewis, these had long ago degenerated into pro forma exercises widely viewed as a bad joke. The only thing "strategic" about them was the strategizing around filling out the Lewis-designed template so as to raise as few questions as possible, to make him go away and leave everyone alone. I once flipped through a stack of SBRs by all of the industry groups and was amazed that for all the data they collected, there was no way to discern a strategy or even tell whether a group was gaining or losing market share to competitors. Now, as if to ensure that gaming the system took even more time, Lewis regularly redesigned the SBR template and proudly disseminated the latest "improvement."

Since the merger of the Media and Telecom Groups, Harland had raised the "strategizing" around preparing these SBRs to a science. As discussed, the data showed a clear if disturbing story. The U.S. telecom business was a disaster. In addition to having dismal market share, the only "growth" to be seen was the growing losses associated with their existing portfolio of junk debt and venture investments. The European telecom business, by contrast, continued to show strength during the bust. The media business was the mirror image of the telecom: the United States was strong, but Europe was weak, although neither was saddled with the over-whelming losses of the U.S. telecom practice. Even a discerning reader of our SBR, however, could never make out these basic facts. Numbers were aggregated across geographies and industry sectors to make them mean-ingless. Or, to give a false sense of transparency, revenues were divided into such narrow subsectors—while mixing the media and the telecom businesses—that it would have required a fair degree of industry know-ledge to reconstruct the basic strategic and financial picture described. To ensure that no one spilled the beans, Harland would send his administra-tive aide around to tell many of us that had historically attended the SBR sessions that our presence would not be required.

On a personal level, each incrementally deeper round of cuts became exponentially more difficult, both for those doing the cutting and for those cut. One of the attributes of internal power and prestige at investment banks is the ability to make sure "your people"—that is, that group of bankers with whom you are formally or informally associated—are "paid" (at year-end bonuswise) and "protected" (when layoffs come around). If the early rounds were relatively easy because of the extent to which much late-boom hiring had applied lower standards, the middle rounds were significantly more difficult because at that point choices on the merits became that much more difficult. Still, in these middle rounds, influential senior bankers could usually ensure that "their people" one way or another were protected: favored in close calls and, in a pinch, given a heads-up that the axe was on its way and quietly found another position elsewhere in the bank before it actually hit. As the retrenchment dragged on into its second full year without any sign of a recovery, the later and more pressured rounds of cuts did not always allow for such highly nuanced management.

The phrase one frequently heard was that it all had become a "numbers game": hitting numbers expected by the Street was going to be challenging for the company, so a precise number of employees needed to be off the books by the last day of the fiscal quarter. This number was then divided up among divisions and then groups. Each group would have to get rid of its assigned number of bankers. Only this time, the number was so large and the amount of remaining fat so meager, there was simply no clever way left to avoid the most painful of decisions.

How, then, to make these decisions? The cuts were already deep into that closely clustered group that constitutes the great middle of the ranks. Individuals had different strengths and weakness, but there was no easy or obvious way to rank by pure merit. This one has stronger technical skills but seems immature and I can't imagine him being a partner. That one is not great on the numbers but clients love him. Should we shoot two associates or one vice president? How well established is the banker at his accounts? Is the area in which she specialized ever going to come back? Intense debates along these lines could be heard throughout these institutions. They were always apparently very logical, but always colored by the question of whose actual ox was being gored. When a speaker at a group managing director meeting on layoffs emphasized the importance of, say, technical skills over marketing savvy, all other minds turned to, "Who is he trying to protect and what will that cost me?" Behind-the-scenes horse trading was relentless. Managing directors closely guarded occasional rumors of openings in other parts of the bank until they could ensure that their most vulnerable acolytes had had a chance to interview. These truly were desperate times.

In this environment, I had a choice. Harland made it clear in any number of ways that he wanted me on the team. He wanted to be associated with my revenues and needed someone to get him up to speed on media.

But he didn't want any of that badly enough to allow me to threaten his broader survival agenda. I could play along, or I could prepare for a war. Comparing Harland's tenure, relationships, and how much the firm had riding on him with my relatively new and modest, if highly profitable, publishing franchise, it was apparent that I had no chance of winning a war. But I had personal reasons for my reluctance to simply roll over.

My decision to confront Harland—on the reassignment of accounts, on the quality of his own business, on the uneven application of the layoffs —rather than reach an accommodation predictably meant that I would be increasingly marginalized in the group. I could tell Harland had begun to try to isolate me, suggesting variously that I couldn't get along with people, that I was covering too many companies or the wrong companies, and that all of the apparent revenues associated with my efforts really were the result of others' efforts—despite the fact that these were overwhelmingly companies and indeed sectors that Morgan Stanley had never done business with prior to my arrival.

Within the newly merged Media and Telecom Groups, each successive round of cuts over the next years followed a similar pattern: Harland would send Tisdale to Cassou and me—pretty much the only time Tisdale found occasion to call either of us—to get our assent to cut relatively busy media bankers and replace them with telecom-trained counterparts whom he insisted were of higher quality. When we would demur, Harland would eventually call to berate us for not being on the "team," warn us of the consequences, and reluctantly agree to something less Draconian than he had originally planned. Although Cassou had been assured of resources to start our West Coast outpost, she eventually only had a single analyst. At some point Harland sent his administrative aide to inform Cassou that an important account he had promised her to justify the West Coast initiative was being reassigned.

The only interruption to this routine was when Ruth Porat, who had joined our group as a senior banker but without any management role to help cover selected large media clients, threatened to quit and join UBS Warburg as a vice chairman. One of Ruth's complaints had been the absolute lack of consultation between Harland and not just we nominal co-heads of media but any of the managing directors in the group. After Ruth agreed to stay, a meeting was scheduled at which we collectively agreed on who would be included in the next round of cuts. Several days later Tisdale appeared at my office with a request from Harland. Notwithstanding what had been agreed, would I be willing to offer up one more media banker in place of one of his telecom bankers? Even I was surprised by how quickly the old routine had resumed.

Much as I would like to paint my resistance to Harland's takeover as the selfless act of a crusader for good against evil in investment banking, I must admit the truth was much more complicated. Even before Harland took over, I had begun to realize that my aspiration to replicate Sidney Weinberg in my little part of the investment banking world was unrealistic. The intense focus on short-term revenue generation and cross-selling multiple products that was sweeping the industry as margins got squeezed and the full-service financial supermarkets became more formidable competitors was inconsistent with my ideal of being the trusted advisor to corporate decision makers.

I had some clients, like the employee-owned Bureau of National Affairs in Washington, whom I had advised for years for a nominal $50,000 annual retainer on the assumption that I would be used should it ever make sense for them to consider a major transaction. Although the company was worth well north of $1 billion, that major transaction might never come. And in the interim the company clearly would have no need of junk debt or, most likely, any other financial products that were being pushed at the moment. To me, this assignment represented the kind of long-term role—advising on best practices for competing against better financed public competitors, responding to unwanted takeover proposals, communicating effectively with employee/shareholders, and framing realistic acquisition strategies—that I thought I was signing up for in leaving my purely deal execution function at Goldman. Yet it was a role that, within a global financial behemoth, seemed to be valued less and less.

In early 2001, I developed a course syllabus for a Media Mergers class and sent it cold to the Columbia Business School. My timing turned out to be fortuitous. The director of adjunct professor hiring for the Finance and Economics Department told me that within a few months of receiving my proposal—after the extent of the downturn became clear and many firms started pushing out older partners—he was deluged with resumes from newly former investment bankers. Luckily, he had already committed to my course.

So my decision to challenge Harland was not made from either an unrealistic expectation of ultimate success or any particular bravery. It was made with one foot out the door.

VIEW FROM THE TOP

I<small>T WAS NOT JUST</small> at the level of inter- and intradepartmental rivalries that one could see bankers, during retrenchment periods, focusing on the political instead of the financial. The phenomenon was visible at the very top of a remarkable number of investment banks during this period. If the troops were disheartened by the kind of political jockeying that Harland and I were engaged in, their concerns could only have been compounded by watching what was playing out within the leadership ranks of these institutions during that time. At Goldman Sachs, Hank Paulson used the opportunity to dispatch his former co-conspirators Thornton and Thain. At Morgan Stanley, the ouster of president and COO John Mack by CEO Phil Purcell revealed the tensions that had simmered at the firm ever since the merger, four years earlier, of the institutions the two men had led.

Ironically, the merger between Morgan Stanley and Dean Witter Discover announced in February 1997 is a textbook case study of a transaction that actually should have worked from a business perspective. And, as Purcell liked to show in analyst presentations after the transaction closed in May 1997, the stock of the combined entity did actually outperform its peers through the boom. But the tongue-twisting moniker that emerged from the combination—Morgan Stanley Dean Witter Discover —was emblematic of how awkwardly the cultures of the two firms fit together.

The business logic of the combination had been clear from the first time the two companies discussed the possibility—in 1993, the first year that Dean Witter Discover was spun off by Sears as an independent company. For

Morgan Stanley, which had traded at a discount compared to its peers since its 1986 IPO because of its relatively volatile earnings, the deal promised both multiple expansion for its stock, and revenue enhancement from the new products that the retail distribution network would allow the investment bank to market more effectively. For Dean Witter Discover, a firm whose customer base in both credit cards and retail brokerage was at the very low end of the socioeconomic demographic for such products, Morgan Stanley represented both an opportunity to upgrade its clientele and a source of proprietary product to market. Logic notwithstanding, no one had ever successfully merged a brokerage culture with an investment banking culture.[1] Indeed, the only successful combination of retail and institutional strength to date had been Merrill Lynch, which had been achieved through painstaking internal growth rather than a merger.[2]

Another key advantage of this deal from Purcell's perspective that hadn't previously been on the table during the on-again off-again talks emerged in 1997: he would be in charge. The previous year Purcell had rejected an attempt by the much larger American Express to purchase Dean Witter Discover.[3] Now, during the intense final negotiations at the Central Park West home of Morgan Stanley's longtime chairman and CEO Richard Fisher, John Mack, Fisher's designated successor, agreed to be the number two at the combined company with no preconditions. In October 1996 it had been announced that Mack would succeed Fisher as CEO as of June 1997. But Mack was willing, over the private objections even of Fisher, to give both the CEO and chairman titles to Purcell in the name of getting the deal done.[4]

. At the time, much of the focus was on the contrasting demographics served by the two institutions. As noted, Dean Witter was not just retail, it was low-end retail. Merrill brokers made on average almost double the commissions of Dean Witter brokers. At one point, Dean Witter actually opened offices in Sears department stores, to the dismay of brokers who had to make their cold calls with the sounds of lost child announcements in the background.[5] Fisher told a story that perfectly captures the extent of the gulf in status between Dean Witter and his former institution. Shortly after the merger Fisher found himself trying to buy his young wife something expensive at a Fifth Avenue boutique using a Discover Card. "I have some bad news," the store manager gravely intoned, when Fisher asked if they accepted the card.

"Not only don't we accept it," the manager continued, "I am afraid we don't serve anybody who has one."

But for all the talk of culture clashes at the time of the merger—headlines like "Class Meets Mass"[6] and "White Shoes Meets White Socks"[7] were typical—the lack of actual business overlap was the very source of the deal's strength. Unlike the disastrous takeover of Donaldson Lufkin and Jenrette by Credit Suisse First Boston, where legions of bankers fought ruthlessly to determine which firm's bankers would survive on a division by division and group by group basis, these institutions were complementary, not competitive.[8] To be sure, Morgan Stanley bankers were horrified by the ridiculous new company name. And they were more horrified when clients would complain that someone claiming to be from Morgan Stanley had recently called trying to hawk stock to them (one banker complained to me that letting Dean Witter brokers have a Morgan Stanley business card is like giving a loaded gun to a child). But aside from such annoyances and occasional snafus, on a day-to-day basis the merger was largely invisible to investment bankers. And to the extent that the deal made investment banking more competitive in selling corporate clients retail-oriented securities, it was a net positive. Even Purcell, who seemed to leave the management of the institutional securities business encompassing investment banking to Mack, was largely invisible after the merger.

Since there was so little interaction between the different parts of the now larger organization, everyone seemed to agree that as long as cultural issues in the executive suite could be managed, there was no reason the merger should not work. As Mack himself said at the time, referring to the unsuccessful American Express transactions, "All mergers are successful from the top. Going back to those mergers, there was a fair amount of disagreement at the top. We don't have that."[9] One can only assume that Mack had no idea of how right and how wrong he was.

As tough as "Mack the Knife"—as he came to be known, not just because of his cost-cutting prowess but his highly direct style—could be, he showed remarkable naïveté in the negotiations with Purcell. For one thing, he didn't use an advisor, reminding one of the adage about a lawyer who represents himself having a fool for a client. Purcell used Bruce Wasserstein. Mack insisted on a split board of seven each from both sides (two insiders and five outsiders from their predecessor companies) but made no provision for who would select new board members.[10]

In a merger negotiation there is no more dangerous combination than naïveté and arrogance, and John Mack had both in abundance. When confronted with concerns by Morgan Stanley executives that they would be reporting to Dean Witter counterparts, Mack is reported to have told his troops that they should not worry:

"Be patient. The cream always rises to the top."[11]

While Mack was being patient, Purcell was picking his pocket. Shortly after John Mack resigned from the firm in 2001, a banking colleague of mine had Phil Purcell do a "walk by" to say hello to the CEO of a new public company Morgan had just underwritten.

"So," said the CEO, "I've never been in a public company before. What should I be focused on?" he asked Purcell.

"The nominating committee," Purcell answered without skipping a beat.[12]

By the time Mack tendered his resignation to Purcell, the board score was Dean Witter–8, Morgan Stanley–3. When an appalled Richard Fisher demanded to speak to the board to convince Mack to reconsider, Purcell confidently told him that the board was not interested in hearing from him.[13] By that time, Fisher was off the board and had been moved off the executive floor. Purcell would shortly have him moved to another building altogether.

It is always hard to know even in retrospect whether the parties to a marriage gone bad had nonetheless entered into it in good faith. Purcell's last-minute insistence on a corporate bylaw change to ensure that neither he nor Mack could be replaced without agreement of three-quarters of the board seems suspicious.[14] At a minimum, Purcell was worried that he himself might be at risk from a Morgan Stanley coup, at least until his control of the nominating committee shifted the balance of power. More incriminating to me was the intensity of the reaction from Purcell to the report that there had been a "handshake agreement" to hand the reins over to Mack after five years. Charles Gasparino, the *Wall Street Journal* correspondent, had broken the story about the existence of such an understanding shortly before Mack resigned.[15]

To any seasoned deal maker, the story appeared ridiculous on its face. It is hard to imagine a negotiation with two more sophisticated parties. If you really want something as part of the deal, you hold out for it. If you still lose the point in negotiations, you may try to comfort your client by trying to get some verbal understanding of the other side's intentions. But no merger professional takes such professions of good will for anything other than the face-saving gesture they are. In this case, both firms publicly denied at the time of the merger that there was any such understanding.[16]

The better part of valor then, particularly once you had forced Mack out, would be to simply let the thing lie. But Purcell became obsessed with quashing the story, because it suggested bad faith on his part from the very moment the companies agreed to combine. He had no more success than he had with the stories about the payments to Christian Curry. But he took the added step of directing then head of Investment Banking, Terry Meguid, to deny the story to the entire assembled Investment Banking Department at the Monday morning meeting immediately following Mack's departure. Purcell and Mack had called the *Wall Street Journal* to deny the story, Meguid said to the assembled troops.

"There was no handshake, Phil and John denied it, and the *Journal* wouldn't print their denial," said a visibly agitated Meguid. So much for the state of contemporary journalistic standards, concluded Meguid.

At the time, I covered Dow Jones, the publisher of the *Journal*, as an investment banker. And this story seemed a little bizarre. Why wouldn't the *Wall Street Journal* print an on-the-record denial from the two parties of the alleged handshake? I happened to have a meeting at Dow Jones the following day and asked. When I related what Meguid had said, the Dow Jones executive started laughing.

"They said they would get Purcell and Mack on the phone to deny it if we promised to kill the story in its entirety," my contact said. In other words, they would deny it on "deep background," that is, not on the record, but only if the *Wall Street Journal* promised in advance to make the whole story go away. With neither man willing to simply deny the story for public consumption, the reporters were understandably skeptical.

"Without the commitment to kill the story, both Purcell and Mack had no comment," he said.

The entire episode left me with a strong impression that Purcell at a minimum felt he had something to hide. I ultimately learned from Richard Fisher that there had been a handshake, but not between Purcell and Mack. Fisher had been so concerned over Mack's insistence on agreeing to the number two position that he had asked Purcell to assure him that it was his intention that Mack would ultimately take over. Purcell did and they shook hands, but the discussion was of a very general nature.

In any case, by 1998, only a year following the merger, Mack appears to have realized that he had made a mistake and began agitating for the co-CEO position. Despite his continuing support of Mack, even Fisher didn't back him in the effort to recut the management deal so soon.[17] Still, Purcell knew he needed to act before sentiment shifted, while consoling Mack that his time would eventually come. As one executive reportedly said of Mack's ongoing efforts at promotion: "Purcell didn't only feel threatened. He was threatened."[18] Just prior to announcing their merger, Mack had announced a major reorganization, splitting the business into securities and asset management divisions. At the head of these two divisions Mack placed his two closest lieutenants, Peter Karches and Jim Allwin, respectively. Mack's campaign to share the top job now put both of their positions at risk.

In 1998, the debt crisis in Russia took a big toll on a number of financial institutions. Morgan Stanley had relatively little exposure compared to many others, particularly the largest commercial banks.[19] The bulk of the Morgan exposure was restricted to a single emerging-markets hedge fund that ultimately reported up to Allwin's asset management division and lost about $300 million that fall. The fund manager involved resigned, while his supervisor took a leave of absence. Everyone assumed this chapter was over. Then in December it was announced that Jim Allwin, all of 45 years old, would be unexpectedly retiring after 22 years at Morgan Stanley.

Despite how well the industry and the firm were doing, on the thirty-ninth floor of 1585 Broadway, where all the senior corporate executives had their offices, daily life reflected a brutal war of attrition interrupted only by sporadic efforts at accommodation. The resulting environment was highly unpleasant. The *Journal* reported that when Purcell approached Peter Karches in early 1999 to find out what he could do to keep Mack happy, Karches responded, "Just leave."[20] It would soon get worse.

In this destructive game of tit for tat, Mack's acolytes saw an opportunity to lay the blame for the Christian Curry scandal at Purcell's feet and dispatch one of his closest lieutenants. One of the biggest surprises when the proposed management team for the combined Morgan Stanley Dean Witter was announced was the appointment of Christine Edwards as general counsel. Left jobless was Morgan Stanley's longtime counsel, Jonathan Clark. Clark had graduated from the University of Virginia Law School where he had served on Law Review and become a distinguished senior partner at Davis Polk and a legend on the Street. Edwards, by contrast, had been a been a management trainee at Sears while she attended night school at the University of Maryland at Baltimore Law School.[21]

If "outsiders were surprised" about Edwards' selection, the *Journal* reported, "many familiar with Dean Witter say it was a certainty Mrs. Edwards would get the top legal job once it became clear Mr. Purcell would take charge of the merged companies."[22] The *Journal* had previously reported that during deal negotiations Purcell had given up a number of other senior positions in order to ensure that Edwards took the general counsel slot.[23] The two both continued to keep their primary residences in Chicago and often commuted to and from New York together on the company plane. The *New York Observer* took note of the growing number of newspaper stories "that also made a few nudge-nudge-poke-poke references to the 'close' relationship between Ms. Edwards and Chief Executive Philip Purcell, . . . both of whom were married."[24] Once the internal investigation revealed that Edwards had indeed been notified beforehand regarding a secret payment to an informant in the Curry case—briefly making Morgan Stanley rather than Curry the target of the prosecutor's interest—it seemed clear that she would need to resign.

Purcell would soon have his revenge, however, in part thanks to the debacle in Morgan's telecom business. In late 2000, for the first time since the merger, Morgan Stanley missed its numbers, causing its stock to fall precipitously. At its September 21 analyst conference call, the firm blamed trading difficulties with its telecom bond portfolio.[25] The stock slide accelerated in October after a Salomon analyst pointed out that Morgan had underwritten the worst performing junk telecom bonds since the beginning of 1998.[26] Starting that summer and continuing through the fall, one after another, almost every key executive from the fixed income side of Morgan Stanley from Peter Karches through Dwight Sipprelle, resigned.[27] John Mack was now totally alone.

Mack's resignation in January 2001 signaled the undeniable ascendancy of the former Dean Witter management. Mack's demise was also representative of the arrogance of investment bankers of the era. Mack had assumed that Morgan Stanley's superior smarts and sophistication would ultimately prevail over the simple folk at Dean Witter. Purcell assumed nothing, kept his eye on the board nominating committee, and bided his time. But having won a critical battle for control within the firm, Purcell still faced a broader war to prosecute in the increasingly competitive marketplace—and legitimate questions about his ability to prosecute it effectively given his largely retail-focused background and the extent to which he had alienated those troops more loyal to the executives he had dispatched.

Nor was the bloodletting over. Shortly after Mack resigned, the fixed income division held their annual conference for institutional high yield investors in Boca Raton. The high yield conference is always something of a big party, with a conservative, male-dominated crowd. Each year the firm springs for a high-profile speaker like Margaret Thatcher and expensive entertainment like Jimmy Buffet. Sometimes things go awry. Like when Margaret Thatcher appeared to have had a little too much to drink at dinner and repeatedly made culturally insensitive comments regarding the developing world. Given the crowd, this probably would have gone over fine. Except when she was finished with the Indians, the Pakistanis, and the Chinese, Thatcher turned to the Argentines. And as Morgan Stanley had done a large high yield offering for Argentina that year, there was a table filled with government officials from that proud nation. They walked out.

No broad public hubbub followed the Thatcher incident. In 2001, however, Morgan Stanley had the distinction of being the first organization to pay now former president Clinton to speak. They actually got a bargain, too. The $100,000 Clinton got was about half of what he would soon generally command in the market. And despite the fact that this was a very Republican crowd and Clinton's talk was a bit rambling and not too interesting, he stuck around and talked to everyone who wanted to speak to him and then partied with the investors late into the evening. It was a big hit.

But because of a circumstance of timing, the event drew negative publicity that stung Morgan Stanley management. Clinton, who had just left office, was drawing heavy flak for his last-minute pardon of financier Mark Rich and the alleged vandalizing and pilfering of the White House by the Clintons and their staff. Commentators were complaining about Clinton "monetizing" his presidency with high-priced speaking gigs. It was a dubious argument, but it lasted a few news cycles before it went away. And before it did, Purcell had issued a public apology for the firm's "insensitivity" in inviting Clinton. A bitter Mike Rankowitz, who had taken over Sipprelle's operation, took responsibility for the apparently improper invitation and now resigned as well. He was replaced by Mitch Petrick, who had run the distressed debt trading desk.

The final shoe to drop in the cleansing of Mack-associated professionals with some connection to the telecom losses was in late 2002, when Anthony Melchiore showed up for work one day to discover that his I.D. no longer worked.[28] As Sipprelle's go-to guy on the trading floor, Melchiore was the person who actually traded the telecom high yield issues Morgan had underwritten. My experience had always been that Melchiore's input on what the market reaction to a prospective issue would be was treated as definitive. Indeed, once I realized that the entire high yield marketing apparatus that gave direction to investment banking simply relied on Tony, I started calling him directly. Tony was a funny, voluble, irreverent trader who had none of the pretensions of the suits whose job it was to manage investment bankers and their clients. As recently as 1999, Melchiore was being lauded in the press as Morgan Stanley's "secret weapon"[29] and one of the four most influential people in the junk bond world.[30]

The implications of Purcell's retail focus are sometimes misunderstood. The simplistic assessment that Mack was associated with the bankers and Purcell the brokers, ignores the fact that Mack had been a bond salesman to institutional accounts, not an investment banker to corporate clients. He had joined in 1972 from a small specialty firm, F. S. Smithers, where he had been a bond trader, as Morgan built its first trading operations. Indeed, the deepest historic schisms within investment banks have been between the fixed income divisions, from which Mack hailed, and the investment banking divisions. And although Purcell had not been heavily involved in calling on corporate banking clients during Mack's tenure, there seems to be some justification for Purcell's claim he steered clear of Mack's areas of responsibility because of the tensions between them. This does not, of course, explain the continuing complaints that Purcell would not make client calls even after Mack departed. Peter Karches continues to contend simply that Purcell "probably is the most incompetent executive in the history of financial services."

What retail does have in common with banking is that it is all about sales. In fact, in my experience, I found that when Purcell actually did go to a client meeting he was in some ways better at it than Mack. Mack was a proud, gruff man. If the CEO you introduced him to was equally proud and gruff, it could go very well or very badly. In the instances that I brought Purcell to meet with a client, he would stick to the script provided and do what it took. As one very senior investment banker told me, "The difference between Phil and John is that Phil understands what business it is we are in. When a client says get down on your knees and suck, Phil is there. John just won't do it."

But the differences between the retail and institutional client bases are very real. The Clinton high yield conference debacle reflects the chasm between these two audiences. The institutional investors for whom the conference was put on had a great time and were thrilled to have met Clinton.

Purcell's decision to apologize was driven by e-mails received by some brokers in the field whose retail customers had read news reports and complained. At the time, I was selling some properties for the controversial conservative newspaper magnate Conrad Black. Black was no Clinton lover, but he was nonetheless appalled that the CEO of a major U.S. corporation would buckle to pressure and publicly apologize for the supposed crime of inviting a former president of the United States to speak.

Bankers often seemed to find themselves apologizing or explaining some aspect of the retail culture that inexplicably crept into the institutional banking business. Once Purcell had control of the board and was rid of Mack, he finally felt secure enough to rename the company what it should obviously have been named in the first place: Morgan Stanley.[31] The problem was that Purcell refused to maintain different brands under this umbrella to target the radically different constituencies served by different parts of the financial behemoth Morgan Stanley had become. When Citigroup subsequently purchased Smith Barney, it did not change the brokers into Citigroup brokers or even Salomon or Travelers brokers. It is still Smith Barney, now a "Citigroup company." Each of those brands mentioned continue to thrive and be directed toward the particular markets they served. The Morgan Stanley business card of a broker in Topeka, however, was now indistinguishable from that of a banker in London. And Morgan Stanley launched a bizarre multimillion-dollar unitary advertising campaign that was meant to simultaneously speak to the strength of the Morgan Stanley brand whether applied to retirees, foreign governments, or corporate CEOs.

There seemed to be no understanding of the fact that although "one client at a time" was certainly broad enough conceptually to cover all of these situations, each market required a level of attention that such a campaign could not deliver. Indeed, the implicit suggestion that Morgan Stanley's skills at helping a middle-American family plan for their kids' college education would translate into the kind of careful strategic advice a CEO would expect on his next major deal fundamentally subverted what was once the strength and prestige of the brand in corporate America. Bankers were ribbed mercilessly by clients about these commercials. The ribbing might be friendly, but it still gave bankers a slightly queasy feeling that maybe their longer-term credibility had been undermined.

Also of concern was the fact that along with Mack's departure, the entire high yield decision-making apparatus was hollowed out. By the end of 2002, the string of names that had been dispatched was long and included not only key decision makers but high yield research analysts and traders. In addition, the sustained and brutally public purge not only robbed the firm of the core of its institutional knowledge base around managing these credits, it made everyone inside and outside the high yield division very nervous about having their fingerprints on any decision that carried any balance-sheet risk.

Given this climate of fear, it is not surprising that during the period following Mack's departure in 2001, in transaction after transaction, even where Morgan was the advisor to the buyer and thus had first dibs on participating in the underwriting, it could not generate an internal consensus to participate. Partly it was having been burnt so badly before. Partly it was the lack of a seasoned internal team to make the relevant credit judgments. In the RHD deal it had been quietly suggested to me that Harland's affiliation had poisoned its chances for approval by the Commitment's Committee because of his track record of failed telecom credits—despite the fact that RHD was obviously a publishing company. Another executive hinted afterwards that there were conversations going on with the credit agencies about Morgan Stanley's own rating that made it cautious about any new credit risk exposures. But mostly all of these situations reflected the climate of fear and uncertainty that lingered after the purge. Harland notwithstanding, it is a lot harder to get fired for not doing a deal, than for doing a deal where losses appear each quarter with your name beside it.

And in 2003 the high yield market came thundering back, which made the timing of this decision-making constipation particularly troublesome. During the biggest high yield boom in history, Morgan finished 2003 ranked a humiliating ninth, behind even much smaller firms like Lehman, in high yield market share. Even where Morgan Stanley itself was the client, the firm could not get out of its own way. When ACG, a portfolio company of Morgan Stanley's own LBO fund arm (called Morgan Stanley Capital Partners or MSCP) wanted to take advantage of the hot high yield market to borrow more money to take out its entire original investment, Morgan's high yield desk said it couldn't be done. Only when in frustration MSCP got competitor First Boston to do the deal did Morgan agree to go along for the ride as a co-financer.

This case also highlights the broader systematic conflicts for a firm between being a supposedly objective financial advisor and being a purveyor of particular financial products. It is the institutional version of the conflict that occurs when a retail financial advisor tries to push his own company's mutual funds because he gets a higher commission. A banker who brings a high yield product specialist to a pitch to work on an acquisition for a client—or even to pitch a straightforward refinancing, as in the case of ACG—must walk a very fine line. A banker who "recommends" its own firm's product—even if its terms are inferior—risks permanently losing client credibility as a source of independent advice. A banker who steers a client to a competitor's products risks internal ostracism or worse.

For all the smug assurances about the benefits to the client of a "one-stop shop," a banker knows that the client's interest is best served by having the cheapest, most certain, and most flexible financing possible. And it is simply not possible for that banker to know whether his own firm's high yield product will ultimately be most competitive. As we have seen in the RHD case, the factors that determine how aggressive a bank will ultimately be when it comes time to make a commitment months later are impossible to predict. Numerous factors affect the willingness of a particular institution to underwrite a particular deal on a particular day. These include that investment bank's level of existing credit exposure to the relevant sector, whether one of the ratings agencies has recently talked to the CFO about the bank's overall risk profile, the level of bullishness or bearishness on the credit and market sector of a wide range of internal constituencies, and the firm's prevailing perspective on the "tone" of the market at that time. Very little of this is knowable by the investment bank, much less the individual investment banker, up front.

And as every banker knows, there is only one thing that secures a client the best terms possible: competition. But advising a client to seek competing financing sources does not make a banker terribly popular within his firm, particularly with the fixed-income division, which is unlikely to get much credit for advisory fees. In addition, if it becomes clear that the financing side of the house will only be willing to underwrite a transaction with less debt than other investment banks—thus limiting how much a client can stretch on price with the bank's continued financing support—pressure can be put on the advisory side of the house to encourage the client to bid a lower price than would otherwise be advisable.

I had once gotten in hot water for waving off a client who was being encouraged to seek equity from a captive private equity arm of the investment banking division called Princess Gate. I merely suggested that the odds of Princess Gate ultimately funding the client's project were only slightly better than those of being hit by lightning. Although statistically speaking I was being generous, and Princess Gate has now mercifully been shut down, at the time this manifestation of "client-centricity" was not appreciated.

So the biggest near-term impact on Morgan Stanley of the departure of Mack and his fixed income acolytes was its loss of market share in high yield specifically, and in the willingness of executives to take financial risk generally. This latter issue was particularly troublesome because it occurred at the very time when all of the "nonbank" investment banks were groping for a response to large commercial bank competitors' aggressive use of their balance sheets to gain share in the post–Glass Steagall world.

Ironically, the only issue of genuine longer-term significance about the power struggle between Purcell and Mack and, indeed, about the struggles at the top of all of the major investment banking houses that transpired during this period, was that none of them were about anything of longer-term significance. As we have seen, struggles at the top were nothing new. Yet these historic struggles seemed to be about something structural or substantive. At Lehman, it was the supremacy of fixed income over investment banking or vice versa.[32] At Kidder Peabody, it was the capital crisis caused by retirements as too many partners pulled out their capital.[33]

This time, however, these power struggles were just that. Power struggles. None of the articles dealing with Purcell and Mack or Thornton and Paulson at Goldman discussed any significant substantive or policy differences at the top. It was as simple as that the number two started agitating to be number one, so he was shot. Indeed, when Mack ultimately took the helm of Morgan Stanley from Purcell in 2005, he steadfastly refused to sell off those businesses—either the Discover credit card or the retail brokerage business—that those who had agitated for Purcell's ouster had promoted.

The closest thing to a substantive dispute underneath the battles for supremacy was a highly parochial geographic one involving New York and Chicago. This was particularly ironic given the increasing hype over the globalization of the decision making at all of these institutions. If this sounds like too petty a topic to be the source of any real tension, think again. The Grumpy Old Men's original March 3, 2005, letter to the Morgan Stanley board seeking Purcell's removal went out of its way to raise the issue.

"While the firm is headquartered in New York, the financial capital of the world," they wrote (to what was certainly an unsympathetic audience at least on this point), "neither the Chairman nor any members of the Board reside in the New York area."

In the cases of both Mack and Thornton, a highly self-confident New York banker agreed to play second fiddle to a Chicagoan whom each was sure could be managed. Instead they were both managed right out of their jobs. Although Mack and Thornton may have been correct about their own relative genius, they were wrong about what skills were required to survive at the top of a public corporation. Certainly one lesson of this period is that the power of a well-managed incumbency cannot be overstated.

There was also a Chicago angle to the jockeying for succession during this period corresponding to the retirement of David Komansky at Merrill Lynch. Although the ultimate victor, Stan O'Neal, had roots in Alabama rather than Illinois, O'Neal owed his promotion to an alliance with what came to be known as the "Chicago Gang" that included some key board members and executives. Specifically, Thomas Patrick, a leading member of the "gang," was CFO during 2002's "bitterly contested horse race" to succeed Komansky.[34] O'Neal's victory came after Patrick made a highly misleading presentation to board members that overstated the profitability of O'Neal's division relative to that of his leading competitor.[35] Even after being exposed, Patrick apologized for an "honest mistake" and went on to dispatch all other contenders to the throne as O'Neal's hatchet man. This story ended as all such stories seemed to do during this era: once Patrick was through, O'Neal dispatched *him*.

In a strange way, the nature of these disputes during the bust reinforced the values that emerged during the boom. If the boom signaled the ascension of a celebrity culture at these firms, the highly personalized brawls that epitomized the bust felt like a logical extension of a new world order in which individual considerations reigned supreme over institutional ones. It had not been so long ago when the interests of the firm and the client really did reign supreme. The boom had called into question these values. The inward focus of the bust had done nothing to restore these values and raised new questions about these institutions' long-term commitment to its employees and clients. As a result, even as the industry now enters a period of renewed growth, it may have lost permanently much of the mystique it once held for both those who worked in it and those who relied on its services.

THE MYTH OF MERITOCRACY

PERSONNEL DECISIONS made during the boom already tested bankers' deeply held belief that their institution was fundamentally a meritocracy. When the smoke cleared after the later rounds of cuts, this myth took another body blow. There were always too many obvious anomalies, and the fingerprints of too many internal rivalries and biases were clearly imprinted on the choices made.

But even the most powerful did not emerge from this period unscathed. And as difficult as it may have been to make these tough choices, it was a lot more difficult for those who for the first times in their lives found themselves unemployed and with little prospect of finding a position of similar social status. Earlier I surmised that many of these bankers were chronic overachievers who had blindly pursued whatever career had been publicly associated with success at the moment regardless of whether it held any independent interest for them. If that surmise is correct, imagine the level of personal psychic devastation being laid off wrought on this population.

These bankers had spent their lives satisfying every expectation of them: good grades, solid SAT scores, the right college, the right postcollege job, a top professional school all culminating in a secure job at a leading investment bank. Now they were on the Street jobless, with only the humiliating prospect of a position at a midtier bank, if even that were available. Those who had left banking during the boom to go to some Internet venture that had since collapsed had the added burden of a somewhat incoherent resume and even bleaker prospects. And now, some were wondering, why did I go into banking in the first place? To the extent that these individuals' sense of intrinsic worth was closely tied to the social standing their jobs in banking afforded them, it is hard to overstate the extent of the change the layoff represented: in the cultural pecking order for professionals of that age, from the pinnacle to the nadir.

There were times during the period from 2001–2003 when helping manage the emotional state of laid-off bankers became a significant part of my job. And it was not just Morgan Stanley bankers. There were periods when every week I would get a call from some guilt-ridden peer from another investment bank. I know you're not hiring, they would invariably start, but there is this great guy who really got screwed and I'd really appreciate it if you would talk to him. A brief explanation of the "screwing" would follow—recently transferred to the group and didn't have a "godfather" yet, some personal conflict with a tyrannical group head, given responsibility for a sector that had disappeared during the bust, whatever. Then finally they'd get around to the expertise they sought from me: the fact I'd done other things in life. Couldn't I just spare a half an hour to help the unfortunate think things through? The banker calling me obviously was tormented by the fact that he had been unable to protect his now-unemployed colleague and had run out of practical ideas.

Of course these meetings were never a half an hour long, and they much more closely resembled psychological counseling sessions than anything else. And they were eerily similar to each other. Each victim insisted on beginning with their well-rehearsed explanation of how it was that they came to be laid off, as if this had any particular bearing on what to do next. And invariably, sometimes at a completely inappropriate moment in the session, they would blurt out, "I am not a failure!" or "I am not a loser!" or, in a peculiarly investment bankerish expression of the same point, "I am not bottom quartile!"

For my part, I got relatively efficient at managing these meetings. After hearing out their stories—that portion of the session could not be managed for time and itself would take up at least the half hour originally scheduled—I told them as gently but directly as I could that no one, but particularly prospective employers, really cared about their problems. In fact, hearing about a stranger's explanations of past problems, conflicts, issues, or injustices, no matter how objectively compelling, makes people very uncomfortable. All people care about is how you can help them. So the first thing you need to do, I would say, is stop looking for sympathy and stop looking for others to solve your problem.

Then I would turn to the good news. It couldn't get any worse! (Of course it could. But to these traumatized individuals whose entire sense of worth had been wrapped up in the status afforded them by their job, it felt like it couldn't.) There should be something incredibly liberating about that, I would suggest. Why don't you think about who you are and what you really want to be rather than what someone else thinks you should be?

At this point I would whip out what I still consider the best career-planning text for young professionals. I came to use German poet Rainer Maria Rilke's *Letters to a Young Poet* as a kind of shock therapy for these broken men and women. I had purchased a stash of copies from Amazon for this purpose. For those of you who don't remember from high school or college, Rilke writes to the poet of the title in order to warn him of the hardship involved in his chosen profession and counsels deep introspection. "[A]sk yourself in the stillest hour of your night: must I write?" If you pause for an instant, Rilke argues, choose something else, "It is enough . . . to feel that one could live without writing, then one must not attempt it at all."

At first glance it might seem extreme to apply Rilke's stringent standards for poets to job selection more broadly. But how many of these professionals would really have become investment bankers in the first place had they first engaged in a little Rilkeesque introspection? And how many of them wished now that they had done so sooner? One of the real benefits of the bust is that it forced new graduates who otherwise would have mindlessly sleepwalked into the hot job of the moment to actually consider what they might genuinely enjoy.[1] The opportunity to really pause, maybe for the first time in a young person's life, and face a world where the expected next step has not been preordained, can be a profoundly cathartic learning experience.

For those who had unreflectively fallen into investment banking during headier times, there was no time like the present to reconsider whether there might not be something else they were meant to do. And to be clear, some number of these recently employed investment bankers really did love banking. They were a small minority, however. For them, the right answer was to make that case to anyone who would listen. They would find a job eventually and do just fine, even if at least initially at a lesser institution than the one they had just departed. The other minority were those who took my advice and started down the long, sometimes lonely, and often frightening road of building a new life and a fuller sense of self. Most were in the great middle who were unsure of whether banking was for them but unwilling to examine what was. When comparing the safety of pursuing more of what they were doing last with the terror of potentially starting over, more often than not safety won out.

For the survivors of the great purges of 2001–2003, life was different in ways big and small. On the small side, fruit baskets and free coffee were long gone from the pantries. And even where the casual dress was not officially altered, the social implications had fundamentally shifted. Where once dressing down implied that a banker had cooler clients than the rest of us, now it implied that a banker had no client meetings to go to at all. And in the era of the great purges, this was not a wise message to telegraph to the community at large. Needless to say, policy or no, suits again became *de rigueur*.

Of course, on a more basic level, the biggest difference was that there was much less business to do. And what business there was to do was much less likely to get done. That is, for almost all of the 1990s any project that walked in the front door of the sausage factory one way or another emerged as sausage a few months later. Now, something less than half of the M&A assignments that were taken on ended up reaching a signed definitive sales agreement with a buyer. And of those that did, probably only about half actually closed, having hit some kind of bump on the road. The two most typical bumps came in the form of an inability to secure the financing or the seller triggering a "material-adverse change," or MAC, clause in the contract by failing to come close to its promised performance.

In the 1990s, it was not unusual for a banker to work on ten or more completed transactions in a given year. Now, for a banker who joined from business school in 2000, it was not unheard of for him or her to become a vice president several years later without having ever worked on a transaction that actually closed. Even ignoring the huge fixed costs associated with these firms' trading and research operations, this suggests why no amount of cost cutting could achieve the profitability of earlier times: there was a dramatic decrease in the efficiency of investment banking. We tried to console young bankers frustrated by endless pitches and deals that never got done by arguing that a difficult environment is the best setting in which to learn. In good times, anybody can get a deal done. It is precisely in tough times that bankers can differentiate themselves and actually make a difference between whether a deal gets done or not. And although there is more than a grain of truth in this observation, the bigger truth is that you can't get good at doing deals without doing deals.

Young bankers might have been more inclined to suck it up and buy the party line if they had either the job security or the financial rewards that they had come to expect from their chosen vocation. Job security was replaced by a constant sense of impending doom, gallows humor, and a remarkably accurate corporate rumor mill fueled by Internet message boards at Yahoo and The Vault. The imagined financial rewards drifted farther and farther off as the pay cuts of 2001 were compounded in 2002. Where once even an average junior vice president could bring home half a million dollars in a year, now there were managing directors who didn't reach that level. And more and more of the compensation was being paid in stock with a vesting schedule that stretched out further and further. All this was compounded by the fact that on a deeper level, the myth of meritocracy, the social compact between banker and bank, and the team culture that had attracted these professionals, were now all under great stress.

· 15 ·

KING OF THE SLCS

A s the end of 2002 approached, a fourth round of cuts was being prepared simultaneously with the dismal bonus allocation. I knew I was in trouble when no one even asked me for my input. Those I had saved from the axe for the three previous rounds would be dispatched.

I had once foolishly assumed that my good luck to have focused on the publishing business, which had continued to show itself to be largely impervious to economic cycles, would protect me. The "information industries"—the sexy name we gave publishing to keep people's attention during the era of Internet hype—included the newly sexy yellow page businesses. But more generally it is made up of a mix of sectors, some of which outperform during boom times (think advertising-driven businesses like newspapers and consumer magazines); others that outperform during bust times (think subscription and other high-recurring, revenue-based businesses like professional legal and scientific publishers, some market research businesses, and, as described, yellow pages); and others that just seem to outperform most of the time (think certain education businesses and ratings businesses like Moody's). Almost all of these businesses have strong cash-flow characteristics, giving companies the flexibility to do deals even in bad times if they were smart enough not to take on too much debt during the good. As we have seen, it also makes them very attractive targets for LBO firms, who rely on the ability to layer debt on top of consistent cash flows to generate high equity returns.

In late 2002, well over a year into the bust, with investment banking still largely dormant, publishing still seemed like a particularly prescient sector to have focused on. Although the publishing industry is over-whelmingly made up of smaller private companies, in 2002 there were only eight announced media M&A deals larger than a billion dollars, and four of them were publishing deals. Our group was involved in two of the four and in many more smaller publishing transactions. In addition to the RHD transaction for Sprint's directories, we were in the process of buying the old Houghton Mifflin textbook publishing business out of Vivendi for a consortium of LBO firms (although, in a series of decisions reminiscent of the firm's posture with respect to the RHD debt offering, Morgan declined to participate in the ultimately highly successful financing of the deal) and buying the Island electronic stock-trading network for Reuters through its Instinet subsidiary. We had just raised $1 billion for Thomson Corp. in one of the biggest equity deals of the year and had been asked by each of Thomson and Moody's to look at important strategic acquisitions on their behalf. The magazine publisher Primedia had asked us to sell *Seventeen* for them, and the Special Committee of the Board of Freedom Communications (publisher of the *Orange County Register* and dozens of other newspapers and assorted TV stations) had asked us to advise them on sorting out a long-simmering dispute among family shareholders. Meanwhile, the telecom side of our group was quiescent, though after three rounds of layoffs it inexplicably had significantly more bankers on the pay-roll than the media side.

But at this point, I was more realistic about my prospects. I assumed Harland was also trying to use this deep cut to be rid of me forever. I had become an investment banker by accident rather than by design, and could hardly believe I was still doing this almost a decade later. I had begun preparing the groundwork for my ultimate departure shortly after the groups merged, even though on any given day it seemed unlikely that I would stumble onto a catalyst for making me move on. Now such a day seemed like it might be imminent. I was enjoying my teaching at Columbia Business School and, through the collection of nonprofit boards on which I served, had developed good relationships with the small cadre of head-hunters who place most nonprofit CEOs, college presidents, and business school deans. I felt that there would be life after banking.

Despite the fact that the job wasn't what it once was, there were legit-imate reasons for my professional inertia. The pay was still ridiculously good, even if a fraction of what it had been during the boom years. With experience, the routine of the job had also become dramatically easier, leaving me with plenty of time to pursue my other interests. My relationships were well established, and building enduring relationships is the most important and time-consuming aspect of a banker's job. I knew the companies and the strategic dynamics that kept their CEOs up at night better than anyone, and I had been around long enough that people trusted me at a time where trust had become possibly the biggest issue facing the industry. And although I had become a banker as something of a lark, by this time I had been calling on many of the same companies and executives for years. In a world where one of the biggest client complaints about bankers is how fast they turn over, I was definitely getting points just for showing up consistently.

For all my initial cynicism about investment banking, and my continuing conflicted feelings about different aspects of the job, I also realized there were deeper substantive reasons for why I stayed. If I honestly performed on myself the same late-night Rilkeesque test I pushed on others, it was the ability to have access to and influence decision makers that had kept me in investment banking so long. Although these bleak years had certainly not been much fun at times, I came to the rather startling conclusion that by this standard, investment banking is about the best job in the world. As an erstwhile policy wonk, I also came to appreciate that CEOs are probably the most important decision makers in contemporary society—certainly as important as the congressmen, senators, and government bureaucrats I dealt with as a lobbyist. Their impact not only on employees but on the economy around them can be more significant than most policy pronouncements from Washington. And investment bankers, unlike, say, lawyers or consultants, get to talk to CEOs about the things that are most important to them on a real-time basis. Short of becoming a decision maker myself, there was no other job out there that provided either the kind of access or the ability to influence that this one did. If directly influencing decision makers on matters of significance is a role you are looking to play, there is no comparable platform to that of investment banking.

For me, despite all that has changed about the practice of investment banking, there is still something uniquely fulfilling about helping a CEO plot a company's strategic course and executing the plan. Whether it involves a recapitalization, a sale of a division, a merger, or, sometimes, just doing nothing, giving good independent advice to boards and senior executives is a great gig. There really is no other like it. And despite the obvious downside of the tough environment, it is precisely in these environments that giving good independent advice can make the biggest difference to a company. I came ultimately to appreciate how strangely fortunate I was to have fallen so unexpectedly into a profession that satisfied this personal need.

I also came to appreciate that the very qualities that had made Morgan such a great place for me in the first few years made it impossible for me to last there much longer. What had attracted me in first place was the latitude it gave its independent industry groups to pursue their businesses as they saw fit. As long as things were going well enough, the group leadership was free to make internal strategic, personnel, and bonus decisions without excessive interference. So while Jeff Sine, Bea Cassou, and I were on the same page, it worked like a dream. The logical corollary of this was that with Harland and me on such different pages, one of us had to go. I did not begrudge the institution for this. I initially reaped the benefits of that decentralized decision making and always understood that were the winds to shift I would have to accept the consequences. As Bob Sillerman might have said, "A d-d-d-deal is a d-d-deal."

Surprisingly to me at the time, Harland was unsuccessful in having me swept up in round four of layoffs (although as I had expected, the balance of those I had previously protected were included). Apparently, I was quietly informed later by members sympathetic to my cause, enough of the Management Committee came to my defense to prevent me from being laid off. Instead, the committee fashioned a bizarre compromise under which I would continue covering many of the companies I had historically, but without formally being in the media group any more. Instead, I would report directly to the head of Corporate Finance and have a new official role. Where I had once been made "King of Publishing," I would now be designated "King of Shitty Little Companies" (hereinafter SLCs).

I understood at least how the elegance of this "solution" appealed to everyone. For Harland, he would lose me both from his official headcount for budgeting purposes and as a political annoyance in my previous role as co-head of Media, but he would retain group revenue credit for the business I continued to bring in. He would also be able over time to peel away from me the handful of larger publishing names and reassign them elsewhere, further undercutting my leverage and influence. For management, it potentially avoided losing a productive banker at a time when there were precious few of them, and it did so without having to restructure yet again the entire media and telecom effort.

While everyone else seemed to be happy with this compromise, I knew that it was destined to failure. To understand why, it is important to consider the difficult history of trying to cover SLCs at major investment banks.

As discussed earlier, "important" bankers like to work on important accounts and important deals. Conversely, it is hard to become an important banker without responsibility for important accounts. "Important" in the investment banking business generally means "big." And with respect to the banking league tables that drive much internal decision making and bestow bragging rights, it is big deals that really make a difference. Nonetheless, a single-minded focus on megadeals and megaclients at the expense of maintaining a strong footprint with companies valued between a few hundred million to a couple of billion dollars—the core of what constitutes SLCs—presents some strategic problems for an investment bank.

First, some key products like junk debt in particular are primarily sold to SLCs. Ensuring that investment banking coverage officers do not ignore the SLCs to which they are assigned is the main reason that a separate high yield marketing effort exists. Their job is primarily to harangue the coverage officers to actually call on these accounts, and to support this effort with materials on these companies' ability to tap the junk debt markets. As we have seen in the case of RHD, these high yield marketing bankers usually have neither formal client responsibility nor authority to actually commit capital, but rather act as ambassadors of the fixed income division assigned to the investment banking division.

Second, a strong franchise among SLCs can mitigate the volatility of investment banking financial results. Some percentage of SLCs sell out or restructure or make an acquisition every year. Although in any given year, big deals represent a disproportionate amount of overall fees, relying exclusively on getting into all the big deals is a high-risk strategy. If you miss, you can end up holding nothing. It is like being a media company that is exclusively invested in hit-driven enterprises like music and film production without the recurring revenue of, say, owning cable channels or a library of previous hit music, movies, or books. Having a portfolio of SLCs under coverage can smooth out the financial results.

Third, the best way to have a dialogue with the big companies in an industry is to know a lot about SLCs. Big companies in an industry tend to know more than a banker ever will about their big peers. But giving them the inside scoop about an SLC that would represent a perfect fill-in acquisition is always viewed as value added. And supplying this information is a great entrée to talk about the really big deals.

The trouble is that it is almost impossible to design an effective SLC coverage strategy. There are two broad approaches.

One is to set up coverage teams just to cover SLCs. The problem with this approach is it is almost impossible to get the best bankers to want to be associated exclusively with SLCs, for the reasons I just mentioned. Merrill Lynch has had a longstanding "midmarket" coverage and execution group based in Chicago, but it is hardly viewed as a training ground for the firm's best and brightest. Goldman at one point thought that calling this effort the "Entrepreneur's Group" would attract more internal interest. Luckily for Goldman, its hiring standards never fell so low that anyone was ever fooled by the euphemism. Sometimes firms have simply given formal coverage responsibility of SLCs to the high yield marketing guys. The problem here is that these bankers usually lose interest unless there is an imminent high yield offering to be done, and by that time it's usually too late to feign genuine interest in the client.

The bigger problem is that SLCs don't think about themselves as "shitty little companies." This is a little like the difficulty faced by the failed magazine launches Mode and, more recently, Grace. These titles were targeted at what are sometimes referred to as plus-size women. In fact, this category describes the vast majority of women who, unlike the anorexic skeletal figures who grace most fashion magazine covers, wisely manage to have three meals a day. The good news is that advertisers are desperate to reach this audience that represents billions of dollars in buying power. The bad news is, no matter how subtle the euphemism used, very few women want to self-identify in this way by purchasing the magazine. Similarly, SLCs want to be covered by something other than the B team of bankers relegated to covering second-class accounts. This is particularly true when the B team has no industry expertise but rather covers a hodgepodge of otherwise unrelated SLCs.

The other approach to SLC coverage is to have the bankers responsible for a particular industry be responsible for all the names in their sector, large and small. This way, the banker has enough industry expertise and personal knowledge of the bigger players to be credible to the SLCs. At the same time, these SLCs are the primary acquisition targets for bigger industry players who will welcome the views of any banker with insights into the strategic intentions of these smaller companies. Although this is a more promising approach, there are problems when it comes to execution. The main one is that this strategy is only as effective as the particular banker. And bankers are notoriously weak at the time-management skills required to effectively cover a large number of SLCs.

Time management, for a banker covering five to ten large companies, is not complicated. You call every week, you constantly think of excuses to be in front of them, you push full bore on all of them all of the time. Covering 30 to 50 SLCs is more complex, particularly if you also cover a handful of big companies. The principle is simple enough. Use your incremental minute of time where it will yield the greatest incremental expected revenue. In practice, this is more complex. It requires a careful assessment of both what the true revenue potential of each SLC is and an honest assessment of the banker's closeness to the account and thus likelihood of securing that business.

It is on the second prong of this test that bankers tend to be extremely poor judges. It is a reflection of the same delusional tendencies that make allocation of "credit" for actual deals so difficult. An account with moderate revenue potential but where you are the CEO's third or fourth call should be largely ignored unless there is some potential catalyst to moving you to the number one or two slot. By contrast, an account with less potential to generate revenue—say, only through the company's ultimate sale, which could happen this year or in three years or maybe never—but where you are the CEO's trusted adviser, is worth investing in even if there is no definite immediate return. A banker who cannot be candid with himself about whether he is tied for first or tied for fourth with an account will of necessity make terrible time-allocation choices in covering SLCs.

As part of the intensive self-examination that Morgan Stanley launched during the bust, the Investment Banking Division had hired its former senior Booz Allen consultant, Richard Foster, to be a kind of internal strategist. What emerged from the various statistics developed regarding Morgan's competitive position was the fact that our share among bronze and silver accounts (their terminology for SLCs) significantly lagged our peers. As the publishing universe was one of the only areas in which we had a leading market share among SLCs, Foster and I got to talking.

In response to Harland's claims that I could not possibly be covering so many companies efficiently, I had coincidentally developed a series of exhibits that placed each company on a matrix reflecting the coverage strategy. The *x* axis indicated the revenue potential and the *y* axis the strength of the client relationship. The recommended strategy was to direct resources toward accounts that were in the quadrant with greatest revenue and relationship strength or where there was strong possibility of being able to move the account into that quadrant. The tool was a simple way both to visually articulate one's coverage strategy and to force bankers to think through how they were prioritizing their accounts. The fact this was consistent with how Foster viewed the issue probably had more to do with my not being laid off with the others in round four than anything else.

There were two ironies here. First, that Harland's poor choice of pretexts to be completely rid of me indirectly resulted in my being given an opportunity to stay. Second, my success at covering SLCs was attributable to pursuing the second approach—namely, using industry expertise and efficient prioritization as a way to effectively maintain a broad client footprint within a sector. The irony was that what was being proposed was for me to extend my "success" to other sectors by applying the first and fundamentally flawed approach to SLC coverage. Namely, attempting to market knowledge of the needs of SLCs across industries as a unique expertise of interest to anyone.

Even if there had been serious resources committed to such an initiative, my view was that it would still be doomed to failure. If my experience in publishing taught me anything, it was that the only way to effectively cover SLCs was by providing appropriate incentives to the thought leaders in each industry sector to take responsibility for these companies as well. The history of previously aborted SLC initiatives had shown that even with that kind of commitment, it was still a challenge to get the staffing needed to execute SLC projects and almost impossible to get research to cover SLCs. As it was, I was being offered no resources, making the effort not only doomed, but farcical as well.

So, in late December 2002, a memo went out to the group that I and Ruth Porat would continue to cover select media accounts but be moving to the General Industrial Group, Ruth to cover selected large accounts and me to cover selected small ones.

The full comic potential of my no-win assignment was apparent at the first meeting at which it was described. In an effort to convince me that this was a real job, I was shown some lists of potential clients. First, I was handed a six-page printout of dozens and dozens of companies in Morgan's database where the coverage officer had visited at most once in the previous year. Flipping through the pages of this list of obscure names, I began to understand why the coverage officers hadn't bothered. Second, to demonstrate the firm's good faith, a number of industry group heads had been personally canvassed for clients I might call on. Naturally, they offered companies that they really didn't care if they covered or not. I was handed the unsurprising fruits of this preliminary effort: a list of 21 unrelated misfit names who either would never do any banking business period or would, because of some historic grudge or conflict of interest, simply never do banking business with Morgan Stanley. I gazed down at this client list from hell, which included such favorites as Price Chopper, a small private chain of discount supermarkets based in upstate New York, and Corrections Corporation of America, a Nashville-based manager of prisons. Finally, I had that catalyst I had been looking for.

"This is just a first cut," I was told reassuringly.

"When you get back from the holidays in January, you can meet with the group heads individually and see what makes sense."

We were now entering the third year of a downturn. We had just completed our fourth round of layoffs. The idea that I would meet with group heads and they would happily offer up promising untapped revenue opportunities was beyond preposterous. But they did make for highly entertaining meetings as each group head tried harder than the next to feign cooperation with this "important" new firm initiative. But at these sessions it was clear that we were both just going through the motions. It was time for me to move on.

· 16 ·

THE LONG GOODBYE

ALTHOUGH I had already begun taking interviews for university and nonprofit jobs, that would be a long, unpredictable road. The obvious and easiest thing would be to just jump ship to another major investment bank. But a funny thing had happened on the way to the bust. Beyond the drama of my little world, the cultural changes described, and even the impact of the ongoing retrenchment, other structural changes in the industry were having unpleasant repercussions for the day-to-day lives of investment bankers and indeed the very role of investment banks. The combined impact of these other changes meant that less of a banker's day was spent actually advising clients and more was spent writing internal memos, talking with compliance officers and lawyers, and making presentations to a blossoming industry of internal committees.

The dirty little secret of investment banking had become that these institutions are unsure of what their business model is and what role they really want to play. The emergence of the financial supermarkets had complicated the lives of investment bankers as Wall Street firms worked through their schizophrenia over what kind of lending businesses they wanted or had to participate in. Just when things looked like they couldn't get worse, Elliot Spitzer showed up at the party. Spitzer, New York state's attorney general, had launched an investigation into whether the reports issued by research analysts, supposedly designed to assist investors in making intelligent stock-buying decisions, were really being manipulated by corporate investment banking clients to pump the value of their shares. The internal e-mails sent by analysts regarding the stocks they were recommending to the public—Henry Blodget famously described one Internet company he was recommending as "a piece of shit" or "POS" for short—uncovered by Spitzer left little question in anyone's mind.

The research scandals further bureaucratized the banker's existence. Although Spitzer did not publicly announce the $1.4 billion settlement with all the major firms until April 2003, his investigation itself had already changed the way business was conducted.

Ironically, the sudden increase in regulatory scrutiny of investment banks' research arms did not stem from any dramatic change in banks' behavior. Institutional investors had long used analysts and their research reports to help them develop independent financial models on companies. Such sophisticated investors never took the recommendations—buy versus sell versus hold—that have been the focus of much criticism seriously and so never complained about them. Indeed, the fact that there was never any correlation between which research analysts won the *Institutional Investor* surveys and stock-picking prowess is further evidence of this fact.

The democratization of share ownership that occurred during the era of stock market euphoria and on-line trading at home, however, made investment banks' equity research reports widely available to the public at large. And giving these research reports with their buy, sell, and hold recommendations to individual investors was a little like arming pilots: it is an accident waiting to happen.

Many senior banking executives were quietly thankful for Spitzer's intervention, as the price of maintaining a superstar roster of research analysts had reached as high as $1 billion annually at some firms. This cost center could be justified during boom times from trading and underwriting profits. But with little equity trading or underwriting in the previous couple of years, many investment banks were relieved to find a way of reducing their cost base that was government–mandated (thus avoiding any charge of interfirm collusion).

But it took another six months after the settlement with the banks —which covered not only financial penalties but how equity research and investment banking are meant to interact—was announced for a court to approve it. And precisely how these rules are implemented varies widely from bank to bank, many of which continue to fine tune their internal procedures. How this will all play out as a practical matter is still very much up in the air. Although the regulatory thrust has assumed that research existed to drive investment banking business, the truth is that this has always been viewed as a side benefit. The real role of equity research is to drive investment banks' enormous trading operations. Trading with investment banks is far more expensive than any number of alternatives available to institutional investors, particularly in the era of low-cost, high-tech electronic trading platforms. Equity research is part of massive "soft dollar" arrangements under which institutional investors are provided with off-setting "value" to compensate for the higher prices. Radically cutting back proprietary research could have significant implications for this engine of trading operations. The bottom line is that, as I write this, no one knows for sure what the new long-term business model—for research specifically and marketing and distributing securities generally—will ultimately look like post-Spitzer.

In the meantime, investment bankers are caught in the middle. On the one hand, rules for how and when they can communicate with research analysts vary among firms but pretty uniformly require the presence of the corporate legal department before most interactions. It is now easier for a banker outside of Morgan Stanley to get information from one of its research analysts about how investors look at a particular company than for a banker who works there. On the other hand, clients still seem to punish and reward bankers based on whether the analyst is sufficiently bullish on their own stocks regardless of whether the clients' actions have any impact on the research. Simply dealing with research issues takes more and more time without any corresponding benefit to the goal of giving "good independent advice."

More generally, the new credit demands and research changes have added yet another level of bureaucracy to a job that had already become rather, well, corporate. As unrealistic as it may be, bankers do like to at least think of themselves as entrepreneurs. And it is in their employer's interest to encourage this illusion—it costs nothing and keeps employees happy. The new heightened degree of bureaucracy being imposed on the job today, however, makes it very hard for the average banker to keep nursing this belief.

By 2002, on top of the internal politics of my own group, I found that I was spending more and more hours of the day negotiating the structural issues described here and elsewhere. I admit that getting older has reduced my patience for spending time on issues not directly related to strategic advice to clients. But even adjusting for my increasingly ornery nature, the internal uncertainty—over what businesses investment banks want to be in and to what extent—is clearly a source of serious distraction to invest-ment bankers who generally do just want to give their clients good advice. The new regulatory overlay combined with the increasingly difficult com-petitive environment has, on the one hand, made it difficult to provide clients the potential benefits of being associated with a major investment bank and, on the other hand, made the pressures to maximize the firm's overall poten-tial revenue, even at the expense of the client, that much greater.

Until the industry and regulatory structure achieve some kind of equi-librium, I think we are likely to see an increasing number of investment bankers—both neophytes and industry veterans—questioning the continu-ing validity of many of the assumptions that initially drew them to the business. And if that equilibrium is a highly corporatized one, the outcome is likely to be the same. It is perhaps no coincidence that investment bank-ing "boutiques" have experienced a renaissance during this period. These small corporate advisory firms offer relief from the bureaucracy of the finan-cial supermarkets to bankers and the promise of independence to clients. Bob Greenhill's modest firm, Greenhill and Co., even managed to go public in May 2004. It actually trades at a substantial premium to either Goldman Sachs or Morgan Stanley. `

Yet despite these changes to the industry and my own increasing marginalization, deciding to leave Morgan Stanley proved surprisingly difficult. Although I liked to think of myself as the consummate outsider, I had not fully confronted the extent to which I had, over time, quietly adopted the values of the industry of which I had been a part for almost a decade. Nor had I been completely honest with myself about the extent to which I had always shared certain personal characteristics with my peers.

For one, I didn't like losing. And I could rationalize what had happened at Morgan Stanley any number of ways, but I certainly had not won. I was actually stunned by the depth of my feelings of competitiveness as I con-templated my departure. I found myself fantasizing about unrealistic strategies to reverse a situation that evidently could not be reversed. I also felt deep shame for abandoning those who had worked closest with me and would face an uncertain future under the new regime.

Having acknowledged that what had attracted me to investment bank-ing was the ability to influence decision makers, I also wondered whether I would regret walking away. No matter how bad things had gotten either within the industry generally or for me personally, I still had to wonder what the alternative was. Could that same level of access to decision makers be available without the institutional armor of a major financial firm? I didn't know the answer to these questions, but I did know that it didn't really matter. For as much as I enjoyed these aspects of this world, it had simply become too small a part of what I did to make it worthwhile. And I had come to feel that the industry changes described here had compromised the service that was being provided.

So I made my decision to leave. I spent my last weeks trying to find jobs for those dispatched in the last round of cuts. Then, in March 2003, I left Morgan to be one of 12 partners at a small corporate advisory and merchant banking boutique where I would no longer need to worry about financings or research or conflicts. It was also understood by my new partners that I would have the flexibility to do more teaching and writing. I had talked to a handful of other investment banks, but these conversations had confirmed my feeling that the larger issues I had observed at Morgan reflected fundamental industrywide phenomena. Although I had initially planned to leave banking altogether, the particular boutique I would be joining was founded by professionals I had known for many years and who had also taught, written, and performed public service. So I hoped their profession of sympathy for my interest in diversifying my interests was genuine. So far, my experience has exceeded my expectations.

My actual departure from Morgan was relatively painless. Very few begrudged my decision and they were visibly relieved that I wasn't going to one of their full-service competitors. The only bit of ugliness came in connection with the largest transaction I was then working on, the $2 billion Freedom Communications recapitalization. As the engagement letter had not been signed, Morgan reluctantly agreed to split the fee with my new firm. As we negotiated the precise division of the fee between us, Morgan offered to make me a personal side payment in exchange for my accepting a lower overall percentage of the fee.[1] Morgan was concerned with the precedent established by the actual percentage and thought by making me more than whole they could persuade me to shortchange my new partners. If I needed any more evidence of the decline in standards of behavior by the investment banks, this certainly more than provided it. I didn't budge and my new firm got the requested share of the fee.[2]

Not surprisingly, Morgan Stanley would never implement a strategy for addressing the SLC market opportunity. In a final irony, almost every other bank on Wall Street did, and 2003 ended up representing a high water mark for deals by SLCs. That year 61 percent of all advisory fees for M&A

around the world ended up coming from transactions of less than $1 billion.[3] Many of these deals now end up being more profitable, even for large investment banks, than much larger transactions because the megadeals now require that the fees are both likely to be heavily negotiated and split among so many different advisers. Despite this newfound interest of some larger institutions, many SLCs still "bristle at the idea of a leading investment bank showing up on the doorstep, cap in hand," according to the *Financial Times*. They are more likely to value their long-term relationship with trusted advisors who more often than not are "boutique investment banks founded by castaways from the New York giants."[4]

EPILOGUE: SEARCHING FOR
SIDNEY WEINBERG

A FEW MONTHS after I left Morgan, the investment banking business seemed to have finally hit bottom. The back half of 2003 showed a modest industry upturn, even as some firms continued to institute additional layoffs. And if 2004 showed evidence of a genuine rebound, 2005 was off the charts with bonuses approaching levels not seen since the heady days of the boom.[1] Total payouts to Wall Street workers were estimated to exceed $20 billion.[2] "It's white truffle season," said one of the partners at the Four Seasons Restaurant, favored by many bankers, "and people are paying as much as $180 for a main course."[3] *Laissez les bons temps rouler!*

The return to financial health has lead some to speculate that the disturbing trends in investment banking that have been the subject of this book were simply temporary anomalies corresponding to an unprecedented market environment. Under this view, investment banking will be able to soon regain its former role and glory, quickly leaving behind the unfortunate but temporary aftermath of the period of boom and bust that came before.

Only time will tell. To be sure, some things swiftly returned to their prebust status well before the 2005 bonus announcements. Investment banking CEO pay, for instance. Even based on 2003's modest rebound, the CEOs of the six largest investment banks took pay hikes of on average 71.5 percent.[4] These increases were so overwhelming that total pay was even greater than at the height of the boom for some Wall Street CEOs.[5] And some of the phenomena described in these pages were clearly transitional in nature. Morgan Stanley seemed to begin to regain its footing in the U.S. high yield business, moving from ninth place in 2003 to a more respectable sixth place in 2004. The firm ranking fell again in 2005, but now with the return of John Mack, Morgan Stanley may be poised to further strengthen this leg of the franchise, although hopefully at less cost than the last aggressive foray into junkland.

But the grumpy old men still seem, well, grumpy. Part of this may be that they have not been exactly welcomed home with open arms. Mack was apparently peeved that they had suggested Bob Scott rather than him when pressed for a proposed successor to Purcell. And Mack has explicitly rejected all of the structural recommendations like the sale of the Discover Card business that the grumpy old men had ultimately proposed during the height of their battle with Purcell. And then there is the painful reality that none of the high-profile Morgan Stanley departees from the period of turmoil the grumpy old men initiated have come back. Joe Perella and Terry Meguid are starting their own boutique—and even attracted Peter Weinberg to join them after he retired from Goldman Sachs. Vikram Pandit, the former head of institutional securities, and John Havens, the former head of equities, are starting their own hedge fund. Ray McGuire left his post as co-head of M&A to lead Citigroup's investment banking efforts. No one has returned. And once bonuses were paid out early in 2006, another wave of departures followed. One analyst noted that Morgan "is expected to have to pay up in order to keep some top producers from jumping ship."[6]

But beyond the continuing travails of Morgan Stanley, their continued grumpiness seems justified. Many of the trends that this book has discussed are likely to have a lasting impact. In my discussions with many investment bankers, at both the junior and senior level, the kind of loyalty to their institutions that was once commonplace is rarely articulated. In its place is an opportunistic attitude toward their current employment that should be of deep concern to their employers. And among CEOs, one finds an unprecedented level of cynicism, suspicion, and distrust of investment banks that should be of even greater concern. There is yet more tangible evidence than my non-scientific sampling of employees and clients to support this hypothesis.

Among employees, during 2004 and 2005 despite the dramatic increases in banking activity and pay, there has been a remarkable increase in voluntary turnover. Among junior ranks, many of the very best employees are going to hedge funds, which seem to be playing the role that Internet companies and venture capital firms did during the boom.[7] In a stunning acknowledgement of the disenchantment among associates, a number of firms, including Credit Suisse First Boston and Bear Stearns, for the first time in recent memory, offered across-the-board financial guarantees early in 2004 for the full year. More disturbing, firms like Goldman, where voluntary departures were once a rarity, have had strong midlevel bankers simply decide to leave without knowing what they were going to do next. This was particularly in evidence once the final tranche of IPO shares vested on June 23, 2004.[8] And among senior bankers, the willingness to move from firm to firm for a better short-term financial deal has never been so great.

Among clients, a telling statistic is the fact that boutique corporate advisory firms have achieved their highest market share ever of M&A business in the current environment. In the abstract, one would have assumed that the increasing prevalence of "pay-to-play" policies of major corporate clients would have hurt the boutiques. "Pay to play" means that to even have the opportunity to pitch new business (i.e., "play") to certain companies an investment bank must first agree to lend (i.e., "pay"). But in fact, it appears that the combined impact of the overall devaluing of the services provided by investment banks and concerns over their objectivity and independence has led more and more CEOs to turn to boutiques as either a preferred advisor or a coadvisor. The result has been a "barbell phenomenon" under which boutiques and full-fledged financial supermarkets, which routinely provide bank credit, have gained M&A share at the expense of traditional pure investment banks. The increase among boutiques has been particularly striking, growing from a 9 percent share of the M&A market in 1998 to 37.9 percent in 2004.[9] This trend appears to have continued.

Old-line Wall Street houses like Morgan Stanley and Goldman Sachs are being squeezed by nimble boutiques without a costly infrastructure on one side and financial supermarkets with huge balance sheets on the other. The *New York Times* quoted a banker as likening this fate to that of a perennially out-of-position tennis player, "stuck in the middle of the court, and not making the put-away shots at the net or winning the deep rallies from the baseline."[10] Furthermore, even with the recent increase in overall business, it appears that the structural changes may have a permanent impact on the margins available to investment banks.[11] These continuing challenges to profitability are likely to make bankers even more transactionally oriented than ever. The cost structure of the full-service investment banks puts relentless pressure on them to complete as many transactions as possible as quickly as possible. It is this transactional focus that has made many clients suspicious about the advice they get from investment banks and limits the kinds of assignment that investment banks are even willing to undertake.

There is not even consensus among the Wall Street houses as to what businesses they are or should be in. Take the diametrically opposite approaches of Morgan Stanley and Goldman Sachs to the LBO fund business. Although Morgan Stanley was one of the earliest of these firms to raise money to invest in leveraged buyouts, in early 2004 it announced that it would spin off these businesses.[12] As these funds have gotten larger and larger, Morgan Stanley found itself competing with clients more and more often for acquisition opportunities. Morgan Stanley and a number of other firms ultimately concluded that there was no practical way to avoid these conflicts short of separating from these businesses entirely.

Goldman Sachs on the other hand concluded that as a $50-billion-plus public company it could not possibly generate an adequate return on its capital by relying primarily on a fee-for-service model. This is particularly true in an environment where advisory and agency margins are becoming thinner as capital markets become more transparent and M&A is becoming more ruthlessly competitive. So Goldman has placed all its capital bets on its trading and principal businesses, which represent over 75 percent of the firm's profits. Goldman's latest LBO fund is one of the world's largest at $8.5 billion, and the firm has been known to decline financing and advisory business for established clients to allow its LBO fund to compete for the asset in question.

Although it secured the top spot again in 2005, whether Goldman will be able to maintain its position as the leading M&A firm given this strategic approach is very much open to question. But the dirty little secret at Goldman is that they have already crossed the Rubicon with respect to this issue. Investment banking now represents barely 5 percent of the profits of Goldman Sachs so that, by definition, is the entirety of their downside risk. And it is a risk they are quite prepared to take. When Goldman president Lloyd Blankfein publicly professes that "it is difficult to overstate the importance of investment banking to our firm," it elicits the same kind of eye rolling that professions of only doing "first-class business in a first-class way" at Morgan Stanley did during the boom.

In fact, both Morgan and Goldman are right. Principal businesses, at least on the scale involved here, do pose an insurmountable conflict to advisory businesses. And there are fewer and fewer unique competitive advantages available in the financing and advisory businesses that might generate a superior return to shareholders over the long run. Indeed, Morgan Stanley, despite having spun off its LBO fund business has now expressed an interest in simply investing its own money alongside LBO clients as an alternative way to juice returns.[13] And CEO Mack has also publicly stated his interest in buying a hedge fund.

None of this seems to have been lost on the latest crop of business school graduates. According to a recent survey of top MBA graduates cited by *Business Week* in its latest review of the best business schools, "[o]nly 10% of the graduates of 11 top-tier business schools wanted to work for investment banks in 2003, . . . the lowest level in nearly a decade."[14] At Harvard Business School, only 8 percent of the class of 2003 took jobs in investment banking, a level comparable to that of the 1970s.

What kinds of policies could redeem the profession and the industry in this time of crisis? Proposing a rule like Sidney Weinberg's of only working with one major corporation in an industry would be about the fastest way a person could get fired in the current environment. Creative client and conflict management and aggressive rationalization of whatever it takes to get the business has been the more recent standard. "Chinese walls" are erected internally to insulate teams simultaneously working at cross-purposes and to maintain plausible deniability when things go horribly wrong. And if such a strict no-conflicts rule would be unwelcome, one could imagine the reaction to the suggestion that we rediscover Weinberg's notion that entire sectors should be viewed as too speculative to sponsor. Weinberg would turn in his grave if he knew that in 2005 Goldman Sachs raised $1 billion in debt and equity for the Weinstein brothers' new asset-free film-production venture and even invested its own money to demonstrate Goldman's confidence in the business model.[15] And if margins are going to continue to be under pressure at the investment banks even during the current upturn, this will only exacerbate this tendency of being too cute by half to justify taking on any available profitable business. And this in turn will accelerate the long-term decline of esteem in which these institutions are held by corporate executives.

In his essay "The Death of the Banker," published just before the period that is the subject of much of this book, Ron Chernow argues that "the entire rationale" for "banker-company alliances" along the old-fashioned relationship model had already "evaporate[d]."[16] His point is that the banker's relevance "depends upon his relative strength compared with that of the providers and consumers of capital."[17] When in the early 1900s huge banks like J. P. Morgan towered over both their clients and a fragmented array of institutional and individual investors, the theory goes, it was in everyone's interest to enter into such long-term associations. But by the 1950s and 60s, "the middleman was dwarfed by the other two pillars of the financial community."[18] On the one hand, Fortune 500 companies had grown to where they "no longer needed a bank's imprimatur."[19] On the other hand, the emergence of huge institutional money managers that pooled the savings of millions of individuals created an industry that should have been able to deal directly with the large corporations with little assistance.

The problem with Chernow's hypothesis is that for decades after they should have stopped if he were correct, these relationships persisted. Chernow explains this "bizarre phenomenon" by comparing these blue-chip corporations to "dim-witted bulls" who simply did not realize that the seismic power shift that had taken place between banker and customer allowed them to burst down the door of their confining long-term relationship.[20]

The trouble with this view is that if you ask senior corporate executives who have been around for many years, they will tell you that they actually miss the ability to trust their investment banker. The kind of role played by Sidney Weinberg was something hugely valued by the companies he served. It is a role that the investment banks certainly do not play now. And the events of the last decade at a minimum call into question whether they can successfully serve that role again. It is also unclear whether these same senior corporate executives would agree to banker exclusivity as the price of returning to the good old days of relationship banking. But this longing of chief executives is palpably present today, more than 50 years after Chernow thinks it should have stopped being the case.

Investment bankers too, particularly young ones entering the field, dream of one day serving in the role of trusted advisor to the titans of industry. The speed with which even those who enter the business for the "right" reasons, rather than simply following the pack, become disillusioned seems to be getting shorter each year.

Chernow is certainly correct about the macroeconomic dynamics that cast a shadow across the investment banker–client relationship. Ironically,

those financing businesses that have become most commoditized are precisely those that are the bread and butter of serving the Fortune 500 companies that investment bankers most long to advise. The only remaining
profitable niches are, he points out, "junk bonds, initial public offerings,
and other forms of financing that primarily cater to smaller and medium-
sized firms without access to the capital markets."[21] In other words, the preferred financing vehicles of the SLCs that investment banks have so much
trouble getting people to cover!

Chernow suggests that the trend is for larger corporations to simply
internalize all of the work once performed by investment banks. The
desire of many senior executives to find a "trusted adviser" suggests that
they appreciate the dangers of the insularity that can result from such wholesale internalization of strategic decision making. Although there are
troubling disincentives in investment banking to giving truly objective
advice, these pale in comparison to the disincentives present within a
large corporate bureaucracy. And corporate bureaucrats generally are not
able to secure—or have an unfortunate tendency to self-servingly color—
the market or competitive intelligence that would allow the key decision-
makers to make fully informed decisions. In some ways, the larger the
corporation the harder it is for the CEO to secure honest, unbiased,
thoughtful, informed input. And it is the resulting profound loneliness
that drives CEOs to continue to yearn for investment bankers to provide
a service that Chernow thinks has passed its expiry date.

At this point it would not be unreasonable for a general reader to
wonder what all the fuss is about. It's fine to romanticize Sidney Weinberg
and the golden age of relationship banking, but why should anybody else
really care about the quality of relationships between investment bankers
and CEOs? After all, both groups make preposterous amounts of money
relative to their social contribution. So what if they can't trust each other?
Nobody else trusts them either!

But there really is something bigger at stake. Investment bankers can
and should play a broader role in giving objective advice to CEOs and to
boards, such as suggesting that a deal is a bad idea or highlighting the market and competitive risks of a course of action. When investment banks
are treated as a commodity service provider, commodity service is precisely
what they provide. Investment bankers then simply enable, for a fee, corporations to do what they had intended anyway. This is what, in many cases,
"fairness opinions" have been reduced to. And that is not good for the

public. The favorite defense of executives in the recent corporate scandals from Enron to WorldCom—whose biggest victims were most often small investors and employees—is that they relied on their advisers: the accountants, the lawyers, the bankers. All of whom were paid to say only what they were told to say. And none of whom had a broad enough sense of their own role and responsibility to say something different.

CEO advice aside, investment banks have over the last century played an important and constructive role in directing the allocation of capital in our economy. That these institutions served us well in this regard did not happen by accident, but because of internal processes that reflected the seriousness of these responsibilities. Today, however, the decision by an investment bank to underwrite an offering no longer represents a sincere institutional judgment that investors *should* hold a security but rather simply a judgment that investors *could* be convinced to hold it at a price. Just as the failure of lawyers to fulfill their role as "officers of the court" rather than simply hired gunslingers has diminished our culture's respect for them and the legal system as a whole, the increasingly mercenary attitude of investment banks undermines confidence in and the efficiency of our financial markets.

European executives whom I talk to view the differences between their cultures and ours as the difference between principle-based behavior, which they favor, and rule-based behavior, which the United States has perfected. This is manifested, they say, in ways big and small. It is the fundamental difference between U.S. Generally Accepted Accounting Principles and International Generally Accepted Accounting Principles. And the justifications provided for even the most heinous corporate scandals in the United States are always couched in terms of an interpretation of some particular rule, regardless of whether the principle being pursued was fundamentally corrupt. One could argue that the initial seed of the entire Enron scandal was planted when Jeff Skilling succeeded in convincing first Enron's Audit Committee and then the SEC to approve the use of mark-to-market accounting in the natural gas industry.[22] Mark-to-market accounting in that context allowed the company to adjust earnings every quarter based on their "estimates" of the future value of natural gas contracts that could run as long as 20 years. Indeed, Skilling made his acceptance of the Enron job contingent on getting that approval, and still contends that everything he did to manage the company's earnings as the company imploded was consistent with that "approved" methodology.

European corporate governance in general is hardly a model we should follow, but the criticism that Americans too often follow the letter of the law at the expense of its spirit rings painfully true. Their point is that in the United States everyone is a lawyer, and a pretty good one at that. The result is that the public, accordingly, is not safe. Unless professionals are guided by professional values, no amount of rule writing will protect us.

This brings us again back to the values epitomized by Sidney Weinberg. The events of the last decade make it all the more difficult to overcome the structural problems, highlighted by Chernow, that make it unlikely we shall recover the golden age of relationship banking. Yet the feeling of loss so palpable among both corporate executives and bankers themselves suggests that there should be a way to recapture at least some of what is now missing. Whether investment banks will find a way to do so, who will fill the void if they can't, and what shape the industry will take in either case are all questions beyond the scope of this book. What I have tried to do is provide a look back at how we got where we are in the hope that we can collectively figure out a way to summon back the spirit of Sidney J. Weinberg.

AFTERWORD

If SIDNEY WEINBERG represents the iconic investment banker in my book, then Henry Ford II represents the iconic client. Ford's status in this regard is not due to the particular assignment he gave Goldman Sachs—which was, after all, highly unusual, involving the restructuring of the family foundation—but simply to the fact that he was a CEO with a problem who needed a banker he could trust, someone with a sophisticated understanding of both the financial markets and the strategic environment the company faced. In today's world of shareholder activism and hedge funds, one could imagine that CEOs would be more interested in obtaining patient, disinterested counsel than ever before.

But it turns out that even within the global financial supermarkets' decreasing portion of business dedicated to serving investment banking clients, less and less of that service is being provided to the corporate CEOs who most need it. Instead, the iconic investment banking client of the modern era has become the LBO fund.

This change has actually accelerated since the end of the boom in 2000. In no industry is the dictum "follow the money" more suitable than in investment banking. In 2001, the top five payers of investment banking fees were all major global corporations. In 2005, only one of them was. The rest were LBO firms. Taking into account the fees paid not only directly by these firms, but by their portfolio companies, the largest LBO firms are responsible for directing between $1 and $2 billion in fees to the street every year.

Since I finished writing *The Accidental Investment Banker* in late 2005, a series of watershed events have further underscored the overwhelming impact of private equity on the financial industry landscape. KKR's 1989 acquisition of RJR Nabisco had stood as the largest LBO for over fifteen years, but it was overtaken twice in 2006. Indeed, it is now the sole transaction among the ten largest LBO deals of all time that did not take place after 2005.[1] With the recent establishment of the first $20 billion LBO fund coming barely a year after the $10 billion fund level had been breeched, more funds and bigger amounts are likely to follow. There is open speculation that the first $50 billion LBO cannot be far away.[2] And for the first time, in 2006, over a quarter of all U.S. M&A deals involved an LBO, or LBO-sponsored firm as the buyer, the seller, or both—almost double the percentage of the previous year.[3]

It is no longer unusual for an investment bank's take from a single LBO firm in one year to run into the hundreds of millions of dollars. And unlike fees obtained from a major corporate client, these investment banking fees are like an annuity. Even if there were the possibility that, in a year of unusually high activity, a corporation could generate a comparable level of fees to its lead investment bank, it could not do so with any consistency. As these LBO firms and funds grow in size and amass a broader array of portfolio companies, that annuity stream is expected to continue to grow.

These phenomena have had significant and interrelated ramifications within investment banks and the corporations that were once their traditional client base.

When I became an investment banker in the early 1990s, covering LBO firms rather than "real" corporate clients was viewed as a second-class, backwater job. Today, the job of managing relationships with LBO firms is viewed as one of the most strategic—and potentially financially rewarding—roles within investment banks. In the early 1990s, a $1 billion fund would command the full attention of those responsible for their investment bank's LBO client coverage; today that same institution might not assign even a mid-level banker to bother with a "mere" $1 billion fund.

There is something culturally subversive about the growing internal importance of bankers to the LBO industry. Bankers responsible for covering LBO firm clients used to be treated as second-class citizens within investment banks because of their lack of industry expertise. A banker to the forest products industry would need to be an expert in forest products, but a banker to the LBO industry would need to be an expert only in finding their clients potential transactions. Generally it is the industry experts who know about potential transactions within their sectors of expertise. In an environment where the banker's intellectual capital was viewed as paramount, it is not surprising that industry experts looked down on banking colleagues whose primary job was to provide LBO firms with access to the bankers who had specialized industry knowledge. LBO firms themselves are full of very smart former investment bankers, many of whom don't think they need help with anything much more than raising money quickly and cheaply. To the extent that this is even somewhat representative of the perspective of the new iconic client, it cannot help but undermine the investment banker's sense of self-worth.

Corporations, for their part, are fully aware of their declining place in the investment-banking-fee hierarchy. This would not make them nearly so queasy were it not for the fact that they have a sometimes uneasy relationship with the LBO firms who have replaced them at the top of that pyramid. Today there are few corporations so large as to be out of the reach of the largest LBO firms—or, increasingly, a consortium of the largest LBO firms. Although most LBO firms eschew hostile bids, in a world where activist shareholders aggressively solicit interest in companies with or without the knowledge of management, the line between friendly and hostile has become blurrier than ever. The hedge fund industry, whose pools of capital are growing faster than even the LBO industry, have no such compunction about hostile activity and are increasingly using their capital to compete with LBO firms for investing opportunities. Given that at any given moment a major investment bank will likely have multiple assignments and solicitations pending with most of the largest LBO firms—and hedge funds represent the biggest clients of their sales and trading operations—the line between what constitutes a conflict and what does not will become blurrier as well.

And then there is still the little question of whether the major investment banks want to be in the LBO business themselves. The landscape on this crucial question has also changed dramatically in the last year. Until then, most major firms, other than Goldman Sachs, had appeared to follow Morgan Stanley's lead: spinning off, or radically scaling back, their principal investing activities. JPMorgan, Citicorp, Credit Suisse and Deutsche Bank had all followed this route. Universally, these initial decisions appear to have been driven not by concerns of conflicts with traditional corporate clients, but rather as a direct response to the anger of LBO clients who complained that the investment banks' captive LBO funds were bidding up prices for deals.

As much as the investment banks do not want to offend their most important source of fees, the size of the LBO investing opportunity has made almost all of them, including Morgan Stanley, to now reconsider their decision to exit this business.[4] LBO firms charge investors as much as 2 percent annually on top of any share in actual gains from investments—a steady stream of revenue that contrasts quite favorably to the cyclicality of the deal businesses that investment banks otherwise rely on. Over half a trillion dollars in LBO funds, raised in just the last couple of years, potentially represents more than $10 billion in fee income annually going to LBO firms before generating any returns to their investors.

But how to participate in the spoils without pissing off the goose responsible for laying the current golden investment banking boom? So far the answer seems to be by pursuing the business in a way that avoids direct competition with large LBO clients.[4] This means limiting investing opportunities to situations either where the investment bank is co-investing with a large LBO firm it is otherwise advising, or where the target company is smaller than those typically of interest to the bigger LBO firms. This approach does not really eliminate potential conflicts even with the large LBO firms.[5] It is also not clear if it represents a sensible business strategy. With respect to being add-on equity to transactions lead by major LBO firms, outside investors are likely to ask why they don't just invest in the major LBO firms' funds directly if the fees are going to be the same. With respect to middle-market transactions below the threshold of interest to major LBO firms, this is the land of the SLC detailed in Chapter Fifteen: precisely the companies that the large investment banks have a competitive disadvantage in identifying and properly servicing. It would be surprising indeed if investment banks nonetheless discovered a previously unknown skill in identifying hidden value by purchasing these companies for their own accounts.

But I am making too much of investment banks's currently articulated strategy for successfully threading the needle between being genuine LBO players themselves on the one hand, and serving as trusted advisors (or at least major sources of capital) to independent LBO players on the other. Wherever the policy ends up, traditional corporate clients are likely to come up short, and be an afterthought in any event. We have seen this movie before, but the script changes with each viewing. As the head of one of the LBO funds spun off from a bulge bracket firm pointed out, "There has always been high turnover and rapid shifts in policy when things don't go well or when conflicts become problematic."

"I don't see any reason why that cycle wouldn't happen again," he concluded.[6]

ACKNOWLEDGEMENTS

As a FIRST-TIME AUTHOR, I have many people to thank. Luckily for the reader, most of them are current and former employees of Goldman Sachs and Morgan Stanley who would prefer not to be cited. Their support and insight were invaluable to this enterprise. For early encouragement and guidance I must also thank Clare Reihill at Harper Collins, Brian Kempner and Peter Kaplan at the *New York Observer*, L. Gordon Crovitz and Paul Ingrassia at Dow Jones, Pat Tierney and Dan Farley at Harcourt, John Sargent and George Witte at Holtzbrinck, and Allison Silver, a long-time friend and editor at the *Los Angeles Times* and *New York Times*. For reading and commenting on various drafts along the way I want to thank Beatrice Cassou, Mark Gerson, Bruce Greenwald, David Knee, Myra Kogen, Chaille Maddox, Lisa McGahan, John Edward Murphy, Jeff Reisenberg, Jason Sobol, and Clyde Spillenger. My two research assistants Nicholas Greenwald and Amani Macaulay kept me grounded in reality. And Stephanie Trocchia and Jeannie Esposito survived and supported my filing system. Finally I want to thank my agent, Elaine Markson, and my editors at Oxford University Press—Tim Bartlett who took it on and others who dragged it across the finish line—for taking a chance on me and for their guidance and confidence. None of these people should be blamed, however, for what I have actually wrought.

NOTES

Preface

1 Andrew Ross Sorkin, "A Wall Street Exposé With an All-Star Index," *New York Times,* July 2, 2006.
2 Michael Lewis, "The Hammering on the Investment Banker's Coffin," Bloomberg .com, September 20, 2006.
3 John C. Coffee, Jr., *Gatekeepers: The Professions and Corporate Governance* (Oxford: 2006), 105.

Introduction

1 Robert Berner and David Kiley, "Annual Report: Global Brands," *Business Week,* August 1, 2005.
2 Langdon Thomas, Jr., "Out of the Tar Pits, Into the House of Morgan," *New York Times,* April 3, 2005.
3 Ibid.
4 Charles Gasparino, "Wall Street: Stand by This Man," *Newsweek,* April 4, 2005.

Chapter 1: A Chicken in Every Pot

1 *SuperMarketing,* March 20, 1987, 32.
2 "Secrets of the City: Survivors—Mergers and Acquisitions," *Times,* April 16, 1992.

Chapter 2: The Accidental Investment Banker

1 Amazingly, a few days after I started in London, I was asked to undergo a hand-

ful of after-the-fact interviews, presumably to complete the Human Resources File on me.

Chapter 3: An Empire of Its Own

1   William Lewis, "Mr. Levy Walks Tall on Wall Street," *Financial Times,* January 23, 1998.

2   Lisa Endlich, *Goldman Sachs: The Culture of Success* (New York: Knopf, 1999), 169. Page number is from the 2000 Touchstone paperback edition.

3   Barry E. Supple, "A Business Elite: German-Jewish Financiers in Nineteenth-Century New York," *Business History Review,* vol. 31, no. 2 (Summer 1957), 145.

4   The first non-Lehman joined the partnership in 1924, almost 70 years after the firm was founded.

5   Michael C. Jensen, *The Financiers: The World of the Great Wall Street Investment Banking Houses* (New York: Weybright and Talley, 1976), 195. The firm's first underwriting was United Cigar earlier that same year, but the Sears offering is credited with establishing Goldman's place in the industry.

6   Neal Gabler, *An Empire of Their Own: How the Jews Invented Hollywood* (New York: Crown, 1988).

7   Jean Strouse, *Morgan: American Financier,* (New York: Random House, 1999), 537–538.

8   Waddill Catchings was not the first nonfamily partner. This distinction belongs to Henry S. Bowers.

9   J. P. Morgan's investment trust fared almost as poorly in the crash, but had been wisely called the United Corp.

10 See Chippendale, Peter and Suzanne Franks, *Dished! The Rise and Fall of British Satellite Broadcasting* (London: Simon & Schuster, 1991); Mathew Horsman, *Sky High: The Amazing Story of BSkyB—and the Egos, Deals and Ambitions that Revolutionised TV Broadcasting* (London: Orion, 1997).

11 Horsman, *Sky High,* 132.

Chapter 4: "Let's Ask Sidney Weinberg"

1   Endlich, *Goldman Sachs,* 124. Page number is from the 2000 Touchstone paperback edition.

2   Odlum, who remained a longtime Goldman client, would soon flip the trust for a profit.

3   Catchings and Goldman were a particular focus of John Kenneth Galbraith, *The Great Crash: 1929* (New York: Houghton Mifflin, 1954), 147.

4   Sidney J. Weinberg, "The Functions of a Corporate Director," address before the Harvard Business School Club of Cleveland, May 31, 1949. The speech is available on the Goldman Web site.

5   Robert Sheehan, " 'Let's Ask Sidney Weinberg,' " *Fortune,* October, 1953.

6   Ibid.

7   E. J. Kahn, Jr., "The Director's Director—I," *New Yorker*, September 8, 1956.
8   Ibid.
9   Ibid.
10 Ron Chernow, *The House of Morgan: An American Banking Dynasty and the Rise of Modern Finance* (New York: Grove, 1990), 513. Page number is from the 2001 Grove paperback edition.
11 E. J. Kahn, Jr., "The Director's Director—I," *New Yorker*, September 8, 1956.
12 Beth McGoldrick, "Inside the Goldman Sachs Culture," *Institutional Investor*, January, 1984.
13 Lynn Cowan, "Deals & Deal Makers: Goldman Sachs CEO Apologizes for Layoff Comments," *Wall Street Journal*, February 4, 2003.

Chapter 5: What Investment Bankers Really Do

1   These three terms are used interchangeably throughout.
2   Sharon Schmickle and Tom Hamburger, "U.S. Justices took trips from West Publishing," *Minneapolis Star-Tribune*, March 5, 1995. See also, Chris Ison, "West calls stories 'tabloid journalism,'" *Minneapolis Star-Tribune*, March 6, 1995.

Chapter 6: The Culture of M&A

1   Cary Reich, *Financier: The Biography of Andre Meyer*, (New York: Wiley, 1983), 234.
2   E. M. Christner, "Goldman Sachs Celebrates Its First 100 Years," *Investment Dealers' Digest*, December 9, 1969.
3   Chernow, *House of Morgan*, 595. Page number is from the 2001 Grove paperback edition.
4   Bruce Wasserstein, *Big Deal: Mergers and Acquisitions in the Digital Age*, (New York: Warner Business, 1998), 560. Page number is from the 2001 paperback edition.
5   Irwin Ross, "How Goldman Sachs Grew and Grew," *Fortune*, July 9, 1984.
6   Ibid.
7   Paul M. Scherer, "Heard on the Street: Goldman Sachs Sees Hostile Bids in New Light," *Dow Jones Business News*, June 10, 1999.
8   Chernow, *House of Morgan*, 597. Page number from the 2001 Grove paperback edition.
9   *House of Morgan*, 597.
10 Michael Peltz, "Wall Street's no-name merger gang," *Institutional Investor*, March, 1996.
11 Endlich, *Goldman Sachs: The Culture of Success*, 61.
12 John C. Whitehead, *A Life in Leadership: From D-Day to Ground Zero* (New York: Basic Books, 2005), 127.
13 Although Jimmy's brother John Livingston married Sue Ann Gotshal of

the Jewish family that founded the well-known law firm Weil Gotshal and Manges, her mother was a Christian Scientist and the family was not practicing.

14 Andrew Barry, "King's Ransom for Lazard: Wasserstein, other insiders benefit royally over new shareholders," *Barron's*, May 9, 2005.

Chapter 7: The Rise of John Thornton

1 The firm went out of its way to communicate its plan to remain independent and private. See Leah Spiro, "Inside The Money Machine: In a big-is-all business, Goldman vows to go it alone," *Business Week*, November, 22, 1997.

2 Anita Raghavan and Michael Siconolfi, "Goldman Sachs Drops Idea of a Public Sale," *Wall Street Journal*, January 21, 1996.

3 Kate Kelly, "Lenzner, Through a Darker Lens," *Time*, July 10, 2000.

4 Andrew Garfield, "Rise of the Goldman Boy," *Independent—London*, March 17, 1999.

5 Anita Raghavan and Patrick McGeehan, "Corzine Resigns as Co-CEO at Goldman Sachs," *Wall Street Journal*, January 12, 1999.

6 Joseph Kahn, "Goldman, Sachs Tries to Soothe Limited Partners," *New York Times*, July 30, 1998.

7 Endlich, *Goldman Sachs*, 267.

8 Corzine was not stupid. He had changed the partnership agreement to require an 80% vote of the Executive Committee to cause a change in the Firm leadership. This means that Paulson, Thornton, and Thain needed to convince Bob Hurst, the other Committee member, to accede to the plan. Clearly, however, if Corzine suspected anything like this was possible, he would never have allowed, some say encouraged, his ally Zuckerberg to resign from the Committee.

9 See Randall Smith, "Going Public Challenges Goldman's Venerable Culture," *Wall Street Journal*, May 1, 2000.

10 Stanley Reed and Joyce Barnathan, "Goldman's 'Dealmaker Supreme,'" *Business Week*, January 25, 1999.

Chapter 8: The House of Morgan

1 Cary Reich, *Financier: The Biography of Andre Meyer: A Story of Money, Power, and the Reshaping of American Business* (New York: Morrow, 1983), 50–51. Page numbers are from the 1997 John Wiley edition.

2 Letter from Russell C. Leffingwell to Franklin Roosevelt cited in Ron Chernow, *The House of Morgan: An American Banking Dynasty and the Rise of Modern Finance*, (New York: Grove, 1990), 386. Page number is from the 2001 Grove paperback edition.

3 Chernow, *House of Morgan*, 500.

4 Chernow, *House of Morgan*, 511.

5 Chernow, *House of Morgan*, 623.

6 Chernow, *House of Morgan*, 24.

7   Beth McGoldrick, "Inside the Goldman Sachs culture," *Institutional Investor*, January 1984.

8   Interview with John Whitehead. In Whitehead's recent autobiography, he tells this story but quotes Weinberg as saying instead "We've had them all along." John C. Whitehead, *A Life in Leadership: From D-Day to Ground Zero* (New York: Basic Books, 2005), 86.

9   Ann Monroe, "Can Joe Perella's New Marriage Work?" *Investment Dealers' Digest*, November 7, 1994.

10 Professor Ashish Nanda of Harvard Business School has lectured widely on the "Producer Manager Dilemma," including to a retreat of managing directors at Morgan Stanley. He is the coauthor of a casebook with former Morgan Stanley's former chief development officer, Thomas Delong. *Professional Services: Text and Cases* (New York: McGraw-Hill/Irwin, 2003).

11 Richard Johnson, "Cigar incites horsey hooliganism," *New York Post*, May 7, 1998.

Chapter 9: Cracks in the Façade

1   Thomson Financial.

2   Chernow, *House of Morgan*, 628.

3   Charles Gasparino and Ann Davis, "Morgan Stanley Case Illustrates Less Tolerance in Bias Claims," *Wall Street Journal*, September 14, 1999.

4   Larry Celona, Adam Miller, and Gersh Kuntzman, "Wall Street Hothead Quizzed in Slaying of Russian Model," *New York Post*, September 15, 1999.

5   Kate Kelly, "Morgan Stanley's Season in Hell," *New York Observer*, September 27, 1999.

6   Lauren's parents did set up a foundation in her name that gives scholarships to deserving students at Smith College.

7   See *Howling at the Moon: The Odyssey of a Monstrous Music Mogul in an Age of Excess* (New York: Broadway Books, 2004) for Walter's own take on his out-of-control antics of the era or Fredric Dannen's *Hit Men: Power Brokers & Fast Money Inside the Music Business* (New York: Random House, 1990) for a less sordid but more balanced appraisal of his reign. While at Goldman, I briefly worked on an assignment to help the cleaned-up Yetnikoff raise money for a new record label, Velvel (Yiddish for, what else, Walter).

8   This fifth commandment is strangely omitted from Whitehead's recent autobiography, which only lists nine. *A Life in Leadership*, 106. Although I suspected that this might have been the equivalent of a grandmother omitting a key ingredient from the official version of a family recipe so it could never be reproduced exactly, Whitehead assures me it was merely an oversight.

9   Elizabeth Douglas, "Another Name at Global Stands Out: Former Chief Executive Thomas Casey was at the helm during the period that is of most interest to investigators," *Los Angeles Times*, October 27, 2002.

10 Steven Lipin, "How a Little Start-Up With No Revenue Attracted an All-Star Board," *Wall Street Journal*, December 14, 1999. Price has since resumed a phenomenally

successful career as an investment banker. See Heidi Moore, "Price Points," *The Deal*, April 12, 2004.

11   Not everyone was delusional. Nina Munk's *Fools Rush In: Steve Case, Jerry Levin and the Unmaking of AOL Time Warner* (New York: Harper Business, 2004), 123–129, is devastating in its depiction of how Case and his advisors schemed as to the most effective use of their overvalued stock and ultimately settled on the hapless Time Warner and the emotionally fragile Jerry Levin.

12   Mary was so dubbed by *Barron's* in an influential December 21, 1998, article by Andrew Barry titled "Net Queen: How Mary Meeker Came to Rule the Internet."

13   De Baubigny later founded a high-end wine storage business in San Francisco, where he continues to work today.

14   This and other similar pages are reproduced in Appendix IX of *The European Internet Report* from June 1999, one of a series of follow-on volumes to the original *Internet Report*. None of these subsequent equity research reports managed to be published commercially.

15   Peter Elkind, "Where Mary Meeker Went Wrong," *Fortune*, May 14, 2001.

16   E.g., Randall Smith, "High Tech Banker Scores Deals With Mule and 'Rocky Raccoon,'" *Wall Street Journal*, September 24, 1999.

17   *Equity Ownership in America, 2002*, Investment Company Institute and the Securities Industry Association.

18   Susan Pulliam and Randall Smith, "Silicon Touch: For Frank Quattrone, With a Fief at CSFB, Tech Was a Gold Mine—Both Banker and Investor, He Made the Most of IPOs and Venture-Capital Ties—Getting in On the Ground Floor," *Wall Street Journal*, May 3, 2001.

19   Andrew P. Madden, "The German Occupation—Frank Quattrone aims to build a new breed of technology investment bank by hitching his wagon to a European powerhouse," *The Red Herring*, May 1, 1996.

20   Ann Monroe, "Under a magnifying glass at Deutsche Morgan Grenfell," *Investment Dealers' Digest*, February 3, 1997.

21   See "Rocky Raccoon" for one documented example of this phenomenon.

22   See "Silicon Touch."

23   Gregg Worth, "Frank Quattrone: Figuring out his next move?," *Investment Dealers' Digest*, May 15, 2000.

24   E. S. Browning, "Party On: Despite Slump, Wall Street Binges on Pay and Perks," *Wall Street Journal*, September 18, 2000.

Chapter 10: Drama of the Gifted Banker

1   "Business Best Sellers," *New York Times*, June 26, 1983, F15.

2   Rakesh Khurana, "The Curse of the Superstar CEO," *Harvard Business Review*, September 2002.

3   Kevin Murphy and Jan Zabojnik, "Managerial Capital and the Market for CEOs," Marshall School of Business, University of Southern California, working paper, December 2003.

4   Pfeffer, J. and Fong, C. T., "The end of business schools? Less success than meets the eye." *Academy of Management Learning and Education*, (2002) 1, 78–95.

5   Katherine Boo, "The Drama of the Gifted Vice President," *Washington Post Magazine*, November 28, 1993.

6   Alice Miller, *The Drama of the Gifted Child: The Search for the True Self*, (New York: Basic Books, 1981) 5–6.

Chapter 11: Take a Walk on the Buy-Side

1   For example, MGM had a very public failed auction for the company. Yvetter Kantrow, "Media Maneuvers: Echo Chamber," *The Daily Deal*, January 18, 2002. That MGM was ultimately able to entice two suitors to offer close to $5 billion in late 2004 suggests that the bust was very much over by then.

2   "R. H. Donnelley Resumes Share Repurchase Program After Suspending Process to Explore Possible Sale of Company," *Business Wire*, December 5, 2000.

3   In February 2002, Morgan Stanley was invited along with every other major institution to respond to a formal RFP from Sprint's assistant vice president for mergers and acquisitions relating to the potential divestiture of its directories. Although one would always prefer to represent the seller rather than one of many potential buyers, because of Morgan Stanley's weak relationships with the established telecom companies that owned the incumbent directories, they were never seriously considered for such an engagement in connection with any of the several directory sales that occurred during this period.

4   Erin E. Arvedlund, "Who Will Buy Bear Stearns?—Dull businesses and scandal taint this odd Wall Street firm," *Barron's*, August 7, 2000.

Chapter 12: "Save the Red Carpet for the Talent"

1   Lauren R. Rublin, "What Now? Some Street seers say the halcyon days of the market are over," *Barron's*, October 16, 2000.

2   Dina Temple-Raston, "Layoff clouds start to gather but surge in last week's numbers may exaggerate actual job losses," *USA Today*, January 29, 2001.

3   Tara Siegel, "Citigroup to Lay Off 'Several Hundred' Workers," *Dow Jones News Service*, April 3, 2001.

4   Roger Lowenstein estimates that the total dollars raised by start-up telecom companies during the boom dwarfed that of start-up Internet companies by a factor of 20 to 1. *Origins of the Crash: The Great Bubble and Its Undoing* (New York: Penguin, 2004), 159.

5   Investment banks do sometimes bid to buy for redistribution large quantities of equity securities in "block trades." This is never done in IPOs and rarely in follow-on offerings, which are the typical means for companies to raise equity capital.

6   Although Harland was nominally global head of the group, European telecoms had long been under the guidance of the talented Paulo Pereira who, unlike Harland,

had focused his efforts on covering the large incumbent telcos in Europe. Pereira's frustration with Harland led him to consider moving to Goldman Sachs, but intervention by senior Morgan management kept him in the fold. See "Morgan Stanley Executive Decides to Stay," *Bloomberg Business News*, October 9, 2001. Earlier this year, Pereira did finally leave Morgan, but not for Goldman. Instead, he followed Joe Perella to the new unnamed boutique investment bank the former Morgan Stanley investment banking chief is building. Carrick Mollenkamp, Jason Singer, and Michael Wang, "Morgan Stanley names new Europe M&A chief—Macdonald tapped as Pereira prepares to join Perella's firm," *Wall Street Journal Europe*, January 27, 2006.

7   Bethany McLean, "Goldman Sachs: Inside the Money Machine," *Fortune*, September 6, 2004.

8   Koenig finally retired in at the end of 2004. See "Observer Column: Restart?" *Financial Times* (U.S.A. edition), December 23, 2004.

Chapter 13: View from the Top

1   The most notable failure had been the attempt by American Express to combine Shearson Loab Rhoades with Lehman Brothers in the 1980s.

2   "One of the things that gets lost in history," Merrill chairman David Komansky said at the time of the merger, "is how long it took Merrill Lynch to build its investment banking business." Tracy Corrigan, "Scenes from a One-Sided Marriage," *Financial Post*, July 25, 1997.

3   See Anita Raghavan and Patrick McGeehan, "Dean Witter's Purcell Gets His Day After Hits and Misses," *Wall Street Journal*, February 13, 1997.

4   Charles Gasparino and Anita Raghavan, "Survivor: How Dean Witter Boss Got the Upper Hand in Merger With Morgan," *Wall Street Journal*, March 22, 2001.

5   See "Purcell Gets His Day."

6   Leah Nathans Spiro, "Class Meets Mass on Wall Street: Morgan Dean Witter could change the balance of power," *Business Week*, February 17, 2001.

7   Leslie Alan Horvitz, "White Shoes Meet White Socks As Morgan Marries Dean Witter," *Insight*, May 26, 1997.

8   Mack would assert that only 250 out of over 40,000 jobs would be cut. See "One-Sided Marriage."

9   Patrick McGeehan and Bridget O'Brian, "The Morgan Stanley/Dean Witter Deal—Conflicts of Cultures Could Occur," *Wall Street Journal*, February 6, 1997.

10 According to press reports, the nominating committee had not been designated at the time the deal had been reached. Anita Raghavan, "Morgan Stanley Puts More in Stock Than in the Title," *Wall Street Journal*, February 7, 1997.

11 See "Survivor."

12 The nominating committee was initially split equally between the sides, but a Dean Witter loyalist was chair. Subsequent events make clear who was running the show.

13 See "Survivor."

14 Ibid.

15 Charles Gasparino, "Will Two Wall Street Reign Makers Cede Their Thrones?—A Handshake Agreement Adds to the Tense Times at Morgan Stanley," *Wall Street Journal*, January 19, 2001.

16 See "Conflicts of Cultures."

17 See "Survivor."

18 Emily Thornton, "Morgan Stanley: Life After Mack," *Business Week*, February 12, 2001.

19 Andy Serwer, "Khrushchev's Revenge," *Fortune*, October 12, 1998.

20 See "Survivor."

21 Laurie P. Cohen, "Morgan Stanley's Top Lawyer Draws Increasing Scrutiny," *Wall Street Journal*, June 4, 1999.

22 Ibid.

23 Patrick McGeehan, "At Dean Witter, Merger Creates Job Limbo," *Wall Street Journal*, February 24, 1997.

24 Kate Kelly, "Morgan Stanley's Season in Hell," *New York Observer*, September 27, 1999.

25 Landon Thomas, Jr., "Morgan Stanley's Hot Guy Folds It Up and Goes Home," *New York Observer*, October 16, 2000. Cites sources claiming, that the firms marked down positions in just three issues were "north of $500 million." Although Morgan repeatedly asserted such claims were greatly exaggerated, total telecom-related losses were ultimately much greater than this.

26 Jonathan Stempel, "Morgan Stanley junk telecom bonds perform worst-analyst," *Reuters News*, October 11, 2000. Salomon ultimately pulled the report at Morgan Stanley's request. Jonathan Stempel, "Salomon pulls Morgan Stanley junk bond analysis," *Reuters News*, October 13, 2000.

27 Randall Smith and Paul Sherer, "Morgan Stanley Bond Executive Resigns After Recent Management Restructuring," *Wall Street Journal*, October 6, 2000.

28 Tom Barkley, "Morgan Stanley Eliminates Head Trader, Others on Junk Bond Team," *Dow Jones Business News*, November 19, 2002.

29 See Pallavi Gogol, "Junk Bond Kings: MSDW's Melchiorre A Jack of All Trades," *Dow Jones News Service*, June 9, 1999. The article makes clear that for all of Anthony's skill as a talented hybrid professional, "part investment banker, a quasi-research analyst, and a master salesman," from a client's perspective it is the " 'huge commitments of capital' " that were the real " 'key to a trader's ability to function.' "

30 Pallavi Gogol, "Four Men Hold Sway Over Junk Bond World," *Wall Street Journal*, June 15, 1999.

31 "Morgan Stanley Changes Parent Company Name," *Business Wire*, June 18, 2002. The "Discover" had been dropped from the corporate moniker in 1998. See "Holders Approve New Morgan Stanley Dean Witter & Co. Name," *Dow Jones News Service*, March 24, 1988.

32 Vividly documented in Ken Auletta's *Greed and Glory on Wall Street: The Fall of the House of Lehman* (New York: Random House, 1986).

33 Charles R. Geisst, *The Last Partnerships: Inside the Great Wall Street Money Dynasties* (New York: McGraw-Hill, 2001), 128.

34   Ann Davis, Randall Smith, and Charles Gasparino, "Merrill Lynch's Cost Cutter Is Out Himself," *Wall Street Journal*, July 30, 2003.
35   Ibid.

Chapter 14: The Myth of Meritocracy

1   Jonathan A. Knee, "Lack of Opportunities May Benefit Graduates," *Atlanta Constitution*, May 28, 2002.

Chapter 16: The Long Goodbye

1   The side payment was to be made in the form of allowing me to keep my unvested stock at Morgan Stanley.
2   And I sadly did not get my unvested stock.
3   James Politi and David Wells, "Wall Street hums a different tune: Investment Banking: Top Financiers are starting to appreciate the merits of the small-time deal," *Financial Times*, August 23, 2004.
4   Ibid.

Epilogue: Searching for Sidney Weinberg

1   Jenny Anderson, "Optimism on Wall Street. Over Size of Bonuses," *New York Times*, November 8, 2005. See also Gene Colter "Wall Street Bonuses Enhance American Dream: In New York, It's 2 BRs and a Meditation Garden," *Wall Street Journal*, January 7, 2006.
2   David Litterick, "Wall Street Life, Scores Score As Payouts Soar While Non-Bankers Suffer Bonus Envy," *Daily Telegraph*, January 14, 2006.
3   Susanne Craig, "Street's Weather: Bonus Showers," *Wall Street Journal*, November 8, 2005.
4   Avital Louria Hahn, "A Rebound Year for CEOs: After taking pay cut in 2002, Wall Street's top executives more than made up for it in 2003," *Investment Dealers' Digest*, March 15, 2004.
5   Patrick McGeehan, "For Wall Street Chiefs, Big Paydays Continue," *New York Times*, March 23, 2004.
6   Langdon Thomas Jr., "Staff Issues Hampering Morgan's Recovery," *New York Times*, November 24, 2005.
7   Carolyn Sargent and Judy McDermott, "This Trader Exodus Has Legs: More and more big names defect from sell side to hedge funds," *Investment Dealers' Digest*, March 14, 2005.
8   Denise Lugo, "Life After Goldman," *Investment Dealers' Digest*, May 24, 2004.
9   Avital Louria Hahn, "Banking the Old Fashioned Way," *Investment Dealers' Digest*, May 17, 2004.
10   Langdon Thomas, Jr., "The Incredible Shrinking Investment Bank: Will Merrill Lynch and Morgan Stanley Become Wall Street Relics?" *New York Times*, October 17, 2004.

11 Robin Sidel, Erik Portanger and Jathon Sapsford, "Investment Banks See Fees Shrink in Battle With New Rules, Rivals," *Wall Street Journal*, May 18, 2004.

12 David Carey and John E. Morris, "Morgan Stanley spins off PE unit," *Daily Deal*, February 27, 2004.

13 A number of investment banks have identified the opportunity of directly "co-investing" in LBO deals as a way to avoid conflicts while benefiting from the returns available in this business. See Randall Smith, "How Merrill CEO Warms to Risk," *Wall Street Journal*, December 8, 2005. The idea is to avoid competing for investors and deals with the major LBO firms that are the investment banks biggest clients by raising their own independent LBO funds. This approach neither provides the same returns nor necessarily eliminates conflicts. A significant portion of LBO economics comes from an annual fee on the billions under management, regardless of the success of deals. And as a co-investor, investment banks will be thrust into difficult negotiations with its advisory "client" over terms and governance rights.

14 Emily Thornton, "Wall Street? Thanks, I'll Pass," *Business Week*, October 18, 2004.

15 David Carr, "Placing Bets On Miramax The Sequel," *New York Times*, October 31, 2005.

16 Ron Chernow, *The Death of the Banker: The Decline and Fall of the Great Financial Dynasties and the Triumph of the Small Investor* (New York: Vintage, 1997), 24.

17 Ibid., 7.

18 Ibid., 49.

19 Ibid., 48.

20 Ibid.

21 Ibid., 73.

22 Bethany McLean and Peter Elkind, *The Smartest Guys in the Room: The Amazing Rise and Scandalous Fall of Enron* (New York: Portfolio, 2003), 39–42.

Afterword

1 R. K. Kirkland, "Private Money," *Fortune*, March 5, 2007.

2 Jason Singer and Henny Sender, "Growing Funds Fuel Buy-out Boom—Already Biggest, Blackstone Will Raise Additional $4.4 Billion as Firms Seek Larger Targets," *Wall Street Journal*, October 26, 2006.

3 Matthew Goldstein, "LBO Fever Stays Hot," The Street.com, December 26, 2006.

4 Julia Werdigier and Dana Cimilluca, "Morgan Stanley Risks M&A Fees by Emulating Goldman Sachs's LBOs," *Bloomberg News*, October 9, 2006.

5 See e.g., Peter Smith, "Credit Suisse Secures $2.1 Billion for Buy-out Fund," *Financial Times*, October 6, 2006.

6 See footnote 13, Epilogue.

7 Ken MacFadyen, "PE Puzzlement: Morgan Stanley's Abrupt 180 Reflects Widespread Indecision about the Role of Private Equity in Investment Banking," *Investment Dealers Digest*, October 2, 2006.

INDEX

JONATHAN A. KNEE is now a partner at a boutique investment banking firm. He is also Adjunct Professor of Finance and Economics and Director of the Media Program at the Columbia Graduate School of Business. His writing has appeared in *The Wall Street Journal, The New York Times, The Washington Post, Los Angeles Times,* and elsewhere.